CW00538688

The Alternative Bible

THE ALTERNATIVE BIBLE

A narrative summary based on
the King James Version

The Old Testament

DAVID VOAS

DUCKWORTH

First published in 1993 by
Gerald Duckworth & Co. Ltd.
The Old Piano Factory
48 Hoxton Square, London N1 6PB
Tel: 071 729 5986
Fax: 071 729 0015

A catalogue record for this book is available
from the British Library

ISBN 0 7156 2466 0

Typeset by Ray Davies
Printed in Great Britain by
Redwood Press Ltd, Melksham

Contents

The Major Prophets

The Twelve Minor Prophets

Introduction

Most people own the Bible. Almost everyone would like to read it, or more accurately, to have read it. Few succeed. Why is this?

Certainly there is no shortage of help. Using a handbook or a commentary, however, means studying the text, not reading it. At the opposite extreme, retold Bible stories are not what the interested adult is after. He or she probably wants to read the classic 'King James' version because of its impact on our language and literature. This text is undoubtedly difficult, but modern translations are scarcely any better: language really is not the main problem. However colloquial you make it, the Bible is still heavy going. The ideas, poetry and action are swamped by names, detail and repetition.

The Alternative Bible offers a new approach. Interweaving quotation and narration, it covers every chapter of every book in the original. The familiar phrases and incidents fall into context in a fast-paced saga alongside some surprising finds. Everything is included – history, law, poetry, wisdom and prophecy – except the bulk. Reduced in length by 80 per cent, the Good Book can become a good read.

What Christians know as the Old Testament (the Hebrew Bible) does not have a narrator. This version supplies one, attempting to see events through the eyes of an expert witness: Michael the Archangel. Being the guardian of the Hebrew people (as the book of Daniel tells us) he is particularly well qualified to tell the story. Respect for his celestial superior does not prevent him from showing a sense of humour.

Caught between God and his people, Michael is as evenhanded as an observer (and occasional participant) can be. He accepts words and events at face value; interpretation is up to the reader.

For anyone wishing to check what the Archangel says with the full text, chapter numbers appear in the margin for reference. Quotations (from the King James Version) are in bold italics; the original punctuation is retained, although poetry is set in verse. An appendix provides a brief survey of the Bible's history.

A few centuries ago, translating scripture was a radical act. What follows is another step towards the same end: to make a great work accessible to all. These days any book, even if essential reading, will gather dust unless it is enjoyable. *The Alternative Bible* aims to meet that challenge.

*

To begin at the beginning (as is only biblical) I must thank my parents. Since I plan to blame them for my failings, which is frowned upon in acknowledgements, it is only fair that they receive credit for whatever elements of education, curiosity and ignorance reacted to produce this book.

My friends Clare Furneaux and Dermot Shields were unfailingly generous with their hospitality, not to mention computer resources, during more visits than they will want to reciprocate. Vicki Briault Manus and Charlotte Ward read the entire text in draft. Their comments, and the more general advice offered by Colin Haycraft, my publisher, made the final version a substantial improvement on the first. I am grateful to Jonathan Earl at Duckworth for suggesting the title.

Finally, my debt to Gwen Morris, most patient of partners, is impossible to measure – or so I hope. She is the heroine of *The Alternative Bible*.

D.V.

1

Genesis

1

In the beginning God created the heaven and the earth. And the earth was without form, and void; and darkness was upon the face of the deep. And the Spirit of God moved upon the face of the waters. And God said, Let there be light: and there was light.

I'm not sure that it was really as easy as that, but it all happened a very long time ago. By his account God needed less than a week to create everything, though with no sun until the fourth day it must have been hard to keep track of the time.

At any rate, Day and Night were created, and ***the evening and the morning were the first day.*** Next God made a vault – which sometimes leaks – to divide the waters above the sky from the waters below: the second day. Then came the dry land, with plants: the third day. ***And God made two great lights; the greater light to rule the day, and the lesser light to rule the night: he made the stars also***: the fourth day. The birds and sea creatures followed: the fifth day. Finally, on the sixth day, came the animals.

And God saw that it was good. And God said, Let us make man in our image, after our likeness. I don't like to appear immodest, but who do you suppose the 'us' refers to? We angels did our best to help. To put the finishing touches on the new being – and it was a marvellous idea – ***male and female created he them. And God blessed them, and God said unto them, Be fruitful, and multiply, and replenish the earth, and subdue it: and have dominion over the fish of the sea, and over the fowl of the air, and over every living thing that moveth upon the earth.*** In retrospect, giving humans *carte blanche* was perhaps unwise.

2

And on the seventh day God ended his work which he had made; and he rested, for once.

There's another angle on the story of Creation; in this version the earth initially lacks vegetation, which might suggest that the third day had not been a success. To put matters right, ***the LORD God formed man of the dust of the ground, and breathed into his nostrils the breath of life; and man became a living soul. And the LORD God planted a garden eastward in Eden***, appointing the man gardener. This was a magical garden, containing such exotic plants as the tree of life, and through it ran a magical river, providing the source of four actual rivers.

God told the man to eat what he liked, ***But of the tree of the knowledge of good and evil, thou shalt not eat of it: for in the day that thou eatest thereof thou shalt surely die.*** That wasn't quite true, as it happens, but then the fellow wouldn't have known what 'death' was anyway.

But before I get ahead of myself, ***the LORD God said, It is not good that the man should be alone; I will make him an help meet for him.*** This hint of domestic service sounded suspect to me, and who needed help in Eden anyway? Still, we came up with a fitting design. Elsewhere, I confess, we showed less imagination: our name for him (Adam, meaning 'Man') was the equivalent of calling a cat Kitty.

So ***the LORD God caused a deep sleep to fall upon Adam, and he slept: and he took one of his ribs, and closed up the flesh instead thereof. And the rib, which the LORD God had taken from man, made he a woman.*** If that doesn't seem an auspicious start, consider that Adam had been made from mud. She was more sophisticated from the outset.

Naturally the man was egotistical enough to declare that ***This is now bone of my bones, and flesh of my flesh: she shall be called Woman.*** And he should have been called Mudthing, the silly dolt.

Making man and woman as he did, God clearly intended them to spend a reasonable amount of time attached. ***Therefore shall a man leave his father and his mother, and shall cleave unto his wife: and they shall be one flesh. And they were both naked, the man and his wife, and were not ashamed.*** Fashion hadn't been invented yet.

3 Now I remember those two in the Garden of Eden, and to be candid they were poor company. Why have a brain if you can't use it? So I wasn't too sorry that the serpent, who ***was more subtil than any beast of the field***, got up to mischief. He just went to the woman and told her the truth, that eating the forbidden fruit wouldn't kill them, that ***Your eyes shall be opened, and ye shall be as gods, knowing good and evil.*** Unfortunately they were not as bright as I had hoped, because immediately after eating the fruit ***they sewed fig leaves together, and made themselves aprons***, or loincloths (or even breeches, according to one account).

You know what followed. ***They heard the voice of the LORD God walking in the garden in the cool of the day.*** Adam tried to hide because it suddenly seemed bad form to appear starkers, God got suspicious, and then the recriminations started. Adam said ***The woman whom thou gavest to be with me, she gave me of the tree, and I did eat. ... And the woman said, The serpent beguiled me, and I did eat.*** But the poor serpent never had a chance.

And the LORD God said unto the serpent, Because thou hast done this, thou art cursed above all cattle, and above every beast of the field; upon thy belly shalt thou go, and dust shalt thou eat all the days of thy life. I felt sorry for him, but frankly, without any legs it made more sense for him to crawl on his belly anyway. Worse was the rupture in relations with humankind; in future, God ordained, ***it shall bruise thy head, and thou shalt bruise his heel.***

The man and woman bore the brunt of divine fury. She was told that ***In sorrow thou shalt bring forth children*** (the little horrors); ***and thy desire shall be to thy husband*** (if you're lucky), ***and he shall rule over thee*** (we'll see about that).

Adam was condemned to hard labour: to toil ***all the days of your life ... In the sweat of thy face shalt thou eat bread, till thou return unto the ground; for out***

of it wast thou taken: for dust thou art, and unto dust shalt thou return. And Adam called his wife's name Eve – that is, 'Life' – ***because she was the mother of all living.*** (Which showed great foresight, as just then she was the mother of no one at all.) In fact they can't have been very popular with other living things, having brought about the end of paradise on earth.

God's comment at the time may seem mysterious unless you realise that it was addressed to me: ***Behold, the man is become as one of us, to know good and evil: and now, lest he put forth his hand, and take also of the tree of life, and eat, and live for ever***, we'll have to throw them out of Eden. Competition was out of the question; having me around was probably bad enough. ***So he drove out the man; and he placed at the east of the garden of Eden Cherubims, and a flaming sword which turned every way, to keep the way of the tree of life.***

STORMY WEATHER

Having left home Adam and Eve started a family, as will happen. They had two sons, Cain and Abel; ***Abel was a keeper of sheep, but Cain was a tiller of the ground.*** Regrettably God played favourites. He was happy with offerings of lamb, while rejecting Cain's vegetarian fare: a traditionalist if ever there was one. 4

Beside himself with fury, Cain killed Abel out in the fields. When God asked where he might find Abel, Cain said ***I know not: Am I my brother's keeper?*** To which God responded, ***What hast thou done? the voice of thy brother's blood crieth unto me from the ground ... a fugitive and a vagabond shalt thou be in the earth.*** God was well and truly cross, because he had no sooner expelled Adam and Eve from one place than he had to deport Cain from the next. At this rate he was going to run out of space before he had a congregation.

Cain protested that ***My punishment is greater than I can bear***; he was terrified of how other people (what other people?) might treat him. Thus ***the LORD set a mark upon Cain, lest any finding him should kill him. And Cain went out from the presence of the LORD, and dwelt in the land of Nod.*** Remarkably enough he found a wife, which just goes to show that no one's cause is hopeless.

The descendants of Cain included ***Jabal: he was the father of such as dwell in tents***, and his brother ***Jubal: he was the father of all such as handle the harp and organ***, and again Tubal-cain, the original blacksmith. As for Adam and Eve, they had another son, named Seth, to replace the one they had lost. After this the begats began in earnest, the genealogy being continued down to Noah with all the men living nine hundred years or more, begetting the whole time. Only poor old Enoch, who ***walked with God***, died prematurely at the age of 365. His son Methuselah, though, became the record holder by surviving to 969. 5

The antediluvian world was an interesting place. ***There were giants in the earth in those days; and also after that, when the sons of God came in unto the daughters of men, and they bare children to them, the same became mighty men*** 6

which were of old, men of renown. It would be more accurate to say 'when the sons of the gods had intercourse' etc. Everyone was in on the act, and that was partly what God didn't like.

Humans had not so far been a big success, but I was taken aback when God decided to exterminate them (with the rest of nature to boot). He simply said ***I will destroy man whom I have created from the face of the earth; both man, and beast, and the creeping thing, and the fowls of the air; for it repenteth me that I have made them.*** These things happen.

God instructed the faithful Noah to ***Make thee an ark of gopher wood***, in which his family and other animals would escape, for ***of every living thing of all flesh,*** 7 ***two of every sort shalt thou bring into the ark.*** Confusingly, though, some favoured species were allowed seven pairs, not just one.

We don't need to linger on events. When the day came ***There went in two and two unto Noah into the ark, the male and the female.*** At the same time as water gushed from the ground, ***the rain was upon the earth forty days and forty nights.*** 8 The entire earth was submerged and it was a year before they could emerge from the ark.

A dove was sent out at weekly intervals after they grounded on a mountain. The first time she ***found no rest for the sole of her foot***, while at the next ***lo, in her mouth was an olive leaf pluckt off***; on the third attempt she did not return. Nonetheless, everyone stayed on board until God gave the all-clear.

Perhaps he felt a twinge of regret: ***The LORD said in his heart, I will not again curse the ground any more for man's sake; for the imagination of man's heart is evil from his youth; neither will I again smite any more every thing living, as I have done. While the earth remaineth, seedtime and harvest, and cold and heat, and summer and winter, and day and night shall not cease.*** Coming from someone who had just annihilated the whole world, I doubt that mention of the evil streak in man went down very well.

9 He told Noah that killing people is wrong. ***At the hand of every man's brother will I require the life of man. Whoso sheddeth man's blood, by man shall his blood be shed: for in the image of God made he man.*** Whereupon he gave instructions that they should be fruitful and multiply, which was where we came in.

God agreed never again to flood the earth, and offered the rainbow as a sign of good faith. ***This is the token of the covenant which I make between me and you and every living creature that is with you, for perpetual generations: I do set my bow in the cloud.***

Noah was supposedly the best man of his generation, which was why he alone had been saved from the Flood. 'Best' clearly didn't mean 'perfect', however. One day his son Ham found him drunk and naked in his tent. Ham – who was rather shocked, his father being over 600 years old – told his two brothers. These two prigs backed into the tent to cover Noah (though on reflection I might avoid looking at a naked 600-year-old myself).

Instead of feeling properly ashamed of himself when he woke up, the old grouch cursed Ham's son Canaan: ***a servant of servants shall he be unto his brethren.*** Not what I would call justice. The descendants of Canaan must have felt the same, because in later years they were always worshipping someone other than God.

Some unexciting genealogies showed the derivation of all the separate nations from the sons of Noah. One of Ham's grandsons is the only name anyone remembers: ***Even as Nimrod the mighty hunter before the LORD.*** 10

At that time ***the whole earth was of one language, and of one speech.*** During their migrations, people settled in a plain where they decided to build a tower ***whose top may reach unto heaven.*** God was not happy with this kind of ambition. He put it to me that ***now nothing will be restrained from them, which they have imagined to do. Go to, let us go down, and there confound their language, that they may not understand one another's speech.*** That was the way to stop construction, and so that's what he did. ***Therefore is the name of it called Babel,*** and henceforth the world was a babble of different languages. 11

ABRAHAM

And so to the patriarchs and matriarchs. God had decided on his strategy: to choose one people, the descendants of one man and one woman, and to protect them in return for their faith and obedience. The founder of the whole clan was a man named Abram, who was later renamed Abraham, and his wife Sarai, who became Sarah. God told him ***Get thee out of thy country, and from thy kindred, and from thy father's house, unto a land that I will shew thee: And I will make of thee a great nation, and I will bless thee, and make thy name great.*** So leave they did, passing through Canaan, which God said would one day be theirs, and on eventually to Egypt. 12

The Egyptians, never in God's good books, were given a foretaste of things to come. Abram had passed off Sarai as his sister, because he feared that he might not live long as the husband of a beautiful woman who was bound to be desired by others. As she was at least 65 years old at the time this seems hard to credit, but subsequent events show that he was not altogether deluded. Pharaoh did indeed come to hear of her, and she was taken into his harem, with Abram being given large gifts. A few God-sent plagues later and Pharaoh was only too ready to send them packing with the reproachful question to Abram: ***why didst thou not tell me that she was thy wife?***

Abram had been travelling with a nephew named Lot. Once back in Canaan Abram suggested that they split up; their flocks were too large to graze on the same land. ***Let there be no strife, I pray thee, between me and thee, and between my herdmen and thy herdmen; for we be brethren.*** Thus he gave Lot his choice of direction. Lot chose the plain of Jordan, towards the cities of Sodom and Gomorrah; it seemed a good idea at the time. ***Abram dwelled in the land of Canaan, and Lot*** 13

dwelled in the cities of the plain, and pitched his tent toward Sodom.

14 As luck would have it, the cities around the Dead Sea, including Sodom, were sacked by their enemies, and Lot was carried off. Abram set out with 318 servants and managed to retake all the goods and people from their captors. The king of Sodom offered Abram the booty, which he declined (somewhat ungraciously: ***I will not take any thing that is thine, lest thou shouldest say, I have made Abram rich***).

15 Abram was not a happy man. God continued to promise him descendants as numerous as the stars, and yet his wife was barren. After asking God to send him a sign, ***a deep sleep fell upon Abram; and, lo, an horror of great darkness fell upon him***; he was given a glimpse of the future of his tribe, as well as the news that he himself would only ***be buried in a good old age***. Given his age at the time, that was of limited reassurance.

16 And still ***Sarai Abram's wife bare him no children***. Finally, in the hope of producing an heir, she suggested that he take her Egyptian handmaid Hagar as his mistress. This he did, and Hagar became pregnant. Regrettably the new arrangement did nothing for domestic harmony. Hagar was insolent to Sarai, Sarai ill-treated Hagar. Hagar even tried to run away, but God sent an angel – me, in fact – to intercept her. I announced that she would have a son, to be called Ishmael, who would be like a wild ass: ***his hand will be against every man, and every man's hand against him***. Not encouraging news, but she did go back.

17 Thirteen years on, God was ready. He told Abram that from henceforth his name would be Abraham, meaning father of a multitude; nations and even kings would descend from him. ***And I will establish my covenant between me and thee and thy seed after thee in their generations for an everlasting covenant, to be a God unto thee, and to thy seed after thee***. The land of Canaan would become their permanent possession. They for their part would circumcise themselves, making a sign of the covenant in their flesh. Normally this would be done to male children eight days after birth, but Abraham had to undergo the operation at the age of 99. That's faith for you.

God went on to rename Sarai 'Sarah', meaning princess, and announced that she would have a son, and be ***a mother of nations***. In those days people weren't always on their best behaviour with God, and Abraham ***fell upon his face, and laughed, and said in his heart, Shall a child be born unto him that is an hundred years old? and shall Sarah, that is ninety years old, bear?*** But God insisted that the following year they would have a son, to be named Isaac. Though Ishmael would also have many descendants, it was through Isaac that the covenant would be fulfilled.

A Trip to Sodom

18 Soon thereafter three strangers appeared while Abraham was sitting in front of his tent. One of them was God in disguise, and another was me. Abraham probably

wasn't fooled, and anyway pressed refreshments on us: ***My Lord, if now I have found favour in thy sight, pass not away, I pray thee, from thy servant.*** Sarah was amused to hear God remark that she would soon have a son. After all, ***Abraham and Sarah were old and well stricken in age; and it ceased to be with Sarah after the manner of women. Therefore Sarah laughed within herself, saying, After I am waxed old shall I have pleasure, my lord being old also?*** Pleasure, by all means; children, generally not.

God scolded her, saying ***Is any thing too hard for the LORD?*** (Perhaps not, but people do wonder why he doesn't exert himself more.) She nervously denied laughing, and he reposted ***Nay, but thou didst laugh.***

As we set out on our way, God decided to tell Abraham what we were up to. He had heard some very poor reports of Sodom and Gomorrah, and was going to see the cities for himself. Knowing what God was like, Abraham immediately feared the worst. What if there were 50 righteous people there? You wouldn't ***slay the righteous with the wicked***, Abraham said, ***Shall not the Judge of all the earth do right?*** God could hardly demur, and so conceded: ***If I find in Sodom fifty righteous within the city, then I will spare all the place for their sakes.***

Abraham didn't lack guts; having gained the principle, he asked – What if there are only 45 good men? Or 40? Or 30? Or 20? And each time God granted that he would then spare the city. Realising that he was on thin ice, Abraham finally blurted out ***Oh let not the Lord be angry, and I will speak yet but this once: Peradventure ten shall be found there.*** To which God said, I will not destroy it for ten's sake. It was a deal.

19

Unfortunately Abraham had been wasting his time: the only man worth saving in Sodom was his nephew Lot. (God didn't seem to want us to count the women.) When we arrived in town Lot urged his hospitality on us. Before we had even gone to bed, though, all the men in Sodom surrounded the house and called on Lot to hand us over for their sexual satisfaction. Heaven knows why they were so desperate. Lot went out, ***And said, I pray you, brethren, do not so wickedly. Behold now, I have two daughters which have not known man; let me, I pray you, bring them out unto you, and do ye to them as is good in your eyes: only unto these men do nothing.***

They didn't like his speech nor, apparently, his daughters, because they proceeded to try to break down the door. We had to pull Lot back in and strike blind everyone outside. At dawn we practically dragged him out of the city with his wife and two daughters – but not his sons-in-law, who thought it was all a joke – telling them on no account to look back. ***Then the LORD rained upon Sodom and upon Gomorrah brimstone and fire***, and that was that. Unfortunately for Lot, who had been so heroic, ***his wife looked back from behind him, and she became a pillar of salt***. God didn't tolerate insubordination.

After their escape from Sodom Lot lived in a mountain cave with his two daughters. The women were quite family-minded, but they lacked men – having come from Sodom, this must have been a familiar problem. Each in turn, therefore, got her father drunk and then went to bed with him. ***Thus were both the daughters of Lot with child by their father***, and both had sons who founded nations.

20 Meanwhile, Abraham continued his travels, still passing off Sarah as his sister. There was another incident of a king claiming her. Once again God stepped in to smooth things over, but this time Abraham had to explain that Sarah really was his sister, or at any rate half-sister: ***she is the daughter of my father, but not the daughter of my mother; and she became my wife***. In this particular period God seemed to be relaxed about incest.

Isaac

21 Sarah had her son Isaac as promised. When the domestic strife continued, Sarah pestered Abraham to send Hagar and Ishmael away. He was reluctant, but God told him to go ahead. Off they went, and so far as I know Abraham never saw them again. Indeed, they only narrowly avoided never being seen by anyone again, coming close to death in the wilderness before God sent me out to save them.

22 Some years passed. God decided to put Abraham to the test, telling him to make a burnt offering of his son Isaac. Abraham didn't say a word; he saddled the ass and set out. When after three days they reached their destination, Abraham gave his son the wood to carry up the mountain.

And Isaac spake unto Abraham his father, and said, My father: and he said, Here am I, my son. And he said, Behold the fire and the wood: but where is the lamb for a burnt offering? And Abraham said, My son, God will provide himself a lamb for a burnt offering: so they went both of them together. And they came to the place which God had told him of; and Abraham built an altar there, and laid the wood in order, and bound Isaac his son, and laid him on the altar upon the wood. And Abraham stretched forth his hand, and took the knife to slay his son. And the angel of the LORD called unto him out of heaven, and said, Abraham, Abraham: and he said, Here am I. And he said, Lay not thine hand upon the lad, neither do thou any thing unto him: for now I know that thou fearest God, seeing thou hast not withheld thy son, thine only son from me. And Abraham lifted up his eyes, and looked, and behold behind him a ram caught in a thicket by his horns: and Abraham went and took the ram, and offered him up for a burnt offering in the stead of his son.

God blessed them, reiterating his promises of future greatness. I couldn't help but be affected by Abraham's terrifying obedience, and if God wanted to stop child sacrifice, the point was made. I was uncomfortable, though, with inflicting that much anguish in bad faith.

23 Sarah died, and Abraham started to feel his age. Isaac was now forty and still
24 unmarried. There were plenty of women in Canaan, but Abraham didn't like the idea of his son marrying out of the tribe. He instructed a servant to go back to the country of his own kin to find a wife for Isaac.

This the servant did, with great success. When he arrived in the city he led his camels to the well, and said to God ***let it come to pass, that the damsel to whom I shall say, Let down thy pitcher, I pray thee, that I may drink; and she shall say, Drink, and I will give thy camels drink also: let the same be she that thou hast appointed for thy servant Isaac.*** The words were hardly out of his mouth when a beautiful virgin named Rebekah, who just happened to be the granddaughter of Abraham's brother, came to the well. The servant was up to her in a flash to ask for a drink from her pitcher, and being a well brought up young woman, she came back with the magic words: ***I will draw water for thy camels also.***

It was smooth sailing from there on in. The servant put a ring in her nose and heavy bracelets around her wrists, and was no doubt tempted to throw her over his camel then and there. In keeping with propriety, however, he went back to her house and put his proposal to the family. Rebekah's father and brother observed that as it hardly seemed to matter what they thought, he had better take her back to Isaac with their blessings.

That was all the messenger needed to hear, and the next morning he suggested that they be off without further ado. Although the prospective in-laws wanted a last few days with their daughter, he wasn't willing to wait. Perhaps he was afraid that his luck might run out.

Back in Canaan the pace didn't let up. Isaac happened to be outside as they approached on the camels. (The authorised version is that ***Isaac went out to meditate in the field at the eventide***, but the original records suggest that he had gone out to relieve himself.) Rebekah barely had time to jump down and put on her veil. ***And Isaac brought her into his mother Sarah's tent, and took Rebekah, and she became his wife; and he loved her: and Isaac was comforted after his mother's death.***

25

Abraham was comforted, too, in marrying another wife, by whom he had six more children. He sent the sons he had had by assorted concubines away to the east, so as not to get in Isaac's way. Finally, at the age of 175, ***Abraham gave up the ghost, and died in a good old age, an old man, and full of years; and was gathered to his people.***

Rebekah suffered from infertility, a chronic problem among the matriarchs. This time God stepped in after a mere twenty years. When Rebekah expressed alarm at the struggling in her womb, he told her that she would have twins, of whom ***the elder shall serve the younger.*** They weren't identical, or even very similar. The first was Esau, red and hairy, who grew up to be ***a cunning hunter, a man of the field.*** The second was Jacob, ***a plain man, dwelling in tents. And Isaac loved Esau, because he did eat of his venison: but Rebekah loved Jacob.***

If Isaac's stomach ruled his heart, Esau's stomach ruled his head. One day when he came in from the fields, faint with hunger, he asked for some of the lentil soup that was cooking. Jacob demanded the inheritance of the first born in return, and Esau was sufficiently rash to agree; ***he sold his birthright unto Jacob. Then Jacob gave Esau bread and pottage of lentiles;*** it was an expensive mess of pottage.

26 Although life was normal enough for Isaac and Rebekah, they relived certain bizarre experiences of Abraham and Sarah. Isaac was passing off his wife as his sister in the very kingdom where his father had done the same; ***And it came to pass, when he had been there a long time, that Abimelech king of the Philistines looked out at a window, and saw, and, behold, Isaac was sporting with Rebekah his wife. And Abimelech called Isaac, and said, Behold, of a surety she is thy wife: and how saidst thou, She is my sister?*** I imagine the poor fellow never believed anyone who claimed to be with his sister again.

In keeping with family tradition Esau didn't marry until he was forty, but then went overboard by taking two wives, both of them Hittites to boot. ***Which were a grief of mind unto Isaac and to Rebekah***, who like many parents had nothing against members of other ethnic groups just so long as they didn't become in-laws.

JACOB HAS FAMILY PROBLEMS

27 Jacob and Rebekah could run rings around the other two in the family. ***When Isaac was old, and his eyes were dim, so that he could not see, he called Esau his eldest son and said unto him ... take, I pray thee, thy weapons, thy quiver and thy bow, and go out to the field, and take me some venison; and make me savoury meat, such as I love, and bring it to me, that I may eat; that my soul may bless thee before I die.*** Rebekah overheard, and devised a plan for Jacob to receive his father's blessing. Jacob pointed out that ***Esau my brother is a hairy man, and I am a smooth man***; smooth in more than ways than one. But Rebekah wasn't going to let that stop her. Having prepared goat meat to taste like venison, she dressed Jacob in Esau's clothes and ***put the skins of the kids of the goats upon his hands, and upon the smooth of his neck.***

Thus attired, and presumably feeling rather ridiculous, Jacob went in to see his father. Isaac was at first suspicious, noting that ***The voice is Jacob's voice, but the hands are the hands of Esau.*** The evidence of his nose persuaded him: ***See, the smell of my son is as the smell of a field which the LORD hath blessed.*** And so Jacob received the blessing: ***Let people serve thee, and nations bow down to thee: be lord over thy brethren, and let thy mother's sons bow down to thee.***

Jacob was hardly out the door when poor dumb Esau walked in with his real venison, asking to be blessed. Consternation: ***Thy brother came with subtilty, and hath taken away thy blessing.*** I expected Isaac to declare it void because fraudulently obtained, but he said that what had been done could not be undone. Esau told himself that ***The days of mourning for my father are at hand; then will I slay my brother Jacob***: they weren't a high-minded lot. Rebekah caught wind of this threat, and told Jacob to go and stay with her brother Laban until things cooled off.

Rebekah put it to Isaac that the local women were awful, and that her life 28 wouldn't be worth living if Jacob married one of them. Isaac told his son to keep things in the family: he should go to visit his uncle Laban and marry one of his daughters. When Esau realised that he had committed a *faux pas* in marrying two women of Canaan, the great clod took as his third wife a daughter of his uncle Ishmael. Being three-quarters Egyptian, it hardly seems likely that this new woman was a greater success with the parents than the first two had been.

On his first night away from home, Jacob slept under the stars with a stone for a pillow. In a dream he saw ***a ladder set up on the earth, and the top of it reached to heaven: and behold the angels of God ascending and descending on it.*** God was above, repeating the promise that one day the whole land would belong to him and to his descendants. ***I will not leave thee, until I have done that which I have spoken to thee of.*** This 'until' worried me; did he intend to leave once the promise had been fulfilled? Time would tell.

Jacob made his pillow into a pillar, and consecrated it, declaring that ***Surely the LORD is in this place; and I knew it not ... this is none other but the house of God, and this is the gate of heaven.*** In the great tradition of 'If you do this, I'll do that' prayer-bargaining, Jacob vowed that if God looked after him, then ***of all that thou shalt give me I will surely give the tenth unto thee.*** Expressed like that it sounds like a bad deal for God ('you give me ten, I'll give you one'), but God needed a labour force and was happy to work on commission.

29

Following in the footsteps of his father's servant, Jacob had to go no further than the local well to meet his future wife. Although the custom of the country was that the stone covering the well would not be rolled back until all the flocks had come in, Jacob no sooner saw his cousin Rachel appear with her sheep than he leapt up and rolled the stone from the well's mouth. Sensitivity to native tradition wasn't one of his virtues.

Laban was happy to take in his nephew. Jacob offered to work seven years in return for the hand of Rachel, Laban's younger daughter, who ***was beautiful and well favoured.*** Laban knew a good deal when he saw one: ***It is better that I give her to thee, than that I should give her to another man: abide with me. And Jacob served seven years for Rachel; and they seemed unto him but a few days, for the love he had to her.***

The great day arrived, and Jacob claimed his reward that night. Not until the following morning did he notice that he had just married, not Rachel, but her elder sister Leah: Laban had tricked him. The whole family could be a trial at times, I must say. When Jacob protested Laban offered the feeble excuse that it would have been improper to provide his younger daughter with a husband before the elder. He proposed to allow Jacob to marry Rachel as well at the end of the week, providing that he agree to work another seven years. Remarkably, Jacob accepted and performed the contract. I wouldn't have blamed him for eloping.

As normal with matriarchs in early married life, Rachel was barren. Still, she was Jacob's favourite, and Leah's only consolation was her fecundity. Thereupon first Rachel, and then Leah, gave Jacob their handmaids on whom to father further children, after which Leah found her fertility renewed, and ultimately even Rachel became pregnant. When the dust settled Jacob had eleven sons and one daughter.

30

Having served his time with Laban, Jacob was starting to think about leaving. Laban urged him to name his terms to stay on. What Jacob proposed, therefore, was that he continue to look after all the flocks, breeding from the black sheep and the spotted goats for himself while leaving all the others for his father-in-law. The deal was done, but then the trickery started again.

Laban removed all the spotted goats and black rams he could lay his hands on, sending them off with his sons. Jacob resorted to what struck me as black magic, though perhaps it was just God being humorous. Peeling the bark from rods of wood to make them striped, he fixed the staves by the watering troughs. Exactly what the sheep and goats did with these rods is fortunately vague, but the result was that more dark, striped and spotted animals were conceived. Jacob became a wealthy man.

31 Family relations were soured, and twenty years after his arrival Jacob decided (with a push from God) that it was time to leave. Without saying good-bye to Laban, he moved out with wives, flocks, and his whole household. Laban set out in hot pursuit, angry at Jacob's lack of civility, and at the theft of his household gods.

Unbeknownst to her husband, Rachel was the culprit. When Jacob invited Laban to search the tent, she hid the idols in a camel bag and sat on it; ***And she said to her father, Let it not displease my lord that I cannot rise up before thee; for the custom of women is upon me. And he searched, but found not the images.*** God seemed to be having only limited success in suppressing idolatry, even among his special clan.

Jacob and Laban consented to a truce based on permanent separation. They gathered a pile of stones to serve as a witness and watch-tower, asking that ***The LORD watch between me and thee, when we are absent one from another.*** Having each agreed to stay on his own side of the tower, they went their separate ways. That's family for you.

JACOB BECOMES ISRAEL

32 Jacob feared the ill-will of another relative: his brother Esau, who apparently was on his way with four hundred men. Jacob divided everyone and everything with him into two groups, reasoning that one might escape even if the other were attacked. In a more positive mood he organised several herds of goats, sheep, camels, cattle and donkeys as an avant-garde, giving orders that when Esau asked about each successive herd to pass, the herders should reply ***They be thy servant Jacob's; it is a present sent unto my lord Esau.*** Appeasement seemed worth a try.

Before the encounter with Esau, we arranged something special for Jacob. His whole household forded a river at night, ***And Jacob was left alone; and there wrestled a man with him until the breaking of the day.*** The unknown assailant struggled without success, first to throw Jacob, and then just to free himself. Jacob said ***I will not let thee go, except thou bless me***, and in turn was told: ***Thy name***

shall be called no more Jacob, but Israel: for as a prince hast thou power with God and with men, and hast prevailed.

Jacob understood: ***I have seen God face to face, and my life is preserved.*** His new name, Israel, meant 'God strove'. God didn't let him get away scot-free, though; he had struck Jacob and dislocated his hip. ***Therefore the children of Israel eat not of the sinew which shrank, which is upon the hollow of the thigh, unto this day: because he touched the hollow of Jacob's thigh in the sinew.***

33

The meeting with his brother seemed an anticlimax. Apparently the grudge had been forgotten, because ***Esau ran to meet him, and embraced him, and fell on his neck, and kissed him: and they wept.*** Esau urged that they continue their journey together. Explaining that his children and flocks could not travel quickly, Jacob said that they would catch up with him. In the event, however, Jacob went and settled somewhere else entirely. So much for the reconciliation.

34

Trouble was never far away. Jacob's only daughter, Dinah, went out visiting; when a son of the local prince ***saw her, he took her, and lay with her, and defiled her. And his soul clave unto Dinah the daughter of Jacob, and he loved the damsel, and spake kindly unto the damsel.*** He wanted to marry her. His father the prince told Jacob's family that they could name their price, take wives from among his people, live and prosper in his country, if they would just let his son marry Dinah.

This offer did nothing to mollify Jacob's sons, who were seething at the seduction of their sister, and they set a trap. The union could only go ahead, they told the prince, if all his men became circumcised. This was readily accepted, and everyone was duly doctored. It's amazing what people will do for love – even someone else's.

Before the effects of the operation had worn off, two of Dinah's brothers came into town and killed every man in it. The other brothers followed; ***And all their wealth, and all their little ones, and their wives took they captive, and spoiled even all that was in the house.***

Jacob was shocked. He saw that his reputation would ***stink among the inhabitants of the land***, putting his own family at risk. His sons could only say, ***Should he deal with our sister as with an harlot?***, ignoring the evident desire to make an honest woman of her.

35

It seemed prudent to move on; the people in the neighbouring towns were too cowed to give them any trouble as they went. At the spot where he had had his dream years earlier, Jacob was again visited by God, who confirmed that ***thy name shall not be called any more Jacob, but Israel ... a nation and a company of nations shall be of thee, and kings shall come out of thy loins.*** All his descendants would belong to this one people (whereas Abraham's sons and grandsons founded different nations). The dramas on the rest of their journey were domestic. First Rachel went into labour and died in childbirth, the baby Benjamin surviving as Jacob's twelfth and last son. Then it came out that Jacob's eldest son Reuben had slept with Rachel's maid, the mother of two of his half-brothers; usurping your father's concubine was a serious matter. There was one more jolt in store for Jacob, for at the age of 180 his father ***Isaac gave up the ghost, and died, and was gathered unto his people, being old and full of days: and his sons Esau and Jacob buried him.***

36 The death of the great man provided an excuse to recount a few genealogies. Just occasionally real life would surface in the midst of the names: there was a certain Anah, for example, and ***this was that Anah that found the mules in the wilderness.*** Nothing else will ever be known about this man, and yet which other mule-finder has had his name recorded for all time?

JOSEPH MAKES A NAME FOR HIMSELF

37 ***And Jacob dwelt in the land wherein his father was a stranger, in the land of Canaan.*** Joseph, the second youngest of Jacob's sons and (with Benjamin) the only other child of Rachel, was 17. ***Now Israel loved Joseph more than all his children, because he was the son of his old age: and he made him a coat of many colours.*** According to my recollection he simply made him a long-sleeved garment, but the misunderstanding is too wonderful to disappear.

His brothers were jealous, and the fact that Joseph was a conceited adolescent didn't help. He would tell them dreams: ***we were binding sheaves in the field, and, lo, my sheaf arose, and also stood upright; and, behold, your sheaves stood round about, and made obeisance to my sheaf.*** To rub it in, he tried out another on his father and eleven brothers: ***behold, the sun and the moon and the eleven stars made obeisance to me.*** Even his father didn't like that one.

Joseph's brothers were a little touchy about all this; the next thing I knew they were conspiring to kill him. One day when he had been sent out with a message from their father, ***they said to one another, Behold, this dreamer cometh. Come now therefore, and let us slay him, and cast him into some pit, and we will say, Some evil beast hath devoured him: and we shall see what will become of his dreams. So they stript Joseph out of his coat, his coat of many colours,*** but thanks to Reuben he was merely thrown into a pit, not murdered.

From there Joseph was taken and sold, for twenty pieces of silver, to a caravan going to Egypt. His brothers dipped his coat in goat's blood before taking it back to their father. ***And Jacob rent his clothes, and put sackcloth upon his loins, and mourned for his son many days ... he refused to be comforted.*** I didn't think much of the sons, to put their father through such misery.

38 They were a tricky lot, though. Judah, one of the brothers, had three sons. ***And Er, Judah's firstborn, was wicked in the sight of the LORD; and the LORD slew him.*** One should only be wicked discreetly. Anyway, Judah told his second son, Onan, to obey custom and to father children on his brother's widow. ***And Onan knew that the seed should not be his; and it came to pass, when he went in unto his brother's wife, that he spilled it on the ground, lest that he should give seed***

to his brother. In God's view using the withdrawal method was not playing the game, ***wherefore he slew him also.*** Suspecting that the prospects for his young third son were none too bright, Judah sent the widow back to her father until the boy had come of age.

That time came and went without Judah sending for the widow. One day, therefore, she posed as a prostitute when he was passing. Judah wasn't bashful, saying ***Go to, I pray thee, let me come in unto thee; (for he knew not that she was his daughter in law.)*** She became pregnant, and before long her father-in-law was told that ***she is with child by whoredom. And Judah said, Bring her forth, and let her be burnt.*** In the best courtroom drama style she thereupon produced various possessions left by her 'client', and Judah confessed that he was most to blame, having not sent her his third son.

39 In Egypt, meanwhile, Joseph was also a victim of sexual intrigue. He had been sold to a captain of Pharaoh's guard named Potiphar who was sufficiently impressed with his talents (for ***the LORD made all that he did to prosper in his hand***) to put him in charge of the household. I believe that Potiphar was a eunuch, which may help to explain why Joseph was sexually harassed by his unfortunate wife. Joseph always excused himself, of course, but one day they were alone in the house. ***And she caught him by his garment, saying, Lie with me: and he left his garment in her hand, and fled, and got him out.*** In revenge for his lack of gallantry she accused him of attempted rape, and Joseph found himself in prison.

40 With him behind bars were Pharaoh's chief butler and baker. One night the butler dreamt that a vine with three branches bore fruit, and that he pressed the grapes into Pharaoh's cup. Joseph told him that the three branches represented three days, within which time he would be released and restored to his position.

Encouraged, the baker described a similar dream in which he carried three baskets on his head, while out of the uppermost basket birds ate the baked goods intended for Pharaoh. The interpretation must have made him wish he had kept quiet: ***within three days shall Pharaoh lift up thy head from off thee, and shall hang thee on a tree; and the birds shall eat thy flesh from off thee.*** And so it happened, to each of them as predicted. Despite this devastating demonstration of psychic power, and his specific request for a good word to Pharaoh on his behalf, ***Yet did not the chief butler remember Joseph, but forgat him.***

41 God has made an early end of people for less, but two years later the butler had a chance to redeem himself. Pharaoh had had two dreams that none of the magicians or wise men in Egypt could interpret. The butler mentioned Joseph, who was brought out, cleaned up and taken to hear Pharaoh's dreams. The first was of seeing seven fat cows grazing, followed by seven scrawny cows; ***And the lean and the ill favoured kine did eat up the first seven fat kine,*** but without becoming any better looking as a result. In the second dream seven good ears of corn were devoured by seven withered ears.

Joseph announced that the two dreams had the same meaning. The plump cows and corn represented seven years of plenty, ***And the seven thin and ill favoured***

kine ... and the seven empty ears blasted with the east wind shall be seven years of famine. The years of bad harvests would follow the good, ***and God will shortly bring it to pass.*** Joseph recommended that Pharaoh appoint someone reliable to oversee the creation of stockpiles during the period of plenty.

In the best tradition of political advice and management consultancy, Joseph was offered the job. Thus, at the age of 30 and a few hours after leaving prison, he became the second most powerful man in the country, for Pharaoh told him ***without thee shall no man lift up his hand or foot in all the land of Egypt ... And Joseph gathered corn as the sand of the sea, very much, until he left numbering.*** He did, however, have time to marry the daughter of an Egyptian priest and to father two sons. When the bad years began the storehouses were opened, and people came from all over to buy food.

The reunion in Egypt

42 ***Now when Jacob saw that there was corn in Egypt*** he sent his sons to buy some, keeping only Benjamin at home. On arriving they bowed down before Joseph without recognising him as their brother. He for his part had no intention of rushing into a reunion. He ***said unto them, Ye are spies; to see the nakedness of the land ye are come***, and threw them into prison. At the end of three days he released all except Simeon, the second-eldest, telling them that if they returned with their youngest brother he would believe their innocence. They left in a sombre mood, made worse by the compromising discovery that the silver used to pay for the food was back in their packs.

Jacob at first refused to let them go back, saying that if anything should happen to Benjamin, ***then shall ye bring down my gray hairs with sorrow to the grave.***
43 Finally, however, the threat of starvation forced him to relent.

When all the brothers returned to Egypt Joseph entertained them royally, while still concealing his identity. They were amazed that he could arrange them in order of age – even spoiling the youngest, for ***Benjamin's mess was five times so much as any of theirs. And they drank, and were merry with him.*** Joseph, however, wanted to test them further.

44 He had his goblet hidden in Benjamin's pack, and this time he had them pursued. The arresting officers asked ***Wherefore have ye rewarded evil for good?***, made a search, and found the goblet. They all offered themselves as slaves, to which Joseph replied ***God forbid that I should do so: but the man in whose hand the cup is found, he shall be my servant; and as for you, get you up in peace unto your father.*** But on this occasion they displayed fraternal devotion.

Judah told of his father's reluctance to let them come, and of his own promise to bring back Benjamin safely. ***Now therefore, I pray thee, let thy servant abide instead of the lad a bondman to my lord; and let the lad go up with his brethren.***
45 Joseph was so touched that he wept, finally telling them ***I am Joseph your brother,***

whom ye sold into Egypt. Now therefore be not grieved, nor angry with yourselves, that ye sold me hither: for God did send me before you to preserve life. If he took such a philosophical view of the matter, I don't know why he had tormented his brothers so.

Joseph warned them that there were five years of famine still to come. He therefore urged his brothers to go back and bring their father, ***And thou shalt dwell in the land of Goshen, and thou shalt be near unto me, thou, and thy children, and thy children's children, and thy flocks, and thy herds, and all that thou hast.*** The thought of the coming reunion was emotional, and Joseph ***fell upon his brother Benjamin's neck, and wept; and Benjamin wept upon his neck.***

When Pharaoh heard who the visitors were he added his welcome: ***I will give you the good of the land of Egypt, and ye shall eat the fat of the land ... Also regard not your stuff,*** because everything will be provided. And so Joseph sent them off, loaded down with gifts, with the instruction ***See that ye fall not out by the way.*** Back in Canaan Jacob was slow to believe the news, but eventually granted: ***It is enough; Joseph my son is yet alive: I will go and see him before I die.***

46

Jacob, otherwise known as Israel, took his enormous family into Egypt. The patriarchs seemed to have a knack for avoiding daughters. Jacob had only had one, in the middle of twelve sons, and of all the grandchildren at this point, only one was female. Since ***all the souls of the house of Jacob, which came into Egypt, were threescore and ten,*** the two women must have wondered whether they were accidents of some kind. Just as surprising was that Benjamin, still a young man – early thirties at the outside – had a son who himself had had time to produce seven sons.

47

And so ***they came into the land of Goshen,*** where Joseph went to meet his father, ***and he fell on his neck, and wept on his neck a good while.*** The family was comfortably established with all its flocks; as an honoured guest, Jacob even had the chance to plague Pharaoh with his grumbles that ***few and evil have the days of the years of my life been.*** It sounded odd coming from a man of his age and advantages, but you have to humour the old folks.

The Twelve Tribes

Meanwhile Joseph continued as chief storemaster, accepting money in payment for bread until all the silver belonged to Pharaoh. Then he took cattle, horses and sheep, until all those were exhausted as well. Finally the people came and said that they had nothing left to offer except their lands and their bodies. ***And Joseph bought all the land of Egypt for Pharaoh; for the Egyptians sold every man his field, because the famine prevailed over them: so the land became Pharaoh's.*** What's more, it was decreed that one fifth of everything grown would be given to Pharaoh.

Joseph hadn't gone soft-hearted. But supposedly the common folk were grateful: ***And they said, Thou hast saved our lives; let us find grace in the sight of my lord, and we will be Pharaoh's servants.*** Fortunately the house of Israel was doing rather better, at least for the moment; ***they had possessions therein, and grew, and multiplied exceedingly.*** As Jacob's death approached at the age of 147 he made Joseph swear not to bury him in Egypt; ***But I will lie with my fathers, and thou shalt carry me out of Egypt, and bury me in their buryingplace.***

48 Before he died Jacob accepted Joseph's two sons as his own, saying that they would also be the founders of tribes. The old usurper had one last trick up his sleeve; he put his right hand on the head of the younger son, and crossed over his left to lay it on the head of the elder, thus reversing the blessings. Jacob was a younger son whose own younger sons were his favourites; he was happy to undermine primogeniture.

49 When his own twelve sons came to receive their blessings, then, I wasn't surprised that Reuben, the eldest, did not come out of it well. His affair with his father's concubine was held against him: ***Unstable as water, thou shalt not excel; because thou wentest up to thy father's bed; then defiledst thou it.*** The next two brothers, Simeon and Levi, were also condemned, in their case because of the atrocities following their sister's seduction. But Judah, the fourth, was rewarded (the episode with his daughter-in-law notwithstanding): ***he couched as a lion, and as an old lion; who shall rouse him up? The sceptre shall not depart from Judah.*** Joseph received a blessing to prevail ***unto the utmost bound of the everlasting hills.***

And so, pausing only to say ***I have waited for thy salvation, O LORD,*** Jacob blessed each of his sons in turn; ***All these are the twelve tribes of Israel.*** Having again directed that he be taken for burial to the cave where Abraham and Isaac lay, ***he gathered up his feet into the bed, and yielded up the ghost, and was gathered unto his people.***

50 The body of Jacob was embalmed, a process lasting forty days. His family and a large company from the royal household took the body back to Canaan, returning to Egypt after the burial.

With their father gone, the other brothers feared that Joseph would take revenge on them. They sent him a message alleging – and I think they might have made this up – that their father's dying wish had been for Joseph to forgive them. In any case they were very contrite, and Joseph repeated that everything had turned out for the best.

When at the age of 110 his time came, ***Joseph said unto his brethren, I die: and God will surely visit you, and bring you out of this land unto the land which he sware to Abraham, to Isaac, and to Jacob.*** The story was only beginning.

2

Exodus

Time passed. ***Now there arose up a new king over Egypt, which knew not Joseph. And he said unto his people, Behold, the people of the children of Israel are more and mightier than we***: the fear of immigrants and their reproductive powers has always been strong. So the Israelites were pressed into hard labour and harshly treated. 1

When this did not succeed in reducing their numbers, the king ordered the Hebrew midwives (apparently there were only two) to kill any male babies. But the midwives, who were godfearing women – and presumably not stupid: what would it do to their careers if they started murdering newborn boys? – ignored him. When called back to explain the undiminished numbers of children, they ***said unto Pharaoh, Because the Hebrew women are not as the Egyptian women; for they are lively, and are delivered ere the midwives come in unto them***. Pharaoh was gullible enough to swallow this story.

Unfortunately he didn't give up, and this time ordered that newborn Hebrew males be thrown into the river. One mother from the house of Levi decided to interpret the command in her own way. When she could no longer hide her baby, ***She took for him an ark of bulrushes, and daubed it with slime and with pitch, and put the child therein***. The basket was floating in the Nile, watched by the baby's sister, when who should find it but one of Pharaoh's daughters, bathing in the river. She realised that it was a Hebrew child, but seemed to have no hesitation in undermining her father's decree. The girl who was keeping a lookout came and asked ***Shall I go and call to thee a nurse of the Hebrew women, that she may nurse the child for thee?*** Pharaoh's daughter must have been either remarkably warm hearted or even more gullible than her father, because she ended up paying the baby's mother to look after her own son. In due course the noble lady adopted the boy, naming him Moses. 2

All went well as he grew into adulthood, until one day Moses saw an Egyptian abusing a Hebrew worker, and killed him. Pharaoh found out, and Moses had to flee the country. In the tradition of his forefathers, he sat down at a well and came away with a woman; having chivalrously assisted seven female shepherds who were not being allowed to water their flocks, he was rewarded by being given a roof and a wife by their father. When their first son was born Moses named him Gershom, meaning 'exiled', ***for he said, I have been a stranger in a strange land.***

But all this time ***the children of Israel sighed by reason of the bondage ... And God heard their groaning, and God remembered his covenant with Abraham,***

with Isaac, and with Jacob. And not before time: I was finally able to go down
3 and get things moving again. One day when Moses was out with the flocks, ***the angel of the LORD appeared unto him in a flame of fire out of the midst of a bush: and he looked, and, behold, the bush burned with fire, and the bush was not consumed.***

Moses was much impressed, I'm glad to say. God made sure of the effect by telling him to ***put off thy shoes from off thy feet, for the place whereon thou standest is holy ground ... And Moses hid his face; for he was afraid to look upon God.*** But God announced the good news: he was going to take the people of Israel out of Egypt, he had come ***to bring them up out of that land unto a good land and large, unto a land flowing with milk and honey.***

And then God told Moses the bad news: ***Come now therefore, and I will send thee unto Pharaoh.*** Moses wasn't keen, and after the usual 'Why me?' response, asked how he was supposed to show his people that he brought a message from God. ***And God said unto Moses, I AM THAT I AM: and he said, Thus shalt thou say unto the children of Israel, I AM hath sent me unto you.***

4 Moses, who was too polite to say that this was not likely to help, merely commented that they might not believe him. To that God provided him with a few magic tricks: he could turn his staff into a snake and back again; he could make his hand white and leprous, and then return it to normal; he could pour water onto the ground where it would become blood.

None of this sounded very useful, but Moses was running out of excuses. He protested that he was no public speaker: ***I am slow of speech, and of a slow tongue.*** God told him not to worry, ***I will be with thy mouth, and teach thee what thou shalt say.*** Moses made one last effort to avoid conscription, and God lost his temper: take your brother Aaron as your spokesman, then, ***and put words in his mouth***, and you'll only have to work the miracles.

There was nothing left to say. Moses went back, asked his father-in-law for permission to return to Egypt, and set out. On the way God told him that when he performed his magic for Pharaoh, ***I will harden his heart, that he shall not let the people go.*** Just what Moses needed to hear.

A bizarre incident during the journey can't have helped Moses' confidence. ***And it came to pass by the way in the inn, that the LORD met him, and sought to kill him.*** His wife got it into her head that the trouble had some connection with their son not being circumcised, so she ***took a sharp stone, and cut off the foreskin of her son, and cast it at his feet, and said, Surely a bloody husband art thou to me.*** That was apparently enough to save Moses from God, though the whole affair still leaves me bewildered.

Moses did meet Aaron, and their discussion with the community elders went
5 well, but then they had to tackle Pharaoh. As expected, it was a disaster. They passed on the message from God, ***Let my people go ... And Pharaoh said, Who is the LORD, that I should obey his voice to let Israel go?*** At that stage Moses was only asking for a religious holiday; he neglected to mention that they planned to

leave the country for good, and who can blame him?

Pharaoh decided that the only way to deal with these lazy foreigners was with firmness, and so he instructed the overseers that ***Ye shall no more give the people straw to make brick, as heretofore: let them go and gather straw for themselves.*** This made it even more difficult to meet the production targets, and they reproached Moses and Aaron for arousing Pharaoh's wrath.

Moses remonstrated with God, who assured him that everything was under control. He was told to go back to the children of Israel with the message ***I am the LORD, and I will bring you out from under the burdens of the Egyptians, and I will rid you out of their bondage.*** The people were not falling for that line again, though, and ***they hearkened not unto Moses.*** Next God told Moses to go back to Pharaoh, this time to ask that everyone be allowed to leave the country. Moses must have been tearing his hair out, and his language started to get more colourful: ***Behold, the children of Israel have not hearkened unto me; how then shall Pharaoh hear me, who am of uncircumcised lips?*** But God didn't pay any attention. 6

Here we paused for genealogical identification. The only thing of much interest to emerge was that the father of Moses had married his own father's sister, hence Moses' mother was also his great aunt. Women still seemed to be thin on the ground.

THE PLAGUES

Anyway, back to Pharaoh. God was looking forward to a showdown, and he didn't want it to seem too easy. ***I will harden Pharaoh's heart, and multiply my signs and my wonders in the land of Egypt. But Pharaoh shall not hearken unto you, that I may lay my hand upon Egypt.*** Moses, who was 80 years old at this point, must have wished that it didn't have to be made so difficult. 7

Things did not get off to a good start. Moses and Aaron did the staff-becomes-a-snake trick for Pharaoh, who was not impressed. He summoned his wise men, sorcerers and magicians, and they all turned their rods into serpents as well – though admittedly God's snake proceeded to eat the others. Next Moses performed the water-into-blood marvel on the Nile. ***And the fish that was in the river died; and the river stank, and the Egyptians could not drink of the water of the river; and there was blood throughout all the land of Egypt.*** For some reason the court magicians felt obliged to repeat this trick as well – quite where I don't recall – and Pharaoh remained unawed. Of course for a whole week the poor ***Egyptians digged round about the river for water to drink.***

As if that hadn't been bad enough, God's next message must have had them squirming: ***Let my people go, that they may serve me. And if thou refuse to let them go, behold, I will smite all thy borders with frogs: and the river shall bring forth frogs abundantly, which shall go up and come into thine house, and into*** 8

thy bedchamber, and upon thy bed, and into the house of thy servants, and upon thy people, and into thine ovens, and into thy kneading-troughs. To make matters worse Pharaoh's magicians were still playing their game of one-upsmanship, so frogs came popping up all over. Pharaoh cried 'uncle', and Moses asked God to wipe out the frogs. The cure was almost as bad as the disease: ***the frogs died out of the houses, out of the villages, and out of the fields. And they gathered them together upon heaps: and the land stank.***

Pharaoh was unwise enough to renege on the deal. In consequence God hit him with a plague of maggots – at which point even his magicians admitted that they were beaten, saying ***This is the finger of God*** – and then flies. Pharaoh again gave

9 in, and then again went back on his word. Next to come was pestilence, ***and all the cattle of Egypt died: but of the cattle of the children of Israel died not one.*** After that it was boils breaking out ***upon man, and upon beast,*** which was odd because there weren't supposed to be any beasts left.

And the LORD hardened the heart of Pharaoh, and he hearkened not unto them. I felt sorry for him; God was beating the stuffing out of him, but not letting him give up. A mammoth hail storm was coming next; God advised the Egyptians to bring in their cattle, for some reason again overlooking the fact that the cattle had already been dealt with. At any rate the hail came, ***Only in the land of Goshen, where the children of Israel were, was there no hail.***

10 To complete the destruction God sent in the locusts, worse than had ever been seen, ***For they covered the face of the whole earth, so that the land was darkened,*** and they ate everything that grew. When Pharaoh was deceitful once more, three days of darkness came as a final warning, ***darkness which may be felt.*** Pharaoh was still not willing to accept Moses' terms, and ordered him never to show his face again, on pain of death.

11 Moses did, though, manage to pass on his last message from God: ***Yet will I bring one plague more upon Pharaoh, and upon Egypt.*** He served notice that ***all the firstborn in the land of Egypt shall die, from the firstborn of Pharaoh that sitteth upon his throne, even unto the firstborn of the maidservant that is behind the mill; and all the firstborn of beasts.*** As before the Israelites would be spared. God had Moses tell his people to borrow gold and silver from the Egyptians. In view of what was to come, the word 'borrow' was being used in the sense of 'plunder'.

12 God gave Moses detailed instructions about how the congregation of Israel should spend its last night in captivity, and celebrate the anniversary thereafter. Each household should take a lamb for the feast, and ***Your lamb shall be without blemish.*** Some of its blood should be spread on the door posts. God proceeded to give cooking directions; he was most particular that the lamb should be roasted – head, legs, guts and all – and not eaten raw or boiled. It should be accompanied by unleavened bread and bitter herbs. God continued his instructions:

And thus shall ye eat it; with your loins girded, your shoes on your feet, and your staff in your hand; and ye shall eat it in haste: it is the LORD's passover.

For I will pass through the land of Egypt this night, and will smite all the firstborn in the land of Egypt, both man and beast; and against all the gods of Egypt I will execute judgment: I am the LORD. And the blood shall be to you for a token upon the houses where ye are: and when I see the blood, I will pass over you, and the plague shall not be upon you to destroy you, when I smite the land of Egypt. And this day shall be unto you for a memorial; and ye shall keep it a feast to the LORD throughout your generations; ye shall keep it a feast by an ordinance for ever. Seven days shall ye eat unleavened bread; even the first day ye shall put away leaven out of your houses.

Moses repeated all the particulars to the elders. ***And it shall come to pass, when your children shall say unto you, What mean ye by this service? That ye shall say, It is the sacrifice of the LORD's passover, who passed over the houses of the children of Israel in Egypt, when he smote the Egyptians.*** And smite the Egyptians he did. As threatened, all the firstborn were killed, ***and there was a great cry in Egypt; for there was not a house where there was not one dead.*** Finally Pharaoh gave in, and told them all to go and be gone.

The migration was massive: six hundred thousand men, not to mention all their dependants and herds. Quite a crowd, even considering that the Israelites had been in Egypt for four hundred and thirty years. There were a few final instructions about the passover feast: none of the meat was to be taken out of the house, none of the bones were to be broken, and ***no uncircumcised person shall eat thereof.***

13

Moses told them to ***Remember this day, in which ye came out from Egypt, out of the house of bondage; for by strength of hand the LORD brought you out from this place.*** Every firstborn creature, animal or man, would belong to God, to be either sacrificed or redeemed. And finally, the record of their deliverance should be worn in phylacteries.

Back to the action, though. God decided on a roundabout route via the Red Sea, rather than the direct way which would bring them into contact with the Philistines. ***Moses took the bones of Joseph with him***, so that he could be returned to the land of his fathers. ***And the LORD went before them by day in a pillar of a cloud, to lead them the way; and by night in a pillar of fire, to give them light.***

THE ESCAPE FROM EGYPT

14

Pharaoh had one last change of heart. He summoned all his chariots, and they set out after his departing labour force. When the Israelites saw that they were being pursued, with their backs to the sea, they became quite sarcastic with Moses: ***Because there were no graves in Egypt, hast thou taken us away to die in the wilderness?*** The whole plan had seemed a bad idea from the start. Moses was blunt: ***The LORD shall fight for you, and ye shall hold your peace.***

Indeed, God was looking forward to a fight. He told Moses ***I will harden the hearts of the Egyptians, and they shall follow them: and I will get me honour.***

Once again he was setting them up so that he could knock them down.

Here I had a role to play: ***the angel of God, which went before the camp of Israel, removed and went behind them; and the pillar of the cloud went from before their face, and stood behind them***; the Egyptians were temporarily in the dark, and God had an extra night to work with. ***And Moses stretched out his hand over the sea; and the LORD caused the sea to go back by a strong east wind all the night, and made the sea dry land, and the waters were divided. And the children of Israel went into the midst of the sea upon the dry ground: and the waters were a wall unto them on their right hand, and on their left. And the Egyptians pursued, and went in after them to the midst of the sea, even all Pharaoh's horses, his chariots, and his horsemen.***

By the time they realised what was happening it was too late. Moses stretched out his hand again, and the sea swallowed up the pursuing forces. The Israelites
15 composed a song in celebration:

I will sing unto the LORD, for he hath triumphed gloriously:
the horse and his rider hath he thrown into the sea.
The LORD is my strength and song, and he is become my salvation:
he is my God, and I will prepare him an habitation;
my father's God, and I will exalt him.
The LORD is a man of war: the LORD is his name. ...
Thy right hand, O LORD, is become glorious in power:
thy right hand, O LORD, hath dashed in pieces the enemy.

The song continued in this bellicose vein, full of jubilation that ***thou sentest forth thy wrath, which consumed them as stubble***, finally concluding: ***The LORD shall reign for ever and ever.*** The women took their tambourines and danced and sang the refrain.

The rejoicing didn't last long, though, when the wandering in the wilderness started. First they were without water for three days, and it took a miracle from
16 God to produce some. Then they ran out of food. People grumbled to Moses ***Would to God we had died by the hand of the LORD in the land of Egypt, when we sat by the flesh pots, and when we did eat bread to the full; for ye have brought us forth into this wilderness, to kill this whole assembly with hunger.***

God saw that dramatic action was needed, so he said ***Behold, I will rain bread from heaven for you.*** To be frank it was not very much like bread, more like little flakes of frost, or white coriander seed, that had to be gathered up every day (except the sabbath, a double supply having come the previous day). Their name for it suggests that people weren't thrilled: Manna, which means 'what is it?' (or by implication, 'you call this food?') In fact ***the taste of it was like wafers made with honey***, but since ***the children of Israel did eat manna forty years ... until they come unto the borders of the land of Canaan***, you can understand that they became sick of it.

There were more problems with water, more mutinous rumblings, and more miracles. There was even an attack by another tribe in which Joshua, about whom we shall hear much more, made his debut as a military commander. Moses stood on a nearby hill during the battle, and God entertained us by giving the advantage to Israel when Moses kept his arms outstretched, and the advantage to their opponents when he dropped his hands. Fortunately Moses had two men with him, who held his arms up before he completely collapsed. Thus supported, Joshua was victorious. 17

Moses received a visit from his father-in-law Jethro, accompanied by the wife and children of Moses from whom (for reasons unknown) he had been separated. They stayed just long enough for Jethro to urge Moses to delegate – advice which he followed, being worn out from doing everything himself. 18

THE LAW IS SET IN STONE

In the third month of their migration, the Israelites reached mount Sinai. On instructions from God, Moses prepared the people – or should I say the men – to receive his commands; they were to clean themselves and their clothes, and to stay away from women. ***And it came to pass on the third day in the morning, that there were thunders and lightnings, and a thick cloud upon the mount, and the voice of the trumpet exceeding loud; so that all the people that was in the camp trembled.*** Everyone was assembled behind barriers at the foot of the mountain, which was shaking and wreathed in smoke. God was adamant that the people should not approach further. Trudging up to the summit for the third time, Moses assured him that nothing could be further from their minds; nevertheless God insisted that he go back down to repeat the order, returning only with Aaron. 19

This is what they heard: 20

Thou shalt have no other gods before me.
Thou shalt not make unto thee any graven image ... for I the LORD thy God am a jealous God, visiting the iniquity of the fathers upon the children unto the third and fourth generation of them that hate me ...
Thou shalt not take the name of the LORD thy God in vain ...
Remember the sabbath day, to keep it holy. Six days shalt thou labour, and do all thy work: But the seventh day is the sabbath of the LORD thy God: in it thou shalt not do any work ...
Honour thy father and thy mother: that thy days may be long upon the land which the LORD thy God giveth thee.
Thou shalt not kill.
Thou shalt not commit adultery.
Thou shalt not steal.
Thou shalt not bear false witness against thy neighbour.

Thou shalt not covet thy neighbour's house, thou shalt not covet thy neighbour's wife, nor his manservant, nor his maidservant, nor his ox, nor his ass, nor any thing that is thy neighbour's.

There was a great deal of thunder and lightning, with trumpets sounding and the mountain smoking. The people were frightened, and they hadn't even heard the commandments yet. They called out to Moses, ***let not God speak with us, lest we die***. But God was just warming up. ***Moses drew near unto the thick darkness where God was***, and heard another few dozen decrees.

These were many and various. To start with the nature of the altar was spelt out: no cut stones could be used, because human tools would sully it. ***Neither shalt thou go up by steps unto mine altar, that thy nakedness be not discovered thereon.*** Wearing trousers rather than skirts would have helped, of course.

21 Then there followed rules for slave owners. Hebrew slaves should be freed automatically after six years of service. Any that had been provided with a wife would have to leave her and their children behind. But ***if the servant shall plainly say, I love my master, my wife, and my children; I will not go out free: Then his master shall ... bring him to the door, or unto the door post; and his master shall bore his ear through with an aul; and he shall serve him for ever***. Not any easy choice.

For women sold into slavery the rules were different. Essentially the master was expected to have sexual relations with the maidservant, as well as to provide her with food and clothing, failing which she should go free. The poor woman was in a bind: if wanting to stay, she might be repudiated at any time, while if wanting to leave, she could be forced to stay – so long as she was regularly raped, of course.

God next outlined the punishment for serious crimes. Murder and kidnapping rated the death penalty. More alarmingly, ***he that curseth his father, or his mother, shall surely be put to death***. The strict implementation of that one might seriously have reduced the population. Still, it would be an interesting threat, if sending the child to bed without dessert proved ineffective.

Beating a male or female slave to death was a punishable offence if the slave died on the spot, but otherwise – for example if he or she managed to survive a day or two – then the death of valuable property was taken to be punishment enough. We tried to promote moderation in all things.

In general, the principle was that ***thou shalt give life for life, eye for eye, tooth for tooth, hand for hand, foot for foot, burning for burning, wound for wound, stripe for stripe***. That said, God immediately provided examples of compensation rather than retribution: hence a man who struck out the eye of his slave should set him free.

An ox would be stoned if it killed a person, but the owner would only be liable to punishment (death or payment of compensation) if the ox had a prior record of violence.

22 A thief would be obliged to replace a stolen ox with five others, or a stolen sheep

with four, even if it meant being sold into slavery. Killing a burglar at night is excusable, but during the day is punishable. ***And if a man entice a maid that is not betrothed, and lie with her, he shall surely endow her to be his wife. If her father utterly refuse to give her unto him, he shall pay money according to the dowry of virgins. Thou shalt not suffer a witch to live. Whosoever lieth with a beast shall surely be put to death.*** The statute book wasn't very organised.

Worshipping false gods warranted a death sentence. From here on, though, many of the edicts were positively humane, dealing *inter alia* with the protection of the poor and the afflicted; for example, if someone pawns a coat, you must return it to him at night, as otherwise how would he sleep?

23 Spreading falsehood, or giving corrupt testimony, is prohibited. ***Thou shalt not follow a multitude to do evil.*** If you see your enemy's animals straying, you must bring them back to him; if someone who hates you needs help, you must help him. Taking bribes is prohibited. ***Also thou shalt not oppress a stranger: for ye know the heart of a stranger, seeing ye were strangers in the land of Egypt.***

Most of the remaining ordinances had to do with observing feast days. As an aside, God mentioned that a kid should not be boiled in its mother's milk, an injunction that later led to no meat and milk being eaten together.

All that out of the way, God gave me my introduction. ***Behold, I send an Angel before thee, to keep thee in the way, and to bring thee into the place which I have prepared.*** Moses went back down the mountain and announced the law to unanimous acclaim. (24) ***And Moses wrote all the words of the LORD*** – he clearly had a good memory – into the book of the covenant. God was by no means finished, though, and so Moses went back up mount Sinai, leaving the people down below.

25 During this session God did nothing but describe in minute detail how he wanted his tabernacle built, how his priests should be dressed, and how sacrifices were to be made. The whole lecture went on for thousands of words, but the gist of it was simple. There should be a wooden ark to hold the tablets God was going to supply, elaborately decorated with gold cherubs, fine linen, etc., etc. (26) This would sit in the Holy of Holies, curtained off from the rest of the tabernacle. (27) The altar was to go in a courtyard: an area surrounded by hangings, where a lamp burned all night. (28) Aaron would be high priest, wearing brightly coloured garments, a turban, and a breastplate with ***the Urim and the Thummim***, sacred objects having mysterious uses in judgment. His sons would also be priests, similarly attired. ***And thou shalt make them linen breeches to cover their nakedness***, so that they're not struck dead when they approach the tabernacle. (29) There were ceremonies for consecrating the priests and the altar, which mainly involved killing animals.

30 At the time of the population census half a shekel should be collected from every man; ***The rich shall not give more, and the poor shall not give less.*** Progressive taxation came later. The money would go to maintain the tabernacle, ***that it may be a memorial unto the children of Israel before the LORD, to make an atonement for your souls.***

To round things off, God supplied recipes for holy anointing oil, consisting of various spices in an olive oil base, and for a holy incense. Anybody using either one for non-sacred purposes ***shall even be cut off from his people.***

31 Fortunately for Moses, God designated a craftsman to make everything he had described. After a final reminder to keep the sabbath, ***he gave unto Moses, when he had made an end of communing with him upon mount Sinai, two tables of testimony, tables of stone, written with the finger of God.***

Breaking the Law

32 Meanwhile, the people down below were becoming impatient. With still no sign of Moses forty days after he disappeared into the thunder and lightning, they figured that the chances of seeing him again were slight. Presumably they thought that Moses and God had vanished together, or else believed that other gods were just as good. In any event they went along to Aaron, saying ***Up, make us gods, which shall go before us; for as for this Moses, the man that brought us up out of the land of Egypt, we wot not what is become of him.***

Considering that Aaron was the brother and chief lieutenant of Moses, his response amazed me. Instead of telling them to get a grip on themselves, he collected all their gold earrings which he then had melted down and remade in the form of a calf. Mind you, his announcement that ***These be thy gods, O Israel, which brought thee up out of the land of Egypt*** sounded so silly that I wondered if he was trying to ridicule the agitators. If so, it didn't work. Everyone felt very jolly; ***the people sat down to eat and to drink, and rose up to play.***

God saw what was going on, and was furious. That's it, he told Moses: ***I have seen this people, and, behold, it is a stiffnecked people: now therefore let me alone, that my wrath may wax hot against them, and that I may consume them: and I will make of thee a great nation.*** Moses realised that he would end up alone unless he could persuade God that mass destruction might not be a good idea. First he used the 'what would people say?' approach: ***Wherefore should the Egyptians speak, and say, For mischief did he bring them out, to slay them in the mountains, and to consume them from the face of the earth?*** Then he followed up with the 'you promised' argument: ***Remember Abraham, Isaac, and Israel, thy servants, to whom thou swarest by thine own self, and saidst unto them, I will multiply your seed as the stars of heaven.*** Fortunately it worked, and God relented.

I have to say, though, that the people were almost as severely punished by Moses as they would have been by God. Moses came down the mountain with the two tablets that ***were the work of God, and the writing was the writing of God,*** when he saw the revelry. He went wild, smashing things up. First he threw the tablets on the ground, where they crumbled; then ***he took the calf which they had made, and burnt it in the fire, and ground it to powder, and strawed it upon the water, and made the children of Israel drink of it.***

The gold dust cocktail was followed by a real killer. ***Moses stood in the gate of***

the camp, and said, Who is on the LORD's side? let him come unto me. The tribe of Levi rallied around. He gave them their orders, apparently from God: ***Put every man his sword by his side, and go in and out from gate to gate throughout the camp, and slay every man his brother, and every man his companion, and every man his neighbour.*** So it went, and about three thousand men died.

33 God decided that he couldn't trust himself not to wipe out the Israelites if he had to deal with them from day to day, and so I was deputised to lead the way: ***I will send an angel before thee ... Unto a land flowing with milk and honey,*** he told Moses. These conversations generally took place in the tabernacle, the meeting tent set up outside the camp. There ***the LORD spake unto Moses face to face, as a man speaketh unto his friend.*** As they were on such close terms, Moses asked God if he would mind appearing as more than a disembodied voice. God replied that ***Thou canst not see my face: for there shall no man see me, and live.*** Instead he offered a view at least as unusual; while you stand there, he said, I ***will cover thee with my hand while I pass by: And I will take away mine hand, and thou shalt see my back parts.***

34 Getting back to business, God told Moses to cut two stone tablets to replace the ones that he had broken. Although God said that he would write on them, in the event it was Moses who had to do the work. God gave Moses the usual lecture about what the people should and shouldn't do. He warned against fraternising with the inhabitants of the promised land, for fear that ***thou take of their daughters unto thy sons, and their daughters go a whoring after their gods, and make thy sons go a whoring after their gods.*** God wasn't a very good host; during the forty days that Moses was being a stonemason, ***he did neither eat bread, nor drink water.***

Eventually Moses came back down with the two replacement tablets, and fortunately everyone had behaved in his absence. This time it was the people who were taken aback by Moses, because ***the skin of his face shone; and they were afraid to come nigh him.*** Moses solved the problem by veiling his face when he talked to the people, and only taking the veil off when he spoke to God. I thought it might have made life easier if he had done it the other way around, but at this point Moses was probably spending more time with God anyway.

35 Then, too, Moses seemed to lack the common touch. When he had assembled all the people to put them to work building the tabernacle, the first thing he told them was that anyone working on the sabbath would be put to death: not really the best way to generate enthusiasm. Perhaps I'm wrong, though, because so many people donated jewellery, linen, skins, spice, oil, etc., that eventually all the craftsmen appealed to Moses to stop the flood of contributions, ***For the stuff they had was sufficient for all the work to make it, and too much.*** 36

37 Nothing daunted, however, the chief craftsman used gold for everything. The ark, the lampstand, the altar and all the other furnishings of the tabernacle were made just as Moses had been instructed. Next they moved on ***and made the holy garments for Aaron,*** who astonishingly had not been disqualified for his part in 38 39

the golden calf episode. When everything was finished it was brought for inspection by Moses, ***and, behold, they had done it as the LORD had commanded, even so had they done it: and Moses blessed them.***

40 The tablets were put in the ark, the priests were anointed, and the whole tabernacle was consecrated. When the Israelites were finally ready to move on, as before I led the way: ***For the cloud of the LORD was upon the tabernacle by day, and fire was on it by night, in the sight of all the house of Israel, throughout all their journeys.***

3

Leviticus

Before following the tribes on their way, it's worth looking through the rule-book on ritual observance. God started with a lecture to Moses on the different kinds of offering, including animal sacrifice. The details can be harrowing; given a turtle-dove, for example, ***the priest shall bring it unto the altar, and wring off his head, and burn it on the altar; and the blood thereof shall be wrung out at the side of the altar.*** Whatever animal is used, whether bullock, sheep or bird, ***it is a burnt sacrifice, an offering made by fire, of a sweet savour unto the LORD.*** To each his own. God preferred savouries to sweets; he didn't want any leaven or honey in the grain offerings, but specified that ***with all thine offerings thou shalt offer salt.*** 1 2

Certain sacrifices were so-called peace offerings, meant to be shared with others. The animal chosen was to be ***without blemish.*** The owner would put his hand on its head, to identify himself with it, kill it in front of the tabernacle, and then have the priest sprinkle its blood on and around the altar. The butchery instructions were graphic: ***the fat thereof, and the whole rump, it shall he take off hard by the backbone; and the fat that covereth the inwards, and all the fat that is upon the inwards, And the two kidneys, and the fat that is upon them, which is by the flanks, and the caul above the liver, with the kidneys, it shall he take away. And the priest shall burn it upon the altar.*** The principle here was that ***all the fat is the LORD's. It shall be a perpetual statute for your generations throughout all your dwellings, that ye eat neither fat nor blood.*** 3

The procedure was much the same for sin offerings, except that more of the blood was sprinkled about. Likewise for guilt offerings, though quite how God distinguished these two wasn't clear to me. 4 5

The general rule of the sin offering was that the priest and his male relatives could and should eat it, but only in the court of the tabernacle. The flesh was sacred, and any clothes stained with blood were to be washed in a holy place. With peace offerings anyone could share in the feast, providing that he hadn't contaminated himself; but ***the soul that shall touch any unclean thing, as the uncleanness of man, or any unclean beast, or any abominable unclean thing, and eat of the flesh of the sacrifice of peace offerings, which pertain unto the LORD, even that soul shall be cut off from his people.*** Speaking of unclean things, God also instructed Moses that an animal that had died of natural causes or had been killed by a wild beast was not to be eaten. 6 7

DEATH IN THE TABERNACLE

8 It was time for the investiture of Aaron and his sons as priests. Apart from putting on all the vestments, the ceremony involved killing a few animals and splashing the blood around. Once a ram had been sacrificed, for example, ***Moses took of the blood of it, and put it upon the tip of Aaron's right ear, and upon the thumb of his right hand, and upon the great toe of his right foot***; he repeated this for Aaron's sons, ***and Moses sprinkled the blood upon the altar round about.*** They stayed in

9 the tabernacle for seven days, and on the eighth day more animals were sacrificed.

So far everything had gone well, and the consecration was drawing to an end.

10 Suddenly disaster struck. ***The sons of Aaron, took either of them his censer, and put fire therein, and put incense thereon, and offered strange fire before the LORD, which he commanded them not. And there went out fire from the LORD, and devoured them, and they died before the LORD.*** I frankly don't know why God suddenly flared up. My guess is that their crime was to improvise, to do something not on the approved list of ceremonial activities.

All Moses could say to Aaron was ***This is it that the LORD spake, saying, I will be sanctified in them that come nigh me, and before all the people I will be glorified. And Aaron held his peace.*** To make matters worse he wasn't even allowed to mourn or attend the funeral, Moses telling him ***ye shall not go out from the door of the tabernacle of the congregation, lest ye die: for the anointing oil of the LORD is upon you.***

God wasn't one for choosing the best moment, either; ***the LORD spake unto Aaron, saying, Do not drink wine nor strong drink, thou, nor thy sons with thee, when ye go into the tabernacle of the congregation, lest ye die: it shall be a statute for ever throughout your generations.*** Moses chipped in with additional instructions for the two surviving sons of Aaron.

Naturally these two sons were too terrified to make a move. Moses discovered that they hadn't eaten a sin offering, as required, and demanded an explanation. Aaron's excuse was too muddled for me to understand, but Moses let them off.

PURITY DEFINED

11 With that drama behind us, God laid down the law on the clean and the unclean. He started with food. ***These are the beasts which ye shall eat among all the beasts that are on the earth. Whatsoever parteth the hoof, and is clovenfooted, and cheweth the cud, among the beasts, that shall ye eat.*** Anything else was off limits, e.g. the camel (chews the cud but padded feet) and pig (cloven hooves but not ruminant).

Ordinary fish from rivers or the sea were fine, but ***Whatsoever hath no fins nor***

scales in the waters, that shall be an abomination unto you: shrimp cocktails were out. As for birds, God presented a list of twenty varieties that were off limits, starting with the eagle and ending with the bat. (I know, it's not a bird, but God is allowed to be careless with taxonomy.) In case anyone was tempted, locusts were deemed edible.

More or less everything else was outlawed, thus ***whatsoever goeth upon his paws, among all manner of beasts that go on all four, those are unclean unto you***. Likewise everything that creeps: rats, lizards, and so on. Apart from not presenting these tempting titbits on the dinner table, people were to avoid contact with any dead specimens they might come across.

12

God then moved on to purification. ***If a woman have conceived seed, and born a man child: then she shall be unclean seven days***. On the eighth day would be the circumcision, ***And she shall then continue in the blood of her purifying three and thirty days; she shall touch no hallowed thing, nor come into the sanctuary, until the days of her purifying be fulfilled***. If the baby was a girl, then the mother would need to double these periods of purification. It was enough to give anyone postnatal depression.

At the end of the period she would present herself to the priest who would – what else – kill an animal. ***And if she be not able to bring a lamb, then she shall bring two turtles, or two young pigeons***; that should read turtle-doves, of course. I could have wished for some more peaceful way of regaining purity.

13

Childbearing was covered in a few sentences, but God took a couple of thousand words to deal with skin disease. It was about as compelling as your average medical text book. He gave detailed descriptions of different symptoms and pronounced the sufferer either clean or unclean. For example, ***The flesh also, in which, even in the skin thereof, was a boil, and is healed, And in the place of the boil there be a white rising, or a bright spot, white, and somewhat reddish, and it be shewed to the priest; And if, when the priest seeth it, behold, it be in sight lower than the skin, and the hair thereof be turned white; the priest shall pronounce him unclean***. And so on, and on, and on.

There were a few lighter moments. God said, ***And the man whose hair is fallen off his head, he is bald; yet is he clean***. That was a relief to many, I'm sure. The diagnosis of malignant skin disease was definitely bad news: ***the leper in whom the plague is, his clothes shall be rent, and his head bare, and he shall put a covering upon his upper lip, and shall cry, Unclean, unclean. All the days wherein the plague shall be in him he shall be defiled; he is unclean: he shall dwell alone; without the camp shall his habitation be***.

14

To be purified, a healed patient was to bring the priest two birds, one of which would be killed. The other was dipped in its blood, but then let loose and allowed to fly away. The lambs brought for the next stage had no such luck, I'm afraid. As for the man, ***he shall shave all his hair off his head and his beard and his eyebrows, even all his hair he shall shave off: and he shall wash his clothes, also he shall wash his flesh in water, and he shall be clean***.

After discoursing on mould and fungus in a house, God was finally finished
15 with this topic. The one he went on to was hardly more appealing, however: bodily discharges. In the first place, ***When any man hath a running issue out of his flesh, because of his issue he is unclean.*** Everything he comes into contact with is contaminated; indeed, ***if he that hath the issue spit upon him that is clean***, then the unlucky victim is unclean all day, despite washing himself and his clothes.

And if any man's seed of copulation go out from him, then he shall wash all his flesh in water, and be unclean until the even. If he was with a woman, the same applies to her. When a woman is menstruating she is impure for seven days; in fact everything she lies or sits on becomes unclean. Just touching the bed, then, makes a man contaminated for the day, ***And if any man lie with her at all, and her flowers be upon him, he shall be unclean seven days.*** With the number of unclean people there must have been walking around, it's a wonder everyone didn't become contaminated.

DOS AND DON'TS

16 Through Moses, God reminded Aaron (as if he needed telling) that trespassing in the tabernacle sanctuary was punishable by death. The appropriate admission procedure involved the usual amounts of blood being tossed about, but with an interesting variation. Aaron was to take two goats; one would be sacrificed after lots were cast, ***But the goat, on which the lot fell to be the scapegoat, shall be presented alive before the LORD, to make an atonement with him, and to let him go for a scapegoat into the wilderness.***

The actual ceremony was to be the following: ***Aaron shall lay both his hands upon the head of the live goat, and confess over him all the iniquities of the children of Israel, and all their transgressions in all their sins, putting them upon the head of the goat, and shall send him away by the hand of a fit man into the wilderness: And the goat shall bear upon him all their iniquities unto a land not inhabited.*** This was to happen annually on a special day of atonement.

17 Still on the subject of sacrifices, God made it clear that he expected all slaughter of animals to be accompanied by offerings in the tabernacle. He also reiterated that the blood was to be drained out of a carcass before eating it, ***For the life of the flesh is in the blood.***

18 Then God launched into a long list of the various combinations of relatives between whom sexual intercourse was outlawed. He prefaced it by saying that they should not follow the ways either of Egypt, where they had been, nor of Canaan, where they were going, but he might equally have ruled out the patriarchs as role models.

Many of the forbidden liaisons were with blood relations: mother, sister, half-sister, granddaughter, aunt. He didn't mention daughter, but I'm sure he meant to. Others were with relatives by marriage: step-mother, aunt, daughter-in-law, sister-in-law. God also prohibited sleeping with both a woman and her daughter, or indeed her granddaughter. As for sisters-in-law, not only your brother's wife but also your wife's sister was off limits: ***Neither shalt thou take a wife to her sister, to vex her, to uncover her nakedness, beside the other in her life time.*** Finally, almost as an afterthought, he remembered plain old adultery: ***Moreover thou shalt not lie carnally with thy neighbour's wife, to defile thyself with her.***

Not content with covering incest, God proscribed (male) homosexuality and bestiality. ***Thou shalt not lie with mankind, as with womankind: it is abomination. Neither shalt thou lie with any beast to defile thyself therewith: neither shall any woman stand before a beast to lie down thereto: it is confusion.*** We must at all costs avoid confusion.

19

Fortunately God moved on to more general commands, many just repeating ones that Moses had already heard. He mentioned that during a harvest the field was not to be gleaned of every last ear or grape; ***thou shalt leave them for the poor and stranger.*** Some of the things he came out with were curious: ***the wages of him that is hired shall not abide with thee all night until the morning. Thou shalt not curse the deaf, nor put a stumblingblock before the blind.*** Well, no. Mostly, though, the decrees were serious and sensible. ***Thou shalt not go up and down as a talebearer among thy people ... Thou shalt not hate thy brother in thine heart.***

God had trouble adjusting to a human sense of proportion; everything was mixed up together. For example, he had no sooner said ***Thou shalt not avenge, nor bear any grudge against the children of thy people, but thou shalt love thy neighbour as thyself*** – the sort of principle you could use to start a whole new religion – than he came out with ***thou shalt not sow thy field with mingled seed: neither shall a garment mingled of linen and woollen come upon thee.*** I tried to work on priorities with him, but it was hopeless.

He even had rules on hairdressing: ***Ye shall not round the corners of your heads, neither shalt thou mar the corners of thy beard.*** I have no idea why he was concerned about that. Self-scarification in mourning, and tattooing, were forbidden. Just when I thought we were on to cosmetics he came out with ***Do not prostitute thy daughter, to cause her to be a whore.*** And that was followed by ***Ye shall keep my sabbaths, and reverence my sanctuary.*** It was enough to make your head spin.

He seemed to be afraid of appearing too gentle. After declaring that ***Thou shalt rise up before the hoary head, and honour the face of the old man,*** and even that ***the stranger that dwelleth with you shall be unto you as one born among you, and thou shalt love him as thyself,*** he hurried to the matter of penalties. Since the verdict was death even for cursing your parents or committing adultery, I wondered what was left for, say, the more unusual sexual liaisons. The same again and worse: ***if a man take a wife and her mother, it is wickedness: they shall be burnt with fire, both he and they; that there be no wickedness among you.*** Encourage people to burn their neighbours alive in order to stamp out wickedness? I'd rather risk a few affairs between men and their mothers-in-law, myself.

20

PRIESTS AND FEASTS

21 God moved on to list his dos and don'ts for priests. Anyone aspiring to be a high priest had to be careful in choosing a partner; ***A widow, or a divorced woman, or profane, or an harlot, these shall he not take: but he shall take a virgin of his own people to wife.*** Mind you, his offspring had to be even more cautious: ***the daughter of any priest, if she profane herself by playing the whore, she profaneth her father: she shall be burnt with fire.***

God was not an equal opportunity employer. Physical disability was a bar to priesthood, ***For whatsoever man he be that hath a blemish, he shall not approach: a blind man, or a lame, or he that hath a flat nose, or any thing superfluous, Or a man that is brokenfooted, or brokenhanded, or crookbackt, or a dwarf, or that hath a blemish in his eye, or be scurvy, or scabbed, or hath his stones broken.*** Fortunately mental handicap wasn't mentioned.

22 A priest had to stay away if he became unclean, through having a discharge, touching a creepy-crawly, or whatever. Even animals with defects weren't welcome as sacrifices; it's just as well they didn't know it, or there might have been an outbreak of feigned lameness among sheep. God stipulated that animals could not be taken from their mothers for sacrifice until a week after birth. ***And whether it be cow or ewe, ye shall not kill it and her young both in one day.*** I'm not sure whether that's a kindness or not.

23 God changed direction and listed the various holidays and feast days that he wanted to be observed. First, of course, there was passover, which started a week of eating unleavened bread. Seven weeks later there was another festival, essentially to make an offering from the harvest. Then ***In the seventh month, in the first day of the month, shall ye have a sabbath, a memorial of blowing of trumpets, an holy convocation.*** On the tenth day of the same month would be the day of atonement. Finally, five days later the week-long feast of tabernacles would start. During this festival ***all that are Israelites born shall dwell in booths: That your generations may know that I made the children of Israel to dwell in booths, when I brought them out of the land of Egypt.***

24 God reminded Moses about the lamp that was to burn in his tabernacle from evening until morning. Also, he asked that every sabbath twelve loaves of bread be set out in the holy place.

Matters were interrupted by a fight between two men, one of whom ***blasphemed the name of the LORD, and cursed.*** He was brought for judgment to Moses, who referred the question to God. The verdict was ***let all the congregation stone him.*** God took the opportunity to repeat his principle of ***breach for breach, eye for eye, tooth for tooth: as he hath caused blemish in a man, so shall it be done to him again. And he that killeth a beast, he shall restore it: and he that killeth a man, he shall be put to death. Ye shall have one manner of law, as well for the stranger,***

as for one of your own country. Applying this principle, the *lex talionis* – the law of retaliation – to the case at hand, I come to a different conclusion. When a man blasphemes the name of the LORD, God should just curse back, surely? No need to start killing people.

25

Even the land had a sabbath: every seventh year it was to lie fallow. Moreover, there was to be an extra sabbath year following seven such cycles; ***ye shall hallow the fiftieth year, and proclaim liberty throughout all the land unto all the inhabitants thereof: it shall be a jubile unto you; and ye shall return every man unto his possession, and ye shall return every man unto his family.*** The point was that land and Israelite slaves were to be regarded as leased, not permanently sold, and all these leases terminated at the jubilee. There were certain exceptions: a house in a walled city could, unlike one in the country, be sold for all time, and foreign slaves would remain family possessions in perpetuity. How God squared this with his pronouncement just before that there should be one law for everyone, I couldn't say.

To God's credit, he made it a duty to help the poor. And if any compatriot fell on such hard times that he was obliged to sell himself, he should nevertheless be treated as a hired hand, not as a slave. As for the heathen, you could ***inherit them for a possession; they shall be your bondmen for ever.*** The reason for the preferential treatment of Israelites worried me; God said that they were his slaves already.

26

God was beginning to wrap up his sermon; it was time to dangle the carrot and wave the stick. If you obey, he said, I will give you rain in due season, and the land shall yield her increase, and the trees of the field shall yield their fruit. If, however, you disobey, there will be terrible afflictions. There will be so little food that ten women will bake their bread in one oven. More horrifying still, ***ye shall eat the flesh of your sons, and the flesh of your daughters shall ye eat.*** Finally, ***upon them that are left alive of you I will send a faintness into their hearts in the lands of their enemies; and the sound of a shaken leaf shall chase them; and they shall flee, as fleeing from a sword; and they shall fall when none pursueth.*** His threats had a wonderful ring to them.

And yet for all that, God declared, I won't break the covenant. Repentance would eventually put things right. Perhaps Moses found that reassuring; for my part, I would have thought more than twice before signing.

27

As an afterthought God laid down a few more rules about the valuation of people and things dedicated to him; depending on age, a female was assessed at between half and two-thirds the notional value of a male. Employers still seem to have the same idea. But there you have it: ***These are the commandments, which the LORD commanded Moses for the children of Israel in mount Sinai.***

4

Numbers

1 God told Moses to take a population census, numbering the able-bodied men aged twenty and up in each of the twelve tribes. (Jacob had had twelve sons, but to confuse matters Joseph counted for two tribes and Levi for none, his descendants being excluded on the grounds that they supplied the priests). The tribes weighed in at between 32,200 and 74,600 each, for a grand total of 603,550.

2 God's order of march required forming a large square. Three tribes were put on each side, with the Levites in the centre looking after the tabernacle. People were to move off one group at a time, starting with the tribes on the east, then the south, west, and finally the north. Since they were in fact headed north from mount Sinai I expected there to be a massive pile-up as the back line overran the front, but somehow they brought it off.

3 God had decreed that the first born of every family, man or beast, belonged to him, by virtue of having spared them during the last great plague in Egypt. Now he announced a deal: ***I have taken the Levites from among the children of Israel instead of all the firstborn***. Moses counted 22,000 Levites of all ages versus 22,273 firstborn males. God said that he'd take five shekels each for the extra 273 firstborn needing to be redeemed, and call it quits.

For once, I think, God was robbed. Judging from the census, there would have been about a million males of all ages; if only 22,273 of these were eldest brothers, the average man had 45 sons (and presumably as many daughters). I wanted God to set up an inquiry, but he let them get away with it.

4 To round off the census-taking God asked for a count of the (male, as always) Levites, by family, between the ages of thirty and fifty. These were the people eligible to work in transporting the tabernacle. With a total of 8,580, I could hardly see that there was enough work to go around.

5 Once numbering the people was out of the way, God went back to law-giving. Apart from instructing that anyone with a skin disease or in recent contact with the dead should be put outside the camp, he was mainly concerned with cases of jealousy. Counselling didn't enter into it; trial by ordeal was his method. Take for example a situation, he said, where there is a women ***And a man lie with her carnally, and it be hid from the eyes of her husband, and be kept close, and she be defiled, and there be no witness against her ... or if the spirit of jealousy come upon him, and he be jealous of his wife, and she be not defiled***, then to sort things out the husband should bring his wife to the priest.

The priest would mix water and dust, uttering dire warnings about what might happen to her, ***and the priest shall write these curses in a book, and he shall blot them out with the bitter water: And he shall cause the woman to drink the bitter water that causeth the curse ... then it shall come to pass, that, if she be defiled, and have done trespass against her husband, that the water that causeth the curse shall enter into her, and become bitter, and her belly shall swell, and her thigh shall rot: and the woman shall be a curse among her people. And if the woman be not defiled, but be clean; then she shall be free, and shall conceive seed.*** Rather a one-way street, this; for the man there was no penalty, for the wife no compensation, attached to false accusations.

There were special rules for anyone who wanted to become a Nazirite, that is a person dedicated to God. In the first place they weren't allowed near wine, grapes, raisins, or anything else from a vine. Secondly, they were not to cut their hair. Finally, corpses were to be avoided at all costs. If a Nazirite was unfortunate enough to have someone drop dead in his lap, he had to shave off his hair and start the period of his vows all over again. 6

God supplied an attractive blessing to be used by Aaron and his sons for the people:

> ***The LORD bless thee, and keep thee:***
> ***The LORD make his face shine upon thee, and be gracious unto thee:***
> ***The LORD lift up his countenance upon thee, and give thee peace.***

For the consecration of the tabernacle, the head of each tribe brought munificent gifts, all identical. God obliged Moses to sit through yet another lecture about the priestly duties of the Levites; this time he gave the starting age for service as twenty-five. He must have realised that serving from age thirty to fifty wasn't much of a career. He also seems to have changed his mind about strangers at passover; he declared that all resident aliens should observe the practice, while previously the uncircumcised were excluded. 7 8 9

Finally, however, some three weeks after the census and over a year after leaving Egypt, the Israelites were able to continue their journey. God signalled when to move and when to camp by raising or lowering the cloud over the tabernacle. Divine assistance notwithstanding, Moses asked his brother-in-law to come along as a guide; you can never have too much help. 10

THE LONG MARCH

Freedom is all very well, but most people think with their stomachs, and the diet was making them long for the good old days. They said ***We remember the fish, which we did eat in Egypt freely; the cucumbers, and the melons, and the leeks, and the onions, and the garlick: But now our soul is dried away: there is nothing at all, beside this manna, before our eyes.*** This ingratitude made God furious and 11

Moses miserable – unreasonably, in my view. Your average Jo(seph) just wants a better life, and that's what he had been promised.

Moses was in such a state (***Have I conceived all this people? Have I begotten them, that thou shouldest say unto me, Carry them in thy bosom, as a nursing father beareth the sucking child …*** ?) that he told God it was all too much for him; ***And if thou deal thus with me, kill me, I pray thee, out of hand.*** A bit melodramatic, really. God was on his side, though, and swore to the people that he'd give them meat not one day, ***nor two days, nor five days, neither ten days, nor twenty days; But even a whole month, until it come out at your nostrils, and it be loathsome unto you.***

That isn't quite what happened, though. God blew quails in from the sea throughout the day, the night, and the following day. There were so many to be gathered that no one came away with fewer than ten donkey loads. But when they sat down to eat, ***And while the flesh was yet between their teeth, ere it was chewed, the wrath of the LORD was kindled against the people, and the LORD smote the people with a very great plague.*** Not exactly fair play, I thought; he had threatened them with indigestion after a month, and then killed them after a day.

12 I felt sorry for Moses, caught between an enormous crowd of unhappy people and a short-tempered boss. God wouldn't even stay out of family quarrels. For example, ***Miriam and Aaron spake against Moses because of the Ethiopian woman whom he had married***, the old mixed marriage problem again. They were out of line, but they were his elder sister and brother after all. God called them to account regardless, told them that Moses was his number one deputy and not to be insulted, ***and, behold, Miriam became leprous, white as snow.*** Once again Aaron escaped scot-free. Poor old Moses ran out and cried ***Heal her now, O God, I beseech thee***, but she still had to spend a week outside the camp.

13 The worst incident followed the return of a party sent to reconnoitre the promised land. Each of the twelve tribes put up one of its senior representatives, ***And Moses sent them to spy out the land of Canaan.*** They came back with a bunch of grapes so large that it had to be carried on a pole supported by two men. Their report was that ***We came unto the land whither thou sentest us, and surely it floweth with milk and honey; and this is the fruit of it. Nevertheless the people be strong that dwell in the land, and the cities are walled, and very great:*** and moreover there were giants.

Two of the explorers, Caleb and Joshua, urged ***Let us go up at once, and possess it; for we are well able to overcome it.*** But this was a minority view, the others claiming that the opposition was too strong, and too tall: ***we were in our own sight as grasshoppers, and so we were in their sight.*** The people were much distressed 14 at the news. If they were going to be killed or enslaved, perhaps it would be better to go back to Egypt.

This was not the kind of talk God liked to hear. He decided to wipe them all out, founding a new nation with Moses as a latter-day Noah. But who could bear the idea of starting all over again from scratch? Anyway, Moses told God that if he destroyed his people everyone else would say that it was just because he hadn't been able to deliver on his promises.

God relented, but not much. To punish their lack of trust in him, he decreed that no one over the age of twenty, except Caleb and Joshua, would see the promised land: ***your carcases, they shall fall in this wilderness. And your children shall wander in the wilderness forty years.*** To get things started, the envoys who returned with the pessimistic reports were fatally stricken with plague there and then.

This caused such consternation that the people set out immediately for Canaan. Moses told them that they were mad, that without God on their side they wouldn't stand a chance. Such was their sense of having nothing to lose, though, that they pressed on without him, only to be defeated in battle as predicted.

15 After these calamities, I hoped that God might give some consolation, or a lecture, or just acknowledge what had happened. In fact his very next words to Moses were additional rules for offerings and sacrifices when the Israelites had reached the promised land! Sensitivity wasn't his strongest quality.

The sensitivity he did have was to disobedience. In one episode ***while the children of Israel were in the wilderness, they found a man that gathered sticks upon the sabbath day.*** Moses wasn't sure what should be done with him, but God was. ***And all the congregation brought him without the camp, and stoned him with stones, and he died; as the LORD commanded Moses.*** To remind the people of their duty of obedience, God told them to put a border of tassels on their clothes. Maybe a few pebbles would have been more to the point.

16 Despite the penalties, rebellion continued. A group challenged the authority of Moses, complaining that he was too high and mighty, and hadn't delivered on his promises to bring them into their inheritance. The next day Moses called on God to show who was boss, ***And the earth opened her mouth, and swallowed them up, and their houses ... They, and all that appertained to them, went down alive into the pit, and the earth closed upon them: and they perished from among the congregation.*** Having thus dealt with the ringleaders, God consumed their 250 followers with fire.

I had hoped that the worst was over, ***But on the morrow all the congregation of the children of Israel murmured against Moses and against Aaron, saying, Ye have killed the people of the LORD.*** God didn't hesitate an instant, and by the time Moses had had a chance to react and make atonement for the people, 14,700 had been struck dead by plague.

17 In an attempt to restore order, God told the leaders of each of the twelve tribes to supply a staff, with Aaron providing one on behalf of the Levites. These staffs were left in the tabernacle overnight, and in the morning ***the rod of Aaron for the house of Levi was budded, and brought forth buds, and bloomed blossoms, and yielded almonds.*** God told Moses to leave this staff on display, to discourage any further complaints. I'm all for symbols, but if killing thousands of people didn't do it, I couldn't feel optimistic about the effectiveness of a flowering stick.

18 Alternating between action and instruction, God went back to lecturing Aaron about the status of the Levites and of the priests among them. They could not inherit, but received all the offerings, including the tithes, made by other Israelites. Of the tithes taken by the Levites, they in turn were to offer a tenth to the priests.

19 A particular ritual was specified for purifying anyone who had come into contact with the dead. A ***red heifer without spot, wherein is no blemish, and upon which never came yoke***, would be brought to a priest. After killing it, ***one shall burn the heifer in his sight; her skin, and her flesh, and her blood, with her dung, shall he burn***. The ashes would be saved for future use in making purifying water.

He that toucheth the dead body of any man shall be unclean seven days. Everything and everyone in the tent of the deceased is likewise contaminated. The purification ritual required mixing some ashes of the burnt heifer in water, ***And a clean person shall take hyssop, and dip it in the water, and sprinkle it upon the tent, and upon all the vessels, and upon the persons that were there, and upon him that touched a bone, or one slain, or one dead, or a grave***. A homeopathic remedy, you might say, using a dead cow to counteract the effect of a dead person. I wondered how doctors, gravediggers and various others ever managed to be clean.

MEETING THE NATIVES

20 Thirty-eight years passed. Miriam died and was buried. The people continued to moan, while Moses struggled to keep the peace, as they wandered in the wilderness.

God was as unpredictable as ever. When the people complained that they had no water, he directed Moses to call everyone together, saying ***thou shalt bring forth to them water out of the rock***. They did just that: ***Moses and Aaron gathered the congregation together before the rock, and he said unto them, Hear now, ye rebels; must we fetch you water out of this rock? And Moses lifted up his hand, and with his rod he smote the rock twice: and the water came out abundantly, and the congregation drank, and their beasts also. And the LORD spake unto Moses and Aaron, Because ye believed me not, to sanctify me in the eyes of the children of Israel, therefore ye shall not bring this congregation into the land which I have given them.***

What had they done wrong? All I can imagine is that Moses failed to give God due credit for this miraculous feat. Honestly, though, to condemn the poor man to die just as forty years of his life were about to pay off is grotesque. It's no wonder God had labour problems.

Moses pressed on, despite this blow. The land became populated as they drew nearer their destination, and the natives were not friendly. Moses asked the king of Edom (the people descended from Jacob's brother Esau) for safe passage, which was refused. Esau's revenge, perhaps; in any case the people of Israel were forced to take a detour.

God decided that it was time for Aaron to die, with his son to succeed him as high priest. He ordered them to the top of a mountain, where ***Moses stripped Aaron of his garments, and put them upon Eleazar his son; and Aaron died there in the top of the mount*** – of exposure, by the sound of it.

When a group of Canaanites got in their way, the congregation said to God ***If thou wilt indeed deliver this people into my hand, then I will utterly destroy their cities.*** It was hard to pass up an offer like that, and so ***the LORD hearkened to the voice of Israel, and delivered up the Canaanites; and they utterly destroyed them and their cities.*** 21

They still couldn't take anything for granted, though. The next time grumbles about food and water were heard, ***the LORD sent fiery serpents among the people, and they bit the people; and much people of Israel died.*** They repented – a little too late, as usual – and God provided an antidote: ***Moses made a serpent of brass, and put it upon a pole, and it came to pass, that if a serpent had bitten any man, when he beheld the serpent of brass, he lived.*** Very slick, but it certainly looked like a graven image to me.

The people went back to making their conquests, and with God on their side it was a great success. When anyone stood in the way, ***Israel smote him with the edge of the sword, and possessed his land.*** With monotonous regularity a king would resist, God would tell Moses that everything was under control, and the Israelites would do battle. That the king was an enemy was enough; ***they smote him, and his sons, and all his people, until there was none left him alive: and they possessed his land.***

The king of Moab tried a different tactic. If military confrontation was unwise, perhaps a curse uttered by a recognised divine would do the trick. He decided to recruit a certain Balaam, who had a reputation for doing things right; as the king put it, ***he whom thou blessest is blessed, and he whom thou cursest is cursed.*** It was a good idea, but God had a word directly with Balaam to warn him off. 22

Balaam sent his regrets to the king. The king insisted, Balaam still demurred, and God behaved strangely again. We had seen it before: he tells X to do Y, X does Y, God gets upset. Thus ***God came unto Balaam at night, and said unto him, If the men come to call thee, rise up, and go with them; but yet the word which I shall say unto thee, that shalt thou do. And Balaam rose up in the morning, and saddled his ass, and went with the princes of Moab. And God's anger was kindled because he went: and the angel of the LORD stood in the way for an adversary against him.***

So there I was, standing in the way of Balaam's donkey. Only the donkey could see me, and Balaam beat her when she turned off the road. I reappeared along a narrow path, where the donkey crushed Balaam's foot against a wall and he beat her again. Finally when I barred the way completely the donkey just lay down, and Balaam really lost his temper with her. ***And the LORD opened the mouth of the ass, and she said unto Balaam, What have I done unto thee, that thou hast smitten me these three times?***

Balaam was a cool customer; faced with a talking donkey he didn't bat an eyelash. He threatened her with further violence, and she suggested that he was being unreasonable. At that point, fortunately, God let Balaam see that I was standing there. I was cross with the man, and let him know it: the donkey had saved him from big trouble. Balaam was properly penitent. I repeated God's instructions that he could go to meet the king, but was only to pass on approved messages.

23 The king was not happy with what he heard. After each set of sacrifices Balaam would deliver a blessing rather than a curse on Israel, and the king kept telling him to try again. The oracles, though, went from bad to worse.

The first concluded with a paean to Jacob: ***Let me die the death of the righteous, and let my last end be like his!*** The next reminded the king that God is not a man, that he should lie, and finished ***What hath God wrought! Behold, the people shall rise up as a great lion, and lift up himself as a young lion: he shall not lie down*** 24 ***until he eat of the prey, and drink the blood of the slain.*** The third was in similar vein: ***How goodly are thy tents, O Jacob, and thy tabernacles, O Israel! As the valleys are they spread forth, as gardens by the river's side.***

The king was furious: ***I called thee to curse mine enemies, and, behold, thou hast altogether blessed them these three times.*** Balaam protested that he could only follow God's command, and before leaving offered one last oracle. It was an apocalyptic vision of the triumph of Israel over all the surrounding peoples: ***there shall come a Star out of Jacob, and a Sceptre shall rise out of Israel, and shall smite the corners of Moab.*** And that was that. There was nothing to do but go home.

25 Notwithstanding such forecasts of lofty destiny, the cycle of sin and retribution never stopped. So, ***the people began to commit whoredom with the daughters of Moab. And they called the people unto the sacrifices of their gods: and the people did eat, and bowed down to their gods.*** Keeping a local girlfriend company at her place of worship was a big mistake: ***the LORD said unto Moses, Take all the heads of the people, and hang them up before the LORD against the sun.***

When one of the Israelites came home with a local women, Aaron's grandson ***rose up from among the congregation, and took a javelin in his hand; And he went after the man of Israel into the tent, and thrust both of them through, the man of Israel, and the woman through her belly.*** God was well pleased with this act of violence, and decided to halt the plague that had killed off 24,000 Israelites.

PREPARING FOR CONQUEST

26 Even God must have wondered if, what with one thing and another, the numbers of his people had been thinned out excessively, because he ordered another census. This time the total for men over twenty able to fight came to 601,730, only slightly less than at the start of the wanderings. This was all the more remarkable in view of the fact that not one of those originally counted was still alive, except for Caleb, Joshua and presumably Moses himself. Since all the rest had, by God's command,

died in the wilderness, the entire population was evidently under the age of sixty. At 120 Moses was therefore twice as old as the next eldest person; that's a generation gap for you.

God ordered that land be parcelled out by lot, but in proportion to the size of the families. He made an interesting ruling along the way. The daughters of a man who had died without a male heir came and asked Moses if they could inherit. God agreed that ***If a man die, and have no son, then ye shall cause his inheritance to pass unto his daughter.*** The rule didn't give women equal rights, but it was a start. 27

The end of the road was not far off. God told Moses that his time was coming: he would be allowed to see the promised land from a mountain top, but then he would die. Moses didn't try to argue. He just asked God to ***set a man over the congregation, Which may go out before them, and which may go in before them, and which may lead them out, and which may bring them in; that the congregation of the LORD be not as sheep which have no shepherd.*** God told him to appoint Joshua as his successor.

After a big decision thoughts turn to food, and so once again God gave long and detailed instructions as to which animals should be sacrificed on which occasions. Just to give the flavour, so to speak, these were the directions for the first day of the holiday known as Tabernacles: ***ye shall offer a burnt offering, a sacrifice made by fire, of a sweet savour unto the LORD; thirteen young bullocks, two rams, and fourteen lambs of the first year; they shall be without blemish: And their meat offering shall be of flour mingled with oil, three tenth deals unto every bullock of the thirteen bullocks, two tenth deals to each ram of the two rams, and a several tenth deal to each lamb of the fourteen lambs: And one kid of the goats for a sin offering; beside the continual burnt offering, his meat offering, and his drink offering.*** Festive Meat Cookery, by God. 28 29

Thus refreshed, God returned to the position of women. When it came to oaths, a man's word was his bond. A woman was likewise responsible, unless the male head of the household actively forbade the oath when he heard it. Failing such repudiation – which in any case did not apply to a widow or divorced woman – she would be held to her vow. 30

It was again time to reduce the local population. The campaign in this area, called Midian, was justified as being God's revenge on the heathen. Every man there was killed – even Balaam, the seer who had sung their praises. ***And the children of Israel took all the women of Midian captives, and their little ones, and took the spoil of all their cattle, and all their flocks, and all their goods. And they burnt all their cities wherein they dwelt, and all their goodly castles, with fire.*** 31

That would have been bad enough, but Moses wasn't satisfied. He blamed the women for seducing the Israelites, and leading them astray. ***Now therefore kill every male among the little ones, and kill every woman that hath known man by lying with him. But all the women children, that have not known a man by lying with him, keep alive for yourselves.*** The booty – thousands of sheep, cows, donkeys and virgins – was divided equally between the army and the whole congregation. On the side of Israel, incidentally, not one man had been lost.

32 As is obvious the twelve tribes were no longer meandering in the desert: they were now on good land. In fact a couple of the tribes suggested that they were happy to go no further, remaining in Gilead, east of the river Jordan. Moses was alarmed. The last time people had been reluctant to press on into the promised land God had made everyone wander in the wilderness for forty years, with the entire older generation wiped out along the way.

The would-be settlers volunteered to help in the campaign without claiming any of the conquered land, if they could come back across the Jordan afterwards. The offer was too good to refuse. If you do what you say, replied Moses, ***this land shall be your possession before the LORD. But if ye will not do so, behold, ye have sinned against the LORD: and be sure your sin will find you out.***

By this stage, though, Moses seemed to be losing his touch. When he went to communicate this deal to Joshua and the other leaders he made it look ridiculous: if the restive tribes come ***every man armed to battle, before the LORD, and the land shall be subdued before you; then ye shall give them the land of Gilead for a possession: But if they will not pass over with you armed, they shall have possessions among you in the land of Canaan.*** In other words, if they help you then the whole of the promised land is yours, but if they don't help then you'll share it with them. The old man wasn't making sense, and I was surprised he got away with it.

33 Moses reviewed the itinerary they had followed through the wilderness. God told him that once across the river Jordan ***ye shall dispossess the inhabitants of the land, and dwell therein: for I have given you the land to possess it. ... But if ye will not drive out the inhabitants of the land from before you; then it shall come to pass, that those which ye let remain of them shall be pricks in your eyes, and thorns in your sides, and shall vex you in the land wherein ye dwell.*** Clearly,

34 there was more bloodshed to come. God defined the boundaries of the land they were to occupy, and Moses assigned the leaders the task of dividing it among the families.

35 The descendants of Levi were strictly speaking not entitled to an inheritance, but 48 cities were to be set aside for them: ***and ye shall give also unto the Levites suburbs for the cities round about them. And the cities shall they have to dwell in; and the suburbs of them shall be for their cattle.*** (They knew even then that suburbs were only fit for cattle.) Six of these cities were to be places of refuge for people who committed manslaughter.

No refuge was available for anyone who deliberately attacked a man and killed him; such a person was guilty of murder and condemned to death. Where the killing had been accidental or without premeditation, the perpetrator would be allowed to remain in one of the designated cities. There he would be protected; elsewhere, the relatives of the victim could kill him with impunity. The curious part was that this banishment lasted not for any fixed term, but until the death of the high priest, after which he could go home. I rather liked this type of amnesty, though the high priest must have lived in fear of being bumped off.

In the field of evidence God was a progressive. A man could be condemned to death as a murderer only where there were witnesses – one was not sufficient – testifying against him. He upheld equality before the law; the death penalty could not be avoided by paying a fine. In his view, justice required capital punishment: ***ye shall not pollute the land wherein ye are: for blood it defileth the land: and the land cannot be cleansed of the blood that is shed therein, but by the blood of him that shed it.*** What is the right amount of blood to act as a cleanser? I'm inclined to believe that more blood means more defilement.

36

When God tackled major issues his judgments had a certain magnificence, but on points of detail he sometimes took bad advice. For example, he compromised his ruling on brotherless women being allowed to inherit after the tribal leaders complained. They argued that any such women who married outside the tribe would take a portion of the patrimony with them. I wanted God to tell them not to add parochialism to their xenophobia, but he was committed to defending the concept of tribal land. Thus he told them that they had a good point, and restricted the women's choice of partners. ***Let them marry to whom they think best; only to the family of the tribe of their father shall they marry.*** There's a contradiction for you.

These are the commandments and the judgments, which the LORD commanded by the hand of Moses unto the children of Israel in the plains of Moab by Jordan near Jericho.

5

Deuteronomy

1 ***And it came to pass in the fortieth year, in the eleventh month, on the first day of the month, that Moses spake unto the children of Israel, according unto all that the LORD had given him in commandment unto them.*** I didn't notice any great enthusiasm among the people at the idea of hearing the law all over again, but Moses wasn't a man to take opinion polls.

In a long prologue, Moses reviewed the history of their journey through the wilderness. He mentioned what I think was one of the high points of his career, the creation of an executive and judicial system in which ***ye shall hear the small as well as the great.***

Moses went on to recall sending the expedition to spy out the promised land, and the disastrous consequences of its report. Their lack of confidence in divine protection condemned everyone of that generation to die in the wilderness. His memory was failing, though; he commented that ***Also the LORD was angry with me for your sakes, saying, Thou also shalt not go in thither***, when in fact God's order came much later, after Moses himself failed in some way. Still, everyone wants somebody else to blame for personal calamities.

2 His memory was also fallible when he reviewed their encounters with foreign peoples. Hence he claimed that they had been given passage through the land of Edom, while in fact they had had to take a long detour to avoid it. The whole area had a colourful history as the home of giants, but they were an endangered species

3 and the Israelites were not great conservationists. Of one such kingdom, ruled by the awesome Og, Moses remarks ***we utterly destroyed them ... the men, women, and children, of every city.*** That would have been the end of the race, because ***only Og king of Bashan remained of the remnant of giants; behold, his bedstead was a bedstead of iron ... nine cubits was the length thereof, and four cubits the breadth of it***, i.e. it measured over four yards long and two wide, roughly speaking.

Moses admitted that he tried to change God's mind about excluding him from the promised land. His appeal had been poignant: ***I pray thee, let me go over, and see the good land that is beyond Jordan, that goodly mountain, and Lebanon. But the LORD was wroth with me for your sakes, and would not hear me: and the LORD said unto me, Let it suffice thee; speak no more unto me of this matter.***

4 Moses always thought that he knew best: perhaps it came from spending time with God. For example, he told the people that ***Ye shall not add unto the word which I command you, neither shall ye diminish ought from it.*** Now certainly God had tried to give him rules for every occasion, but you can't just assume that

nothing will ever change. It was all very well to ask rhetorically ***what nation is there so great, that hath statutes and judgments so righteous as all this law, which I set before you this day?*** – it was probably true, at the time – but you shouldn't be complacent.

Being an old man, Moses rambled on about this and that. He seemed to forget that God had kept everyone waiting down below while he alone heard the ten commandments; he said ***the LORD spake unto you out of the midst of the fire: ye heard the voice of the words, but saw no similitude; only ye heard a voice.*** The fact that God didn't show his face prompted the thought that no one should make a likeness of any living creature. I wanted to warn him that he might find art useful one day, but it was too late.

Despite all that I found Moses eloquent, and was touched when he spoke of not going ***in unto that good land, which the LORD thy God giveth thee for an inheritance: But I must die in this land, I must not go over Jordan: but ye shall go over, and possess that good land.*** He warned them, though, that future generations could fall into idolatry; ***I call heaven and earth to witness against you this day.*** They would be driven out, to ***serve gods, the work of men's hands, wood and stone, which neither see, nor hear, nor eat, nor smell. But if from thence thou shalt seek the LORD thy God, thou shalt find him, if thou seek him with all thy heart and with all thy soul.***

THE COMMANDMENTS

After this long preamble, Moses finally embarked on his overview of the law. He began, needless to say, by repeating the ten commandments. Interestingly, he didn't seem to treat them as carved in stone – which they were. He introduced slight variations in the wording here and there. 5

The injunction to keep the sabbath was made to sound less like a duty to God and more like a duty to fellow men and women; he explained the prohibition against anyone in the household working as so ***that thy manservant and thy maidservant may rest as well as thou.*** Moreover, while on mount Sinai he was told that the sabbath commemorates the seventh day of creation, Moses wanted everyone to ***remember that thou wast a servant in the land of Egypt ... therefore the LORD thy God commanded thee to keep the sabbath day.*** This may be a *non sequitur*, but the sentiment seemed admirable.

The other variation Moses made, bless him, suggested that he wasn't too old to recognise injustice. The tenth commandment had stated ***Thou shalt not covet thy neighbour's house, thou shalt not covet thy neighbour's wife, nor his*** etc., etc. The wife sounded just like a piece of property. By changing the order Moses was able to make it seem less offensive: ***Neither shalt thou desire thy neighbour's wife, neither shalt thou covet thy neighbour's house, his field,*** etc. At least she came top of the list of possessions.

6 The real highlight followed. Moses offered a grand summary of the whole enterprise: ***Hear, O Israel: The LORD our God is one LORD: And thou shalt love the LORD thy God with all thine heart, and with all thy soul, and with all thy might. And these words, which I command thee this day, shall be in thine heart: And thou shalt teach them diligently unto thy children, and shalt talk of them when thou sittest in thine house, and when thou walkest by the way, and when thou liest down, and when thou risest up. And thou shalt bind them for a sign upon thine hand, and they shall be as frontlets between thine eyes. And thou shalt write them upon the posts of thy house, and on thy gates.***

This great commandment was splendid, though stern old Moses might have been surprised had he known that his words would be the foundation for a whole theology of love. Then, too, I wasn't sure what to make of the opening proclamation: ***The LORD our God is one LORD***; Jehovah our God is one Jehovah. It's like saying 'Michael the Archangel is one Michael'.

Moses went on to say ***Ye shall not go after other gods, of the gods of the people which are round about you***; our God is jealous. Because of that violent streak, ***Ye shall not tempt the LORD your God.*** He didn't need much tempting to get out the cane. Moses tactfully referred to the period when the ***LORD shewed signs and wonders, great and sore, upon Egypt, upon Pharaoh, and upon all his household, before our eyes,*** but he could as well have mentioned the signs and wonders that disposed of thousands of Israelites in the wilderness.

7 There was every reason to believe that God would continue to be muscular. According to Moses, he was going to expel any nations in the path of Israel, ***And when the LORD thy God shall deliver them before thee; thou shalt smite them, and utterly destroy them; thou shalt make no covenant with them, nor shew mercy unto them: Neither shalt thou make marriages with them; thy daughter thou shalt not give unto his son, nor his daughter shalt thou take unto thy son.*** It didn't sound as though there would be anyone left to marry anyway.

As we know, the children of Israel enjoyed a unique relationship with God. As Moses put it, ***thou art an holy people unto the LORD thy God: the LORD thy God hath chosen thee to be a special people unto himself, above all people that are upon the face of the earth.*** Becoming carried away, he even promised that no one would ever be sick or childless.

8 In the wilderness God had beaten them with one hand and fed them with the other; the lesson was that ***man doth not live by bread only, but by every word that proceedeth out of the mouth of the LORD.*** God's intention was for the people to walk in his ways, and to fear him. (Little problem there, one would think.)

Moses continued his enraptured delivery: ***For the LORD thy God bringeth thee into a good land, a land of brooks of water, of fountains and depths that spring out of valleys and hills; A land of wheat, and barley, and vines, and fig trees, and pomegranates; a land of oil olive, and honey; A land wherein thou shalt eat bread without scarceness, thou shalt not lack any thing in it; a land whose stones are iron, and out of whose hills thou mayest dig brass.*** He was bringing them to an earthly paradise; all would be well if they obeyed the rules, and all would be lost if they didn't.

The episode of the golden calf was mentioned as a reminder of their past sins. 9 Modesty did not get in the way of Moses giving himself credit for saving their skins, though he changed a few of the details to make himself sound less cruel and more self-sacrificing. For example he recalled having ground the statue into dust and casting it into the river; in reality, of course, he had mixed the dust with water and made people drink it. Instead of mentioning that he ordered the massacre of three thousand sinners, he now claimed that he went forty days and nights without food or water praying that everyone be forgiven.

After breaking the first set of tablets, Moses had had to produce the copies 10 himself. In his retelling of the story, however, God did the writing, just as he had done on the originals. All God wants is total obedience, Moses said: to be loved, feared and served with proper enthusiasm. Unfortunately his conclusion wasn't easy to follow, being a very mixed metaphor: ***Circumcise therefore the foreskin of your heart, and be no more stiffnecked.*** As for Moses, he wanted God to be all things to all men, both terrible and mighty, and the protector of widows and orphans. The qualities that made for success as a national god, however, weren't necessarily those you sought in a personal god.

Moses wound up his exhortation by once again offering a vision of their 11 destination. In those more down-to-earth days the virtuous were not expected to find their rewards internally, or in another world; compensation on the spot was expected. Of course, God used both a carrot and a stick, or as Moses said, ***a blessing and a curse; A blessing, if ye obey the commandments of the LORD your God, which I command you this day: And a curse, if ye will not obey the commandments of the LORD your God, but turn aside out of the way which I command you this day, to go after other gods, which ye have not known.***

THE LAW BOOK

At this point Moses launched into the detail of the law, not the most inspiring 12 material for his valedictory address. You won't be surprised when I tell you that the first topic on the list was killing animals. God wanted to relax the rules for slaughter; it wasn't necessary that it always be done at the altar. Although he still expected the burnt offerings, ***Notwithstanding thou mayest kill and eat flesh in all thy gates, whatsoever thy soul lusteth after.***

God intended the Israelites to conquer, and he certainly did not support the maxim 'When in Rome ...' The people were put on their guard, ***that thou enquire not after their gods, saying, How did these nations serve their gods? even so will I do likewise.*** God wasn't interested in new and exotic forms of devotion. For him, the old-fashioned ways were always best.

He also didn't plan to tolerate any nonsense. ***If there arise among you a*** 13

prophet, or a dreamer of dreams, and giveth thee a sign or a wonder, you should stay well clear. In fact, ***If thy brother, the son of thy mother, or thy son, or thy daughter, or the wife of thy bosom, or thy friend, which is as thine own soul, entice thee secretly, saying, Let us go and serve other gods ... thou shalt surely kill him; thine hand shall be first upon him to put him to death, and afterwards the hand of all the people. And thou shalt stone him with stones, that he die.*** A city that has been subverted by heathens should be destroyed and left as a ruin in perpetuity. To my mind, he was too rough; if you're going to be number one, you should act secure.

14 In reviewing all the dietary restrictions, Moses put anything that had died of its own accord off limits. The carcass should be given to a resident alien, or sold to a foreigner. I hope they knew what they were getting.

God was prepared to see people let their hair down, fortunately. A proportion of the crop was to be set aside for special feasts in the consecrated places. If these were far away, the tithe could be converted into cash, and once the journey was made ***thou shalt bestow that money for whatsoever thy soul lusteth after, for oxen, or for sheep, or for wine, or for strong drink, or for whatsoever thy soul desireth: and thou shalt eat there before the LORD thy God, and thou shalt rejoice, thou, and thine household.*** I wish everyone could have seen that jollier side of God more often.

This arrangement was not such good news for the Levites. Previously they had been given the tithe as of right, and now Moses was saying that they would only receive it every third year. Perhaps he was talking about an additional tithe, but that wasn't the way I heard it.

15 In talking about duties to the poor, Moses was in a muddle. He wanted to preserve his vision of a land without poverty, but recognised that ***the poor shall never cease out of the land: therefore I command thee, saying, Thou shalt open thine hand wide unto thy brother, to thy poor, and to thy needy, in thy land.*** Every seventh year all debts were to be forgiven and all slaves freed. God had provided, though, that any slave wishing to remain would have his or her ear pierced against the door with an awl, and would henceforth belong to the master in perpetuity.

16 As he descended into the minutiae of the law Moses became increasingly garrulous. He described all the festivals yet again. He prescribed the death penalty

17 for heretics yet again. (The sentence would be stoning, and the witnesses would cast the first stones.) He was on the point of detailing the remuneration of priests when he did just happen to let it slip that the people might wish to appoint a king in due course. Oddly, God's first warning was that ***he shall not multiply horses to himself***, apparently because they would have to come from Egypt, which was out of bounds. But then ***Neither shall he multiply wives to himself, that his heart turn not away: neither shall he greatly multiply to himself silver and gold.*** Moreover, the king was to make a copy of the law and read it every day, ***That his heart be not lifted up above his brethren.*** A worthy thought, if hard to picture.

18 After that contribution to political philosophy, Moses slipped back into review-

ing what share of the sacrifices belonged to the priests and other Levites. More esoteric still was his acquaintance with the remarkable variety of occult practice, concerning which he emphasised that ***There shall not be found among you any one that maketh his son or his daughter to pass through the fire, or that useth divination, or an observer of times, or an enchanter, or a witch, Or a charmer, or a consulter with familiar spirits, or a wizard, or a necromancer.*** God enjoyed the occasional bit of magic himself, of course, but some people went too far.

While depriving the people of sorcerers, God declared that he would send another prophet like Moses to pass on his commands. There was an awkward dilemma, though; people ignoring a real prophet would be punished, but a false prophet would die. Credulity seemed to be the safest course, since only sceptics and impostors were at risk. God's answer to the problem of identification was that failed prophecies revealed the false prophet. That was clear enough, but it didn't help if the pretender avoided predictions, or was lucky enough to get them right.

19

Moses returned to the beaten track, outlining the need for cities of refuge where people who killed without malice could escape vengeance. He even provided a picturesque illustration: ***when a man goeth into the wood with his neighbour to hew wood, and his hand fetcheth a stroke with the axe to cut down the tree, and the head slippeth from the helve, and lighteth upon his neighbour, that he die; he shall flee unto one of those cities, and live.*** I wasn't much impressed with this example: surely in such cases of purely accidental death there should never be any question of a blood feud. You need to distinguish not only murder and manslaughter, but manslaughter and bad luck.

Perjury was to be punished by inflicting whatever penalty the person hoped to impose on his adversary. This was another application, then, of the principle that ***life shall go for life, eye for eye, tooth for tooth***, etc.

20

In any battle against enemy forces, however large, victory was guaranteed. That said, there were a number of remarkable exemptions available from military service. Anyone who had built a new house and not yet dedicated it, or planted a new vineyard and not yet had fruit from it, was instructed to stay at home. Likewise the officers should ask ***what man is there that hath betrothed a wife, and hath not taken her? let him go and return unto his house, lest he die in the battle, and another man take her.*** But the most surprising provision was that anyone who was ***fearful and fainthearted*** would be excused, on the grounds that he might otherwise be a risk to morale. Conscription obviously did not have God's approval.

When it came to the opposing side, however, the rules of warfare were far from generous. If a besieged city surrendered then its inhabitants would lose their freedom but not their lives. If they resisted, all the men would be killed, while the women, children, livestock and property would be divided among the victors. In the case where the city was one of those in the land God had earmarked for the Israelites, then ***thou shalt save alive nothing that breatheth.*** The purpose of this annihilation was supposed to be the avoidance of religious contamination, but I don't know that God helped his cause in the long run by being so extreme.

21 God gave close attention to sex and violence. There were rituals to be followed for an unsolved murder, and rules for conducting a hanging. He went into some detail about what to do when you have been to war ***And seest among the captives a beautiful woman, and hast a desire unto her, that thou wouldest have her to thy wife; Then thou shalt bring her home to thine house; and she shall shave her head, and pare her nails; And she shall put the raiment of her captivity from off her, and shall remain in thine house, and bewail her father and her mother a full month: and after that thou shalt go in unto her, and be her husband, and she shall be thy wife. And it shall be, if thou have no delight in her, then thou shalt let her go whither she will; but thou shalt not sell her at all for money, thou shalt not make merchandise of her, because thou hast humbled her.***

One law that God had not previously taken very seriously was that of primogeniture. Now, though, he said that the firstborn son shouldn't be slighted just because a later son was the offspring of a favourite wife. Perhaps he realised that the patriarchs had set a poor example of family life.

When it came to discipline, God was an enthusiast. If a son was persistently disobedient, the parents ***shall say unto the elders of his city, This our son is stubborn and rebellious, he will not obey our voice; he is a glutton, and a drunkard. And all the men of his city shall stone him with stones, that he die.*** That's what I call tough love.

22 Obviously the permissive society wouldn't have lasted long with God in charge. One of the prohibitions was on cross-dressing: ***The woman shall not wear that which pertaineth unto a man, neither shall a man put on a woman's garment: for all that do so are abomination unto the LORD thy God.*** The variety of issues that God set his mind to was quite bewildering; in quick succession, he ruled that you could take a bird's nest, so long as you let the bird itself go free; you should have a parapet on your roof terrace; you shouldn't use your vineyard for planting anything else; ***Thou shalt not plow with an ox and an ass together. Thou shalt not wear a garment of divers sorts, as of woollen and linen together.*** Sometimes I wondered how he thought these things up.

Without changing gear, God went back to sex. What should be done when a man claims that his newlywed wife did not come to him a virgin? The woman's parents could take evidence of her wedding-night chastity, a blood-stained cloth, to the elders. As punishment for the slander the husband would be obliged to pay damages to his father-in-law, and more oddly, prohibited from ever seeking a divorce. ***But if this thing be true, and the tokens of virginity be not found for the damsel: Then they shall bring out the damsel to the door of her father's house, and the men of her city shall stone her with stones that she die.*** The most blameless of virgins must have been terrified of not bleeding sufficiently.

Naturally anyone guilty of adultery or fornication was condemned to die. Remarkably, though, the rape of a virgin not yet betrothed was to be punished not by death but by marriage. Although the perpetrator was obliged to pay a fine to the woman's father, it was only half as large as the fine payable in the prior case of slander. Perhaps accusations of unchastity were more serious than rape because they reflected badly on the father?

God's tendency to machismo was underlined by the exclusion of men who had suffered unfortunate accidents below the belt: ***He that is wounded in the stones, or hath his privy member cut off, shall not enter into the congregation of the LORD.*** I was never aware of any checks being made, thank heavens. Various other groups of people were disqualified from joining God's team, generally on ethnic grounds. 23

God had rather quaint concerns for the purity of men in military camps. Any nocturnal emissions were to result in self-banishment during the following day. Furthermore everyone was supposed to carry a small shovel, the delicately-put idea being that ***when thou wilt ease thyself abroad, thou shalt dig therewith, and shalt turn back and cover that which cometh from thee: For the LORD thy God walketh in the midst of thy camp***, and doesn't want to step in anything unpleasant.

As before, though, just when you thought God was being prim he'd come out with something striking. In this instance, he showed real compassion towards runaway slaves: they were not to be turned over to their masters, but given sanctuary in a place of their choosing. For that matter, his ruling against the institution of temple prostitution, among men or women, was forward looking. In economics he was less strong, as evidenced by the prohibition on charging interest, except to foreigners. You don't encourage investment if a person is obliged to lend the fruits of his labour without compensation.

The laws became somewhat miscellaneous at this point. There was to be no recycling of partners; if a woman remarried following a divorce, then even if her second marriage ended her first husband would not be free to take her back as a wife: that would be an ***abomination***. 24

Brushing up on his image, God repeated his humanitarian statutes. The poor should not be made to suffer unduly when they borrowed. ***The fathers shall not be put to death for the children, neither shall the children be put to death for the fathers: every man shall be put to death for his own sin.*** After a harvest the widows, orphans and foreigners should be given generous opportunities to glean the fields.

No one was to be given more than forty lashes. ***Thou shalt not muzzle the ox when he treadeth out the corn.*** If two brothers live together and one of them dies childless, the other must marry his widow. Should he refuse, and persist in refusing, ***Then shall his brother's wife come unto him in the presence of the elders, and loose his shoe from off his foot, and spit in his face, and shall answer and say, So shall it be done unto that man that will not build up his brother's house. And his name shall be called in Israel, The house of him that hath his shoe loosed.*** Well, there are worst things to be called. 25

Any woman becoming mixed up in a fight between men, even if she was just trying to break it up, had to keep her hands well clear of sensitive regions: ***When men strive together one with another, and the wife of the one draweth near for***

to deliver her husband out of the hand of him that smiteth him, and putteth forth her hand, and taketh him by the secrets: Then thou shalt cut off her hand, thine eye shall not pity her. That's robust refereeing.

That more or less wrapped up the recital of the law; I confess that my attention 26 was flagging. Moses gave a reminder that the first fruits were to be offered to God, that the Israelites were God's own people and thus expected to be obedient, and so on.

Moses blesses and curses

27 Just to make sure that it had all sunk in, Moses offered a series of curses, blessings, and more curses. As usual I never knew quite what to expect; he threw in curses on people who gave bad directions to the blind, on those who moved their neighbour's boundary stones, etc., as well as on the perpetrators of more exotic sins: ***Cursed be he that lieth with any manner of beast. And all the people shall say, Amen.*** We again heard ***Cursed be he that lieth with his mother in law,*** which it's hard to imagine was ever much of a problem.

28 The blessings for compliance were more predictable: wealth, offspring, power – nothing very spiritual, I'm afraid. The promises had a fine cadence to them, though: ***Blessed shalt thou be when thou comest in, and blessed shalt thou be when thou goest out. The LORD shall cause thine enemies that rise up against thee to be smitten before thy face: they shall come out against thee one way, and flee before thee seven ways.***

We only heard a few more of the blessings in store before being warned what would happen if the commandments were not obeyed. God didn't like to waste time describing the carrot when he could be waving the stick, and this list of curses was truly monumental. Among the milder threats was ***Thou shalt betroth a wife, and another man shall lie with her: thou shalt build a house, and thou shalt not dwell therein: thou shalt plant a vineyard, and shalt not gather the grapes thereof.*** Some were heartrending: ***Thy sons and thy daughters shall be given unto another people, and thine eyes shall look, and fail with longing for them all the day long: and there shall be no might in thine hand.*** The Israelites would become famous, not as the people God had chosen, but as the one he had afflicted. ***And thou shalt become an astonishment, a proverb, and a byword, among all nations whither the LORD shall lead thee.***

I was already feeling uncomfortable, but God was only just warming up. He repeated the warning of death and disaster to come, ***Because thou servedst not the LORD thy God with joyfulness*** – is it any wonder? The curses became ever more horrifying. In their besieged cities, delicate women would be reduced to eating the newly born.

In every conceivable way, then (as well as some only barely conceivable) God promised to make their lives miserable unless they took the commandments to heart. He put it quite well: ***In the morning thou shalt say, Would God it were even! and at even thou shalt say, Would God it were morning!*** The final curse was bizarre, the ultimate indignity: you will return to Egypt for sale as slaves, but no one will buy you.

29 Having transmitted these dire warnings, Moses returned to speaking in his own voice to cajole the people. He told them that ***Ye stand this day all of you before the LORD your God ... from the hewer of thy wood unto the drawer of thy water: That thou shouldest enter into covenant with the LORD thy God.*** After yet more visions of a blighted future, he stated one of the fundamental principles of theology: ***The secret things belong unto the LORD our God: but those things which are revealed belong unto us and to our children for ever, that we may do all the words of this law.***

THE DEATH OF MOSES

30 Moses continued to urge obedience among his listeners, but he knew that anything he said would be an anticlimax. His only new argument was that it would be easy; the law was there before them. And so he summed up with the declaration ***I call heaven and earth to record this day against you, that I have set before you life and death, blessing and cursing: therefore choose life, that both thou and thy seed may live.*** 31 Finally, with a reference to his age (120) and his agility (not what it was), he announced that his time had come. Joshua would lead them across the Jordan where, with God's help, they would defeat their enemies.

God invested Joshua with command, ***and said, Be strong and of a good courage: for thou shalt bring the children of Israel into the land which I sware unto them: and I will be with thee.*** Meanwhile Moses had turned over the law to the priests, and prepared, somewhat against character, to recite a couple of long poems to the people.

32 I don't know what got into him, because it certainly didn't sound like the Moses I knew. His thunder had gone; in fact he said as much himself in the first sentence: ***My doctrine shall drop as the rain, my speech shall distil as the dew, as the small rain upon the tender herb, and as the showers upon the grass.*** Of course, it was only ever the people he criticised; as for God, ***He is the Rock, his work is perfect: for all his ways are judgment: a God of truth and without iniquity, just and right is he.***

In his poetic discourse, Moses once more offered an historical overview. The starting point was Jacob, because when nations were being formed God ***kept him as the apple of his eye.*** But the people of Israel ***waxed fat, and kicked ... he forsook God which made him, and lightly esteemed the Rock of his salvation.*** Being wicked, they would come to a bad end, one described in unpleasant detail.

God was just as abrupt with Moses as with everyone else. ***And the LORD spake unto Moses that selfsame day, saying, Get thee up into this mountain ... And die***

in the mount whither thou goest up. Instead of expressing some appreciation for all that the man had done, God brought out the old tale of transgression and told him to drop dead.

33 Still, Moses blessed the various tribes of Israel before he went. He even offered the last group the wistful hope of an old man: ***as thy days, so shall thy strength be.*** But to all, he declared that ***The eternal God is thy refuge***.

34 Moses had his one glimpse of the promised land, a first and last look. ***And the LORD said unto him, This is the land which I sware unto Abraham, unto Isaac, and unto Jacob, saying, I will give it unto thy seed: I have caused thee to see it with thine eyes, but thou shalt not go over thither. So Moses the servant of the LORD died there in the land of Moab, according to the word of the LORD.*** There he was buried, and unlike the patriarchs ***no man knoweth of his sepulchre unto this day.*** The greatest of the prophets lies in an unknown grave outside the land of his people's inheritance; a sad end for a man who never had a home.

6

Joshua

Joshua was now in charge. God promised him that ***as I was with Moses, so I will be with thee***, which must have seemed a mixed blessing. But God did his best to be reassuring, saying repeatedly ***Be strong and of a good courage; be not afraid, neither be thou dismayed: for the LORD thy God is with thee whithersoever thou goest.*** 1

From his headquarters in the unattractively-named Shittim, Joshua planned his campaign. Once across the river Jordan they would need to capture the city of Jericho. ***And Joshua the son of Nun sent out of Shittim two men to spy secretly, saying, Go view the land, even Jericho. And they went, and came into an harlot's house, named Rahab, and lodged there.*** I trust they weren't mixing business with pleasure. 2

The counter-espionage forces were soon alerted, but Rahab hid the spies and sent their adversaries off towards the city gate, saying ***pursue after them quickly, for ye shall overtake them.*** She thus became one of the first to fill the role of the good bad woman, risking her life to help a man in trouble.

Rahab made a deal with Joshua's men; in return for her help and discretion she asked them to guarantee the safety of her family when the Israelites arrived. The men agreed, giving her a ***line of scarlet thread*** to mark the house.

With the spies safely back, Joshua prepared to move. God made a nice gesture; to show that he backed Joshua as enthusiastically as he had Moses, he decided to part the river Jordan just as he had done with the Red Sea. When the priests carrying the ark reached the river the water coming downstream piled up, ***And the priests that bare the ark of the covenant of the LORD stood firm on dry ground in the midst of Jordan, and all the Israelites passed over on dry ground, until all the people were passed clean over Jordan.*** In all their journeys they never had to get their feet wet. 3

To remind future generations of this event Joshua made a pile of twelve stones, one for each of the twelve tribes. The whole country is so rocky, though, that I doubt a few stones ever attracted any attention. Joshua put another pile on the spot in the riverbed where the priests stood, and presumably those have been underwater ever since. He should have taken some advice on memorial-building, in my opinion. 4

The order of battle was another puzzle. The two and a half tribes hoping to return to land east of the Jordan fielded some forty thousand men, not much more than a third of the census figure. I suspect that their support was less than wholehearted.

5 Before getting on with the campaign, Joshua stopped to circumcise all the men. For some reason nobody had been done during all the years of wandering, so there was a lot of catching up to do. That was probably the way they felt about eating, too, since the manna stopped once food became available in Canaan. Variety at last.

God appeared before Joshua in the guise of a warrior, which made a major impression. When Joshua, prostrate, asked what message he had come to give, he merely said ***Loose thy shoe from off thy foot; for the place whereon thou standest is holy.***

6 Still, God did get around to suggesting some highly novel tactics to Joshua. ***Now Jericho was straitly shut up because of the children of Israel: none went out, and none came in.*** The plan was to march once around the city every day for six days. On the seventh day they would do seven circuits, unleash a blast from the ram's-horn trumpets and give a great shout, and that would be the end of the city. As psychological warfare it was brilliantly conceived; I imagine the inhabitants of Jericho were so unnerved by the ominous circling that a small peep would have finished them off.

So the people shouted when the priests blew with the trumpets: and it came to pass, when the people heard the sound of the trumpet, and the people shouted with a great shout, that the wall fell down flat, so that the people went up into the city, every man straight before him, and they took the city. And they utterly destroyed all that was in the city, both man and woman, young and old, and ox, and sheep, and ass, with the edge of the sword. To finish the job properly, Joshua (whose ***fame was noised throughout all the country***) put a curse on anyone attempting to rebuild the city. At least the family of Rahab was spared, though.

7 God had wanted Jericho to serve as a giant sacrifice; all looting and pillaging was to be strictly for his benefit alone. One of the Israelites took a souvenir that he thought wouldn't be noticed, which was a big mistake.

In the next encounter with the enemy the Israelites were routed, and God said that they had only themselves to blame. Condemned merchandise had been taken, he revealed; ***they have put it even among their own stuff.*** God devised a theatrical method of indicating the guilty party: the tribes would be put on parade, and he would choose one; and then the clans from within that tribe, the households from the chosen clan, and finally each man of the selected household, would come forward. I expected nerves to crack, but in fact the culprit held out until the end.

Joshua was very paternal: ***My son, give, I pray thee, glory to the LORD God of Israel, and make confession unto him; and tell me now what thou hast done; hide it not from me.*** The man came clean, saying ***Indeed I have sinned against the LORD God of Israel, and thus and thus have I done: When I saw among the spoils a goodly Babylonish garment, and two hundred shekels of silver, and a wedge of gold of fifty shekels weight, then I coveted them, and took them.*** This being a show trial, however, confession was followed by a messy end. He was taken with his booty, his children, his animals and all his possessions, and despatched with a comment in doubtful taste: ***Joshua said, Why hast thou troubled us? the LORD shall trouble thee this day. And all Israel stoned him with stones, and burned them with fire, after they had stoned them with stones.***

THE CONQUEST

8 Thus purified of corrupting influences, they were able to resume the conquest. In taking the next town Joshua used a new strategy; part of his army – first he ***chose out thirty thousand mighty men of valour***, and then confusingly ***he took about five thousand men*** – was told to sneak behind the town; the force making the frontal attack pretended to flee, drawing out the defenders, and the waiting troops took the city unopposed. All the inhabitants were duly slaughtered and the city reduced to a heap, and this time God let them keep the loot.

9 The locals were in a quandary, because the Israelites were clearly determined to wipe them all out. One group from the town of Gibeon had sufficient ingenuity to find a solution. Wearing their worst clothes and oldest shoes, carrying mouldy bread and split wine containers, they came to Joshua ***and said unto him, and to the men of Israel, We be come from a far country: now therefore make ye a league with us.*** Their well-travelled appearance seemed to back up this story, and so without seeking God's advice ***Joshua made peace with them, and made a league with them, to let them live***. A few days later it came out that these were local people in disguise, but the oath had been made.

Joshua wasn't going to take this lying down. He had promised not to kill the people of Gibeon, but declared ***Now therefore ye are cursed, and there shall none of you be freed from being bondmen, and hewers of wood and drawers of water for the house of my God.*** He seemed outraged by their deceit, but they replied very reasonably that since ***the LORD thy God commanded his servant Moses to give you all the land, and to destroy all the inhabitants of the land from before you, therefore we were sore afraid of our lives because of you, and have done this thing.*** I give them a lot of credit.

10 The king of Jerusalem and his allies were not pleased by this defection, and decided that attacking Gibeon was the next best thing to taking on the Israelites. It was not a wise move. Joshua, who had no intention of letting his slave colony be overrun, marched all night to come to its aid. The enemy was defeated; ***the LORD discomfited them before Israel, and slew them with a great slaughter at Gibeon***, to use a mixture of understatement and hyperbole. God finished them off with hailstones; indeed, ***they were more which died with hailstones than they whom the children of Israel slew with the sword.***

Not wanting to run out of time, Joshua commanded
Sun, stand thou still upon Gibeon;
and thou, Moon, in the valley of Ajalon.

And the sun stood still, and the moon stayed, until the people had avenged themselves upon their enemies. Is not this written in the book of Jasher? So the sun stood still in the midst of heaven, and hasted not to go down about a whole day. And there was no day like that before it or after it, that the LORD hearkened unto the voice of a man: for the LORD fought for Israel. I wouldn't place a lot of credence in the book of Jasher, which no one even bothered to save, but I'm sure it seemed like a long day to the other side.

The kings of the defeated cities were brought before Joshua, who told his commanders to put their feet on the necks of the captives. This is what we shall do to all our enemies, he said, ***And afterward Joshua smote them, and slew them, and hanged them on five trees: and they were hanging upon the trees until the evening.*** As a neighbour he left something to be desired. ***So Joshua smote all the country of the hills, and of the south, and of the vale, and of the springs, and all their kings: he left none remaining, but utterly destroyed all that breathed, as the LORD God of Israel commanded.*** Just following orders, you might say.

11 Having conquered the south, Joshua turned to the north. Once again the local rulers were determined to fight, but as before God was against them. He ordered not just that the enemy be killed to the last man and their chariots burnt, but also that their horses be hamstrung – I hadn't realised that they were guilty. To be honest, God didn't want the inhabitants of Canaan to make peace; on the contrary, ***it was of the LORD to harden their hearts, that they should come against Israel***
12 ***in battle, that he might destroy them utterly.*** At the final count Joshua had notched up thirty-one kings dead, with all their land and cities captured.

DIVISION OF THE SPOILS

13 ***Now Joshua was old and stricken in years; and the LORD said unto him, Thou art old and stricken in years, and there remaineth yet very much land to be possessed.*** God wasn't easy to satisfy. Then again, he possibly felt that all was not so rosy as everyone had been led to believe; the Israelites did not, in fact, have complete control, and some groups had not been expelled. Nonetheless he told Joshua to parcel out the land among the tribes.

14 Provision had already been made for two and a half tribes to settle east of the river Jordan, and on account of their priestly duties the tribe of Levi had no inheritance ***save cities to dwell in, with their suburbs for their cattle and for their substance.*** The new land would be distributed to the others, supposedly by lot. I wasn't surprised, though, when the string-pulling started. Caleb put in the first bid, claiming his reward for loyal service when he was sent on the first expedition into the promised land forty-five years previously: ***Now therefore give me this mountain, whereof the LORD spake in that day.*** I frankly didn't remember God promising Caleb anything except his life, but Joshua gave him what he wanted: the city of Hebron.

In fairness I should say that Caleb had to drive out the people living there at the time, but that didn't take him long. The conquest of a neighbouring city he subcontracted, offering whoever could capture it his daughter's hand in marriage. The city was duly taken and the daughter handed over. Being treated as a prize can't do much for easy family relationships; she certainly had a very odd way of asking her father for things. One day she came up to him on a donkey and made a (rude?) noise, and when asked to explain herself said ***Give me a blessing; for thou hast given me a south land; give me also springs of water. And he gave her the upper springs, and the nether springs.*** They could be very mysterious at times. 15

They could also be very boring, as when someone decided to list every single village given to the tribe of Judah. Not even the person who made it could have been very interested, because after mentioning thirty-six different towns he declared the total to be twenty-nine; he then gave a further fifteen names and said that he listed fourteen. From there on, though, the arithmetic got better.

The two tribes descended from Joseph were assigned their territories. As you might expect, the people bickered and complained like children examining their portions of pudding. When one group protested that they deserved more, ***Joshua answered them, If thou be a great people, then get thee up to the wood country, and cut down for thyself there.*** The people were getting on his nerves; he was starting to sound as testy as Moses. 16 17

Joshua decided that they needed a lecture. For the occasion ***the whole congregation of the children of Israel assembled together at Shiloh, and set up the tabernacle of the congregation there.*** He told them that they were lazy; the land had been conquered, and they hadn't yet settled down. He ordered that the land be surveyed by a team drawn from the seven tribes yet to be allotted an inheritance. That done, he said, ***bring the description hither to me, that I may cast lots for you here before the LORD our God.*** 18

The remaining land was duly described and distributed. It must have been decided that Judah had received more than their fair share, because some of their territory was given to Simeon. Otherwise it was all straightforward, except that once again the lists of cities became so dull that in a few instances people lost count of how many they had been given. ***So they made an end of dividing the country.*** 19

Six cities were designated as refuges for ***the slayer that killeth any person unawares and unwittingly.*** Forty-eight cities were given to the Levites, who were thus scattered among the other tribes. Rather embarrassingly the children of Aaron pulled rank on Caleb, relieving him of Hebron, though he was able to keep the surrounding area. Needless to say all the cities were listed, along with the donor tribes. 20 21

The conquest having come to a successful conclusion, Joshua told the two and a half tribes which had their land across the Jordan that they could go back to Gilead. On their way home they built a large altar by the river, an act interpreted by the other tribes as evidence of budding heathenism: there was supposed to be only one altar for sacrifices, in the tabernacle. A delegation was sent to warn the 22 errant brethren that disobedience meant death. In reply, the people of the two and a half tribes swore by ***the LORD God of gods*** that the altar was intended purely as a sign of their faith, ***not for burnt offerings, nor for sacrifices; but it is a witness between us and you. God forbid that we should rebel against the LORD***. Fortunately the explanation was accepted, because the last thing we needed was a civil war.

23 ***And it came to pass a long time after that the LORD had given rest unto Israel from all their enemies round about, that Joshua waxed old and stricken in age***. To be more accurate one might say that Canaan had been given a rest from the Israelites. In any event, we knew that Joshua's farewell address was coming. He knew it, too: ***behold, this day I am going the way of all the earth***. Through him,

24 God reminded the people that he expected gratitude, not least for providing a windfall: ***I have given you a land for which ye did not labour, and cities which ye built not, and ye dwell in them; of the vineyards and olive-yards which ye planted not do ye eat.*** I don't know about you, Joshua said, ***but as for me and my house, we will serve the LORD. And the people answered and said, God forbid that we should forsake the LORD, to serve other gods.***

And so the covenant was renewed. At the age of 110, his task complete, Joshua died.

7

Judges

Now after the death of Joshua it came to pass, that the children of Israel asked the LORD, saying, Who shall go up for us against the Canaanites first, to fight against them? They were starting to recognise, I think, that the land was not so completely subdued as some had made out. 1

So the battles continued. When the king of one defeated group fled he was pursued, caught, and deprived of his thumbs and big toes. I didn't like to see our people engaging in mutilation, but he himself accepted it as divine justice: *Three-score and ten kings, having their thumbs and their great toes cut off, gathered their meat under my table: as I have done, so God hath requited me.* A very sporting attitude: too bad he died.

Everything was much the same as before; the story of Caleb and his daughter even came around again. Now, though, no one was making claims of total victory. Generally the Israelites had to coexist with the local inhabitants; at best *they put the Canaanites to tribute, and did not utterly drive them out.*

God wasn't happy with what he saw, and I was sent to the people to pass on his message: *I will not drive them out from before you; but they shall be as thorns in your sides, and their gods shall be a snare unto you. And it came to pass, when the angel of the LORD spake these words unto all the children of Israel, that the people lifted up their voice, and wept.* You'd think I had taken food out of their mouths. 2

As predicted the religion of Canaan was seductive. The worship of Baal and Ashtaroth, gods of nature and fertility, could be quite a party; I admit that we found it difficult to compete. Of course God was furious when the people went astray, and the whole period was a constant round of punishment, repentance, and backsliding. When they were sufficiently chastised *the LORD raised up judges, which delivered them out of the hand of those that spoiled them.* Unfortunately *it came to pass, when the judge was dead, that they returned, and corrupted themselves more than their fathers, in following other gods to serve them*, and so on and on it went.

The first judge was Othniel, the nephew (and son-in-law) of Caleb. All anyone remembers about him is that he won his battle, but for the next judge, Ehud, everyone knows the details. He was a daring man, though in retrospect his assassination of the local tyrant looks like a mob hit; the title 'judge' didn't really suit him. 3

To appreciate the story you have to know that Ehud was left-handed and so could draw a weapon concealed on his right side, and also that the king ***was a very fat man.*** When Ehud came to pay the tribute extorted from the Israelites he asked to have a word with the king in private. ***Ehud said, I have a message from God unto thee. And he arose out of his seat. And Ehud put forth his left hand, and took the dagger from his right thigh, and thrust it into his belly: And the haft also went in after the blade; and the fat closed upon the blade, so that he could not draw the dagger out of his belly; and the dirt came out. Then Ehud went forth through the porch, and shut the doors of the parlour upon him, and locked them.*** The king's servants assumed that their master was relieving himself behind the locked doors; by the time they went in and found the body, Ehud was long gone. The Israelites rallied around Ehud, going on to conquer the kingdom in the usual fashion. ***And the land had rest fourscore years. And after him was Shamgar the son of Anath, which slew of the Philistines six hundred men with an ox goad: and he also delivered Israel.*** He was the fastest ox goad in the territory.

DEBORAH

4 ***And the children of Israel again did evil in the sight of the LORD***, so God again made them suffer. This time their saviour was a woman, the prophetess Deborah. She was a formidable figure; after ordering her military commander to prepare an attack, he ***said unto her, If thou wilt go with me, then I will go: but if thou wilt not go with me, then I will not go.*** It didn't seem a very military response to me. While agreeing to come, Deborah said that Sisera, the enemy captain, would be delivered into the hands of a woman. At the time I thought that she was referring to herself, but I was wrong.

The enemy was routed in battle, despite having ***nine hundred chariots of iron***; Sisera, though, managed to escape on foot to the tent of a woman named Jael whose household was neutral in the conflict. She came out to meet him, saying ***Turn in, my lord, turn in to me; fear not. And when he had turned in unto her into the tent, she covered him with a mantle. And he said unto her, Give me, I pray thee, a little water to drink; for I am thirsty. And she opened a bottle of milk, and gave him drink, and covered him.*** Before falling asleep he asked her to keep his presence a secret. That much she did, but otherwise the hospitality left something to be desired. Jael ***took a nail of the tent, and took an hammer in her hand, and went softly unto him, and smote the nail into his temples, and fastened it into the ground: for he was fast asleep and weary. So he died.***

5 Such a glorious victory deserved a song, and Deborah provided one. It described the sorry state of affairs before

> ***I Deborah arose,***
> ***that I arose a mother in Israel.***

The troops were roused,

kings came and fought ...
They fought from heaven;
the stars in their courses fought against Sisera.

As for his slayer,

blessed shall she be above women in the tent.
He asked water, and she gave him milk;
she brought forth butter in a lordly dish.

When she struck her blow,

At her feet he bowed, he fell, he lay down:
at her feet he bowed, he fell:
where he bowed, there he fell down dead.
The mother of Sisera looked out at a window,
and cried through the lattice,
Why is his chariot so long in coming?
why tarry the wheels of his chariots?
Her wise ladies answered her,
yea, she returned answer to herself,
Have they not sped? have they not divided the prey;
to every man a damsel or two ... ?

Sadly for them, the explanation was different.

GIDEON

For forty years all was well, but it couldn't last. ***The children of Israel did evil in the sight of the LORD: and the LORD delivered them into the hand of Midian seven years.*** The stage was set for another hero to step forward, and I was sent to summon him. 6

His name was Gideon, and I must tell you that he was a sorry sight. Afraid of being seen by the Midianites, he was actually threshing wheat in a winepress when I arrived. It was with a wry smile that I announced ***The LORD is with thee, thou mighty man of valour.*** He wasn't easy to convince, and when I finally established my credibility with some magic, he got it into his head that death was around the corner. I'm all for equal opportunity, but you had to wonder if this fellow was really the man for the job.

Following God's command, Gideon replaced his father's altar to Baal with a proper one. Being fearful he did it at night, but he was found out anyway. His father saved Gideon from the mob, saying ***unto all that stood against him, Will ye plead for Baal? ... if he be a god, let him plead for himself.*** A very sensible view, I thought.

Despite this unpromising start, Gideon managed to become the rallying point when the enemy next threatened; ***the Spirit of the LORD came upon Gideon, and he blew a trumpet.*** He still needed a lot of reassurance, and before consenting to go to war said to God, ***Behold, I will put a fleece of wool in the floor; and if the dew be on the fleece only, and it be dry upon all the earth beside, then shall I know that thou wilt save Israel by mine hand, as thou hast said. And it was so: for he rose up early on the morrow, and thrust the fleece together, and wringed the dew out of the fleece, a bowl full of water. And Gideon said unto God, Let not thine anger be hot against me, and I will speak but this once: let me prove, I pray thee, but this once with the fleece; let it now be dry only upon the fleece, and upon all the ground let there be dew. And God did so that night.*** I didn't much appreciate Gideon's lack of confidence, but at least he showed some grasp of scientific method.

7 In any case, God was always happy to demonstrate his power. When Gideon turned up with thirty-two thousand men God said that he didn't want such a large force, lest the army take too much credit. Firstly, therefore, they announced that ***Whosoever is fearful and afraid, let him return and depart***; twenty-two thousand were honest enough to take the opportunity. As a second test Gideon led the men down to the river. All bar three hundred got down on their hands and knees to drink, and were discharged. God didn't explain why he chose those who drank out of cupped hands, but one assumes that it was because they were more watchful and soldierly.

Before the coming battle, when ***the host of Midian was beneath him in the valley***, Gideon skirted the enemy camp to hear what they were saying. Morale didn't appear to be good; one man was interpreting the dream of another in a highly defeatist manner.

Gathering his three hundred for the attack, Gideon ***put a trumpet in every man's hand, with empty pitchers, and lamps within the pitchers. And he said unto them … When I blow with a trumpet, I and all that are with me, then blow ye the trumpets also on every side of all the camp, and say, The sword of the LORD, and of Gideon.*** They crept up, surrounded the camp, and then blew their trumpets and broke the pitchers to reveal the torches. The enemy was thrown into great confusion. The Israelites must have been in some confusion themselves, with their hands full of torches, swords, and trumpets, trying to shout and blow at the same time. Still, it was a rout, and Gideon sent messengers to the other tribes asking for help in the pursuit.

Among those to respond was the tribe of Ephraim. Though two of the enemy
8 princes fell into their hands, they were unhappy that Gideon – who belonged to the clan of Abiezer – had not invited them to join in earlier. In a diplomatic response he offered one of the first proverbs; ***he said unto them, What have I done now in comparison of you? Is not the gleaning of the grapes of Ephraim better than the vintage of Abiezer?*** This wasn't completely honest – the killing of two princes hardly compared with the defeat of the entire army – but it appeased them.

You couldn't be neutral in those days. During the time his small company was ***faint, yet pursuing*** the Midianites, two groups declined to supply them. The battle won, Gideon returned to take revenge. The 77 elders of the first group he scourged with thorns and briars, and in the other town he destroyed the fortifications and killed the men.

The Israelites invited Gideon to become their hereditary ruler; he refused, saying ***I will not rule over you: the LORD shall rule over you.*** This was a fine sentiment, but he proceeded to use the gold from the spoils of war to make a graven image; ***all Israel went thither a whoring after it: which thing became a snare unto Gideon, and to his house.*** None the less Gideon lived to a ripe old age, having fathered 70 sons by his many wives. He had also had a son named Abimelech by a concubine – a big mistake.

ABIMELECH, JEPHTHAH, AND THEIR UNLUCKY FAMILIES

Abimelech sought the support of his mother's family in overthrowing the rule of his father's clan. They provided him with 70 pieces of silver, ***wherewith Abimelech hired vain and light persons, which followed him***, though it would be more accurate to describe them as murderous thugs. Abimelech proceeded to butcher his half-brothers ***upon one stone***; only the youngest escaped. 9

Abimelech became king. The sole survivor of the massacre took refuge in another land, but before leaving told a fable about trees selecting a king with the moral that if you think Abimelech is the right choice, be glad, but if not, prepare to be devoured: ***let fire come out of the bramble, and devour the cedars of Lebanon.***

In time there was a rebellion against Abimelech, which he suppressed with the ruthlessness one would expect of a man who had murdered 69 members of his own family, setting fire, for example, to a fort being used by refugees. The death toll was ***about a thousand men and women.*** Eventually, however, he came to a nasty end. While he was preparing to burn another rebel stronghold, a woman dropped a millstone on his head. Dying but not dead, ***he called hastily unto the young man his armourbearer, and said unto him, Draw thy sword, and slay me, that men say not of me, A woman slew him. And his young man thrust him through, and he died.*** The woman still gets the credit, in my view.

And after Abimilech there arose to defend Israel Tola the son of Puah, the son of Dodo; they don't name them like that any more. He ruled as judge for 23 years, followed for 22 years more by Jair. ***And the children of Israel did evil again in the sight of the LORD, and served Baalim, and Ashtaroth, and the gods of Syria, and the gods of Zidon, and the gods of Moab, and the gods of the children of Ammon, and the gods of the Philistines, and forsook the LORD, and served not him. And the anger of the LORD was hot against Israel, and he sold them into the hands of the Philistines, and into the hands of the children of Ammon.*** 10

Hedging your bets can be dangerous.

With the enemy camped in Gilead, the people looked around for a leader. The best candidate was Jephthah, the son of a prostitute who had been chased out of the country years before. The elders showed a good deal of nerve in asking for his help, but he agreed to return – provided that victory would make him ruler. His terms were accepted.

11

The dispute with Ammon was over territory, and Jephthah attempted to persuade them that it rightfully belonged to Israel. His historical case was shaky, however, and ultimately the dispute was between rival national deities: what God gave the Israelites we defended, and what their god gave them, they defended.

In return for God's full support in the coming battle Jephthah vowed to make a burnt offering of the first living thing to emerge from his house when he returned. Jephthah was playing with fire, and I could see what was coming. The slaughter of the Ammonites duly accomplished he returned home, and ***behold, his daughter came out to meet him with timbrels and with dances: and she was his only child; beside her he had neither son nor daughter.***

She was remarkably philosophical about her fate, asking only ***let me alone two months, that I may go up and down upon the mountains, and bewail my virginity***, so sad was it to meet death a virgin. At the end of the two months she came back to die. People praise Jephthah's will, but I didn't hear him offer to sacrifice himself. It was his daughter who paid his debts.

12

Like Gideon, Jephthah had a dispute with the men of Ephraim, but unlike him had little talent for diplomacy. To their protests about lack of consultation, he complained that in taking on the enemy ***I put my life in my hands***, with no help from them. War broke out as the insults flew, and Jephthah's forces seized the crossing points on the river Jordan. To identify any Ephraimites wanting to ford the river ***Then said they unto him, Say now Shibboleth: and he said Sibboleth: for he could not frame to pronounce it right. Then they took him, and slew him at the passages of Jordan: and there fell at that time of the Ephraimites forty and two thousand.*** Which just goes to show the importance of proper elocution.

Jephthah judged Israel six years, followed by Ibzan, Elon, and Abdon. The only thing anyone remembers about these last three was that Abdon ***had forty sons and thirty nephews, that rode on threescore and ten ass colts***. It's not much of a mark to make in the history books, but I suspect that the less we now recall the more content people were at the time.

Samson

13

And the children of Israel did evil again in the sight of the LORD; and the LORD delivered them into the hand of the Philistines forty years. This time God decided to raise his champion from birth; a childless woman from the tribe of Dan was identified, and I was sent down with the good news: ***the angel of the LORD***

appeared unto the woman, and said unto her, Behold now, thou art barren, and bearest not: but thou shalt conceive, and bear a son. He was to be a Nazirite, that is to say dedicated to God, obeying special requirements of purity, and leaving his hair uncut. ***And the woman bare a son, and called his name Samson: and the child grew, and the LORD blessed him.***

It shouldn't be supposed, however, that he was particularly holy: rather the reverse. For one thing he liked to consort with foreign women, to the despair of his parents. ***His father and his mother said unto him, Is there never a woman among the daughters of thy brethren, or amongst all my people, that thou goest to take a wife of the uncircumcised Philistines?*** But Samson let nothing stop his visits to his mistress, not even a lion which he tore to pieces with his bare hands. ***After a time he returned to take her, and he turned aside to see the carcase of the lion: and, behold, there was a swarm of bees and honey in the carcase of the lion.*** 14

A marriage was finally arranged with the Philistine woman. Samson made a wager with the men of his wedding escort that they could not answer his riddle before the end of the seven-day feast: ***Out of the eater came forth meat, and out of the strong came forth sweetness.*** Since no one knew of the lion it wasn't a very sporting bet, but then the others didn't act much like gentlemen either; ***they said unto Samson's wife, Entice thy husband, that he may declare unto us the riddle, lest we burn thee and thy father's house with fire.*** So she pleaded and cajoled until finally, prefiguring the manner of his eventual downfall, he told her the answer.

She was quick to pass it on, ***And the men of the city said unto him on the seventh day before the sun went down, What is sweeter than honey? and what is stronger than a lion? And he said unto them, If ye had not plowed with my heifer, ye had not found out my riddle.*** This crass reference to his own wife was only the start, however, as Samson set new standards as a bad loser; he murdered and robbed thirty men in order to settle his wager.

The marriage was completed with one of the other men taking Samson's place, and he was turned away the next time he came to visit. In revenge, ***Samson went and caught three hundred foxes, and took firebrands, and turned tail to tail, and put a firebrand in the midst between two tails.*** He set the torch-bearing animals loose in the fields, utterly destroying the Philistines' crops (not to mention the blameless foxes). On learning what had started the havoc, they in turn burnt his would-be wife and father-in-law. I wasn't sure if the idea was to appease Samson or to punish him, but it only provoked more violence; ***he smote them hip and thigh with a great slaughter.*** 15

The Philistines pursued him into the land of Judah. The people of Judah were none too pleased to be overrun on his account, and they came to turn him over to his pursuers. He simply said ***As they did unto me, so have I done unto them***, and agreed to go quietly. Once among the Philistines, however, he burst out of the ropes with which he had been tied, seizing a fresh jawbone as a weapon. ***And Samson***

said, With the jawbone of an ass, heaps upon heaps, with the jaw of an ass have I slain a thousand men. It was thirsty work, and God was sufficiently impressed to create a new spring for him.

16 ***Then went Samson to Gaza, and saw there an harlot, and went in unto her.*** His enemies decided to ambush him, but he was too wily. In the middle of the night he stole away, taking the doors of the city gate with him.

In the end, though, his womanising did him in. He was unlucky enough to find a woman, Delilah, who was as persistent as he was powerful. When the affair started ***the lords of the Philistines came up unto her, and said unto her, Entice him, and see wherein his great strength lieth, and by what means we may prevail against him, that we may bind him to afflict him: and we will give thee every one of us eleven hundred pieces of silver. And Delilah said to Samson, Tell me, I pray thee, wherein thy great strength lieth, and wherewith thou mightest be bound to afflict thee.*** Her strength, clearly, did not lie in subtlety.

Samson wasn't a fool, and told her that the secret was to bind him with undried bowstrings. It didn't take Delilah long to get the material, and he woke up to hear her cry ***The Philistines be upon thee, Samson.*** But he freed himself without the least difficulty.

A wise man would have found a new mistress, especially after she tried twice more to betray him. (He had told her that new ropes would do the trick, and then that his hair should be woven into the loom.) Unless he had a death wish, she must have had some remarkable appeal I couldn't spot. The daily interrogations finally wore him down, and he revealed the secret: ***if I be shaven, then my strength will go from me, and I shall become weak, and be like any other man.***

So one night ***she made him sleep upon her knees; and she called for a man, and she caused him to shave off the seven locks of his head***, and this time he was powerless against his enemies; ***he wist not that the LORD was departed from him. But the Philistines took him, and put out his eyes, and brought him down to Gaza, and bound him with fetters of brass; and he did grind in the prison house.*** That might have been the end of the story, except that his hair slowly grew back.

One evening during a great celebration the blind Samson was brought up from the prison, to be mocked as entertainment. The temple was filled with people. ***And Samson called unto the LORD, and said, O LORD God, remember me, I pray thee, and strengthen me, I pray thee, only this once, O God, that I may be at once avenged of the Philistines for my two eyes. And Samson took hold of the two middle pillars upon which the house stood, and on which it was borne up, of the one with his right hand, and of the other with his left. And Samson said, Let me die with the Philistines. And he bowed himself with all his might; and the house fell upon the lords, and upon all the people that were therein. So the dead which he slew at his death were more than they which he slew in his life.***

Bad times

Given the outlandish behaviour of the judges, it should be no surprise that life was precarious and the state of morality low. Two stories illustrate the point. The first concerns a man named Micah, who had stolen 1100 shekels from his own mother. Alarmed by the curse she put on the thief he returned the money, and in thanksgiving she ***took two hundred shekels of silver, and gave them to the founder, who made thereof a graven image and a molten image.*** Micah even managed to recruit a passing Levite to administer this domestic sanctuary; he put great stock in having the best that money could buy. His view was that ***Now know I that the LORD will do me good, seeing I have a Levite to my priest.*** 17

Unfortunately for him, the Levite got a better offer. A group from the tribe of Dan, migrating northwards, came and relieved him of both his priest and his religious paraphernalia. When he chased after them with his neighbours they turned and asked ***What aileth thee, that thou comest with such a company? And he said, Ye have taken away my gods which I made.*** Being a large, well-armed force, they told him to run off home before something unfortunate happened. 18

Micah could, in fact, count himself lucky that he had only been robbed and insulted. The men of Dan took the land they wanted to settle with utter ruthlessness. They came ***unto a people that were at quiet and secure: and they smote them with the edge of the sword, and burnt the city with fire.*** God had given them *carte blanche*, in their view.

The second story is even more startling. A Levite travelling with his concubine stopped in Gibeah, a town belonging to the tribe of Benjamin. The people showed no hospitality, but ultimately an old man took them in. The sequel was identical to my experience at Sodom; men surrounded the house and called for the visitor to be brought out for their carnal pleasure; the host refused, offering his virgin daughter as a substitute. ***But the men would not hearken to him: so the man took his concubine, and brought her forth unto them; and they knew her, and abused her all the night until the morning: and when the day began to spring, they let her go.*** When the doors were opened, the man found her lifeless on the threshold. 19

The Levite's response to this gang rape and murder was nearly as horrifying as the event itself. ***When he was come into his house, he took a knife, and laid hold on his concubine, and divided her, together with her bones, into twelve pieces, and sent her into all the coasts of Israel.*** Everyone agreed with his messengers that the crime was unprecedented.

Then all the children of Israel went out, and the congregation was gathered together as one man, from Dan even to Beer-sheba, to consider what should be done. ***And all the people arose as one man,*** calling for punishment of the guilty men. The Benjamites refused to hand the criminals over for execution, gathering their forces, 26,000 strong, at Gibeah. Against them were 400,000 troops from all the other tribes. Surprisingly enough the first two days of fighting went in favour 20 of Benjamin, but on the third day there was annihilation. Of all the people in the entire tribe, only 600 men escaped death.

21 Even the victors were shocked at the carnage, and lamented the disappearance of one of the tribes of Israel. They decided that the surviving Benjamites must be encouraged to reproduce, but asked ***How shall we do for wives for them that remain, seeing we have sworn by the LORD that we will not give them of our daughters to wives?*** The answer in the first instance was to attack a town that had not participated in the conflict, killing ***every male, and every woman that hath lain by man.*** That left four hundred young virgins: a good start, but not sufficient.

Thinking of the annual festival at Shiloh, ***they commanded the children of Benjamin, saying, Go and lie in wait in the vineyards; And see, and, behold, if the daughters of Shiloh come out to dance in dances, then come ye out of the vineyards, and catch you every man his wife of the daughters of Shiloh, and go to the land of Benjamin.*** So having killed tens of thousands of men, women and children in retaliation for the rape and murder of the concubine, the victors authorised the vanquished to abduct hundreds of young girls. A curious business.

I doubt that I was the only one waiting for better leadership. ***In those days there was no king in Israel: every man did that which was right in his own eyes.***

8

Ruth

Now it came to pass in the days when the judges ruled, that there was a famine in the land. [1] Hoping to find a better life, one man took his wife and their two sons out of Judah into the land of Moab. There he died, but his sons found wives and stayed.

After some ten years disaster struck: both sons died, leaving their mother Naomi without male support. Although she decided to return to Judah, she urged her two widowed daughters-in-law, Orpah and Ruth, to remain and remarry. ***And they said unto her, Surely we will return with thee unto thy people.***

Naomi insisted, however, that to come would mean sacrificing any hopes of marriage and children, and Orpah reluctantly turned back. For her part, Ruth responded with the finest expression of loyalty and affection I had heard for a very long time. ***Ruth said, Intreat me not to leave thee, or to return from following after thee: for whither thou goest, I will go; and where thou lodgest, I will lodge: thy people shall be my people, and thy God my God: Where thou diest, will I die, and there will I be buried.*** Her mind was made up. ***So they two went until they came to Bethlehem.***

I wish I could say that the double blessing of this homecoming and Ruth's devotion filled Naomi with joy. In fact she was sorry for herself, bitter with God and ungrateful to her daughter-in-law. Ruth, to her credit, showed no signs of [2] impatience, but worked to support them both, asking the men in the fields to ***let me glean and gather after the reapers among the sheaves.***

This was what Ruth was doing when she happened to be noticed by Boaz, a solid citizen and a man of property. He approached and told her to stay on his land, where she would be well treated throughout the harvest.

Ruth asked him ***Why have I found grace in thine eyes, that thou shouldest take knowledge of me, seeing I am a stranger? And Boaz answered and said unto her, It hath fully been shewed me, all that thou hast done unto thy mother in law since the death of thine husband.*** The fact that she was not an Israelite by birth made her all the more praiseworthy, in his view.

To ensure that Ruth was successful without compromising her self-reliance, Boaz told his reapers to leave a generous amount behind for her to pick up; that night she went home with a bushel of barley. Naomi was yet more pleased to hear the name of Ruth's benefactor, because Boaz was related to her late husband. ***Blessed be he of the LORD,*** she said, ***who hath not left off his kindness to the living and to the dead.*** Naomi, though, had no intention of leaving everything to

God. She was quite right; events need to be helped along the right course.

3 When a man died childless his nearest kin were responsibile for ensuring that his widow did not do likewise. Naomi thought that Boaz was well equipped to take her son's place, and only needed reminding of his duty. A night he was spending in his threshing room seemed an ideal opportunity, and she was ready with instructions for Ruth. ***Wash thyself therefore, and anoint thee, and put thy raiment upon thee, and get thee down to the floor: but make not thyself known unto the man, until he shall have done eating and drinking. And it shall be, when he lieth down, that thou shalt mark the place where he shall lie, and thou shalt go in, and uncover his feet, and lay thee down; and he will tell thee what thou shalt do.*** Who says women can't take the initiative?

In the middle of the night Boaz stirred and ***behold, a woman lay at his feet. And he said, Who art thou? And she answered, I am Ruth thine handmaid: spread therefore thy skirt over thine handmaid; for thou art a near kinsman.*** Boaz, however, showed his colours as a true gentleman. He pointed out that someone more closely related to her husband had prior rights, promising to make the necessary enquiries in the morning. Until they had resolved the question her place was back at home. He filled her mantle with barley, saying ***Go not empty unto thy mother in law*** – always good advice.

4 Boaz went to sit by the city gate, where eventually he spotted the man he had mentioned. Having found ten elders to act as witnesses he laid out the situation: Naomi wanted to sell land to a relative, and she was entitled to expect the purchaser to produce children with Ruth in the name of her dead husband. As it happened the man with first option would have been interested in the land, but was unwilling to meet the conditions of sale. ***Now this was the manner in former time in Israel concerning redeeming and concerning changing, for to confirm all things; a man plucked off his shoe, and gave it to his neighbour: and this was a testimony in Israel. Therefore the kinsman said unto Boaz, Buy it for thee. So he drew off his shoe.*** I can't remember what Boaz did with the shoe, but he took the land and the woman.

And all the people that were in the gate, and the elders, said, We are witnesses. The LORD make the woman that is come into thine house like Rachel and like Leah, which two did build the house of Israel. It was an extravagant blessing, but reality didn't fall wide of the mark. Ruth had a son, who had a son; and one of that man's sons was David, about whom we shall hear a great deal.

Naomi was congratulated by all on her good fortune in having a grandson, and ***for thy daughter in law, which loveth thee, which is better to thee than seven sons.*** The woman from Moab was now well and truly a member of the family of Israel. If more of God's people had shown the virtues of Ruth and Boaz their story might have been altogether more peaceful.

9

The First Book of Samuel

1

The promised land was occupied; the time of glory was approaching. God needed a man to usher in that age, to serve as the last of the judges, the first (after Moses) of the prophets. To produce this man he required a woman, and happily a good candidate was not hard to find.

The woman was named Hannah. She was childless, which made her an object of derision to her husband's other wife. During the family's annual visit to the tabernacle at Shiloh, Hannah, in great distress, prayed for a son. She vowed that the boy would be a Nazirite – one dedicated to God – all his life.

Eli, the priest, was present while she prayed. ***Now Hannah, she spake in her heart; only her lips moved, but her voice was not heard: therefore Eli thought she had been drunken. And Eli said unto her, How long wilt thou be drunken? put away thy wine from thee. And Hannah answered and said, No, my lord, I am a woman of a sorrowful spirit: I have drunk neither wine nor strong drink, but have poured out my soul before the LORD. ... Then Eli answered and said, Go in peace: and the God of Israel grant thee thy petition that thou hast asked of him.***

Hannah conceived and bore a son, whom she named Samuel. When he was weaned she brought him back to Shiloh, entrusting him to Eli in fulfilment of her vow to God. This time she prayed in thanksgiving: nothing is like God;

2

The adversaries of the LORD shall be broken to pieces;
out of heaven shall he thunder upon them:
the LORD shall judge the ends of the earth;
and he shall give strength unto his king,
and exalt the horn of his anointed.

In the circumstances I found it rather belligerent, and her reference to a king was unexpected, to say the least. God liked it, though; he even made it possible for Hannah to have five more children.

Samuel grew up a fine young man, which was more than could be said of Eli's own sons, even allowing for the natural wildness of children of the clergy. Preferring steaks to stew, they demanded raw meat from people making sacrifices, not even waiting for the fat to be burnt. This sacrilege was compounded by sexual misconduct. ***Now Eli was very old, and heard all that his sons did unto all Israel; and how they lay with the women that assembled at the door of the tabernacle***

of the congregation. And he said unto them, Why do ye such things? Being foolish, they ignored him.

God warned Eli what was coming: ***there shall not be an old man in thine house for ever ... all the increase of thine house shall die in the flower of their age.***

3 Even Samuel was used as a messenger. One night while he was sleeping ***the LORD called Samuel: and he answered, Here am I. And he ran unto Eli, and said, Here am I; for thou calledst me. And he said, I called not; lie down again.*** But Samuel heard a second call, and then a third. Eli finally realised that Samuel must be hearing the voice of God, and told him next time to answer ***Speak, LORD; for thy servant heareth.***

So it went, and ***the LORD said to Samuel, Behold, I will do a thing in Israel, at which both the ears of every one that heareth it shall tingle.*** I didn't think the news was quite so ear-tingling as all that, just being confirmation that Eli's descendants were doomed – a judgment that Eli accepted calmly.

4 Now around this time the Israelites were at war with the Philistines. After losing one battle they came up with an idea (in retrospect, a very bad one): ***Let us fetch the ark of the covenant of the LORD out of Shiloh unto us, that, when it cometh among us, it may save us out of the hand of our enemies.*** As this was an abuse of God's goodwill, I wasn't surprised when the Philistines recovered from their initial fear and, rallying to the cry ***Be strong, and quit yourselves like men,*** slaughtered thirty thousand of our people (including the sons of Eli) and captured the ark.

The news was too much for Eli: ***he fell from off the seat backward by the side of the gate, and his neck brake, and he died: for he was an old man, and heavy.*** His pregnant daughter-in-law went into labour and died in childbirth; the prophesied fall of Eli's family was well under way. But the people had other concerns; as one woman said, ***The glory is departed from Israel: for the ark of God is taken.***

5 If losing the ark was a catastrophe for the Israelites, winning it was equally bad for the Philistines. They laid the trophy in front of their own god, Dagon, only to come back the next morning to find that ***behold, Dagon was fallen upon his face.*** They propped him up, but the following day he had not only fallen over, ***the head of Dagon and both the palms of his hands were cut off upon the threshold; only the stump of Dagon was left to him.*** Being alone in a dark room with God had not been a happy experience.

The Philistines themselves did not escape; they moved the ark from one town to another, but in each place people were afflicted with haemorrhoids and worse. ***And it was so, that, after they had carried it about, the hand of the LORD was against the city with a very great destruction: and he smote the men of the city, both small and great, and they had emerods in their secret parts.*** God could be such a rascal.

6 After all this the Philistines were only too happy to send the ark back, along with compensation of ***Five golden emerods, and five golden mice.*** As a test of whether their misfortunes really were due to God rather than bad luck the ark was

loaded onto a wagon drawn by two untrained milch-cows: when the cows headed straight for the land of Israel, the answer was apparent.

The ark returned to great celebration. Not everyone rejoiced sufficiently, however, and God struck down somewhere between 70 and 50,070 people, depending on which source you prefer. Even the local Israelites found the ark too hot to handle, and were glad to have it taken away and turned over to the care of a priest. 7

Twenty years passed. The Israelites were ripe for a religious revival, and Samuel promised that if they served God alone he would take care of them. Duly (if only temporarily) reformed, the people were ready; when an attack came ***the LORD thundered with a great thunder on that day upon the Philistines, and discomfited them; and they were smitten before Israel.*** Smitten they might have been, but they didn't stay that way. The Philistines would plague the Israelites for some time yet.

THE FIRST KING OF ISRAEL

8 ***And it came to pass, when Samuel was old, that he made his sons judges over Israel.*** Sadly there were the familiar problems; ***his sons walked not in his ways, but turned aside after lucre, and took bribes, and perverted judgment. Then all the elders of Israel gathered themselves together, and came to Samuel … And said unto him, Behold, thou art old, and thy sons walk not in thy ways: now make us a king to judge us like all the nations.***

Samuel wasn't happy with this suggestion. He warned the people that a king would conscript their children, requisition their property and ultimately enslave them all. ***Nevertheless the people refused to obey the voice of Samuel;*** they wanted a king to ***fight our battles,*** which shows how little they understood the respective roles of kings and subjects. God felt that they were rejecting his leadership, but he told Samuel to go ahead and find them a king.

9 The future king, meanwhile, was trying to find his father's donkeys. His name was Saul, ***and there was not among the children of Israel a goodlier person than he: from his shoulders and upward he was higher than any of the people.*** (But was he higher-minded, I wondered?) These donkeys, anyway, had vanished, and Saul was searching far and wide for them.

He was about to turn back when his servant suggested that they ask the local seer for help. Saul got more help than he had bargained for. The whole situation was comical: Saul just trying to find his donkeys, Samuel telling him that they were safe and, by the way, you are now king of Israel. ***Samuel took a vial of oil, and poured it upon his head, and kissed him.*** 10

On the homeward journey Saul was inspired with prophecy, and ***the people said one to another, What is this that is come unto the son of Kish? Is Saul also among the prophets?*** When he got home his uncle said ***Tell me, I pray thee, what Samuel said unto you. And Saul said unto his uncle, He told us plainly that the asses***

were found. But of the matter of the kingdom, whereof Samuel spake, he told him not. Otherwise, I imagine, he might have found himself under very close observation.

Samuel gathered the people together for the public designation of their king. He used the technique of picking first a tribe, and then a family, and then a man, and the lots fell on Benjamin, narrowed down to the reluctant winner. Saul vanished, but God gave him away: ***Behold, he hath hid himself among the stuff. And they ran and fetched him thence.*** Samuel declared that Saul was one of a kind, and ***all the people shouted, and said, God save the king.*** A few, if truth be told, were less enthusiastic. Not seeing that a king would improve their fortunes, ***they despised him, and brought him no presents. But he held his peace.*** He would soon be in a position to give himself all the presents he wanted.

11 The enemy surrounded a town, which expressed its readiness to surrender. The leader of the besiegers replied ***On this condition will I make a covenant with you, that I may thrust out all your right eyes, and lay it for a reproach upon all Israel.*** This was not an attractive offer, but they despaired of obtaining better terms. When Saul heard the news, however, he chopped up some oxen, sending the pieces to every corner of the land with the message that a similar fate awaited the oxen of anyone not enlisting in the army; he thereby succeeded in recruiting 330,000 men. The Israelites prevailed, as troops in fear of losing their oxen rescued people in fear of losing their eyes.

12 To ask for a king when God should rule was wickedness, Samuel continued to believe. Nevertheless, if they remained obedient then both king and country would be safe. ***As for me, God forbid that I should sin against the LORD in ceasing to pray for you: but I will teach you the good and the right way.*** The pessimism characteristic of prophets was creeping into his tone, however.

13 The new king continued the military campaign, aided by his son Jonathan. ***Saul blew the trumpet throughout all the land, saying, Let the Hebrews hear.*** People rallied to him, but at the same time the Philistines were gathering their 30,000 chariots and countless troops, ***as the sand which is on the sea shore in multitude.*** Worried that time was running out and unwilling to wait any longer for Samuel to arrive, Saul went ahead and performed the sacrifices himself.

When Samuel finally turned up he was far from pleased at this usurpation of his priestly authority. He told Saul that previously he might have expected to keep the throne in his family forever, ***But now thy kingdom shall not continue: the LORD hath sought him a man after his own heart.*** I wasn't convinced that God had made the punishment fit the crime, but Saul was now living on borrowed time.

As an arms control measure the Philistines had managed to prevent any blacksmith from working in the land of Israel. In consequence ***there was neither sword nor spear found in the hand of any of the people***, and only Saul and Jonathan were equipped. It's a wonder how they managed.

14 Perhaps it was this that inspired Jonathan to take on the Philistines almost single-handedly, coming into the open accompanied only by his armour-bearer. If,

he decided, the Philistines told them not to move when they emerged it would be a sign from God that they were out of luck, while if the Philistines told them to come forward then God would be signalling that victory was theirs for the taking. Jonathan made up these rules himself, but God was apparently willing to go along.

So ***the men of the garrison answered Jonathan and his armour-bearer, and said, Come up to us, and we will shew you a thing.*** Jonathan himself had it in mind to show them a thing or two. Together with his faithful servant he cut them down, slaughtering some twenty men. On seeing the uproar, where ***every man's sword was against his fellow,*** Saul sent the whole army into the fray. The Philistines were routed.

Notwithstanding this victory, ***the men of Israel were distressed that day: for Saul had adjured the people, saying, Cursed be the man that eateth any food until evening.*** Jonathan, however, hadn't heard the orders, ***wherefore he put forth the end of the rod that was in his hand, and dipped it in an honeycomb, and put his hand to his mouth; and his eyes were enlightened.*** As he pointed out when told about his father's curse, everyone would have fought better had they not been faint with hunger. Perhaps the intention had been to safeguard the first fruits of victory for God, but the men were so famished that they ***flew upon the spoil, and took sheep, and oxen, and calves, and slew them on the ground: and the people did eat them with the blood*** – not the approved procedure.

When it became clear that someone had sinned, Saul cast lots to find the guilty person in a process of divination by elimination. First he and Jonathan stood on one side, with the people on the other; the two of them were selected, which made the rest a great deal faster. When he was picked out, Jonathan said ***I did but taste a little honey with the end of the rod that was in mine hand, and, lo, I must die.*** This was very willing of him, but the people wouldn't hear of it. He was the day's hero, and everyone insisted that ***there shall not one hair of his head fall to the ground.***

15 The next military episode followed a message from God concerning one of their traditional enemies: ***Now go and smite Amalek, and utterly destroy all that they have, and spare them not; but slay both man and woman, infant and suckling, ox and sheep, camel and ass.*** At least we wouldn't have any problems with widows and orphans. In the event, the opposing king was taken captive and the best animals were saved for sacrifice instead of being butchered on the spot. Samuel was livid; he insisted that God's commands should be carried out to the letter: ***Because thou hast rejected the word of the LORD, he hath also rejected thee from being king.***

Saul was contrite, but Samuel replied that God's mind was made up: ***he is not a man, that he should repent***; a better person would be made king. To take care of unfinished business, Samuel called for Agag, the captured king, to be brought in. Ignoring his suggestion that they put the past behind them, ***Samuel said, As thy sword hath made women childless, so shall thy mother be childless among women. And Samuel hewed Agag in pieces before the LORD.*** This memorable occasion was the last that Saul and Samuel saw of each other. ***And the LORD***

repented that he had made Saul king over Israel. Hadn't Samuel just said that being God meant never having to repent?

THE RIVAL

16 God had by now chosen Saul's successor; he sent Samuel to Bethlehem to seek out the sons of a man named Jesse. Needless to say God rejected the eldest son, telling Samuel ***Look not on his countenance, or on the height of his stature; because I have refused him: for the LORD seeth not as man seeth; for man looketh on the outward appearance, but the LORD looketh on the heart.*** Seven sons later God was still looking, and Samuel asked Jesse if he didn't have another hidden away somewhere. There is the youngest, he replied, ***he keepeth the sheep.***

The boy was brought in, and of course he was the one they were after: his name was David. He was good looking, red-cheeked and bright-eyed, God's claim that he ignored appearances notwithstanding. ***Then Samuel took the horn of oil, and anointed him in the midst of his brethren: and the Spirit of the LORD came upon David from that day forward.***

None of this was known to Saul, who was being afflicted by less agreeable spirits. On the advice of his servants he decided to appoint a musician, someone to play soothing music on the harp. Who should be recommended but David, the simple shepherd, remarkably enough described as ***cunning in playing, and a mighty valiant man, and a man of war, and prudent in matters, and a comely person, and the LORD is with him.*** I always did find job references exaggerated.

Fortunately David turned out to be a great success, even becoming Saul's armour-bearer. ***And it came to pass, when the spirit from God was upon Saul, that David took an harp, and played with his hand: so Saul was refreshed, and was well, and the evil spirit departed from him.***

17 The next confrontation with the Philistines provided David with his big break. The two armies were camped in the hills on opposite sides of a valley. Among the enemy was a man nearly ten feet tall named Goliath, who wore bronze armour and carried an enormous spear. Every day for forty days he taunted the Israelites, challenging anyone who dared to single combat. Saul offered large rewards, including his daughter (did kings produce daughters just for these situations?), to the man who succeeded in killing him.

When David appeared on the battlefield, his eldest brother could see that something was up; ***I know thy pride, and the naughtiness of thine heart.*** David certainly didn't lack confidence, saying to Saul about Goliath, ***Let no man's heart fail because of him; ... Thy servant slew both the lion and the bear: and this uncircumcised Philistine shall be as one of them, seeing he hath defied the armies of the living God.*** Though sceptical, ***Saul said unto David, Go, and the LORD be with thee.***

Saul buckled him into his own armour, but David was uncomfortable and took it off. ***And he took his staff in his hand, and chose him five smooth stones out of the brook, and put them in a shepherd's bag***. Goliath wasn't impressed at the sight of a youth carrying a sling. ***And the Philistine said unto David, Am I a dog, that thou comest to me with staves? And the Philistine cursed David by his gods. And the Philistine said to David, Come to me, and I will give thy flesh unto the fowls of the air, and to the beasts of the field. Then said David to the Philistine, Thou comest to me with a sword, and with a spear, and with a shield: but I come to thee in the name of the LORD of hosts, the God of the armies of Israel, whom thou hast defied.***

After a few more threats they each advanced. ***David put his hand in his bag, and took thence a stone, and slang it, and smote the Philistine in his forehead, that the stone sunk into his forehead; and he fell upon his face to the earth. ... David ran, and stood upon the Philistine, and took his sword, and drew it out of the sheath thereof, and slew him, and cut off his head therewith. And when the Philistines saw their champion was dead, they fled.*** The Israelites set off in hot pursuit. ***David took the head of the Philistine, and brought it to Jerusalem***, which having not yet been captured was a very odd place to take it. Even stranger was the fact that Saul didn't seem to know who he was, asking ***Whose son art thou, thou young man?*** Somebody was mixed up.

18 It was around this time ***that the soul of Jonathan was knit with the soul of David, and Jonathan loved him as his own soul.*** They made a pact to confirm their mutual love, with Jonathan giving David ***his garments, even to his sword, and to his bow, and to his girdle***. His father, however, was becoming envious of David's success. On their way back from war women danced and sang

Saul hath slain his thousands,
and David his ten thousands.

Highly displeased with this comparison, Saul asked ***what can he have more but the kingdom?*** The answer, indeed, was nothing, except perhaps his daughter.

Saul twice went as far as to hurl a javelin at David while he was playing the harp. He gave him command of a thousand troops, but David's success continued. Finally he decided to use his youngest daughter as bait, letting it be known that ***The king desireth not any dowry, but an hundred foreskins of the Philistines, to be avenged of the king's enemies. But Saul thought to make David fall by the hand of the Philistines.*** Certainly the Philistines weren't going to surrender something so precious without a fight.

In the event David and his men killed not one but two hundred Philistines, taking from each the trophy demanded. He didn't ask Saul to take his word for it, either; he counted them out in front of him. Thus David became Saul's son-in-law.

19 From then on it was one murder attempt after another, with David escaping, often as not, thanks to help from one of Saul's own children. Jonathan persuaded his father to swear that David wouldn't be killed, but that didn't prevent Saul from

throwing a spear at him. David was helped to escape by his wife – Saul's daughter – who made a decoy in the bed and claimed that he was ill. The ruse was discovered when Saul sent his men back, ***saying, Bring him up to me in the bed, that I may slay him.*** Chivalry wasn't much in evidence, I'm afraid.

David found refuge with Samuel and his holy men. Everyone Saul sent after him fell under the spell of religious enchantment; when ultimately Saul decided to go himself, ***he stripped off his clothes also, and prophesied before Samuel in like manner, and lay down naked all that day and all that night. Wherefore they say, Is Saul also among the prophets?*** I should imagine that was the least they said.

20 David returned to ask Jonathan for help. Jonathan, who ***loved him as he loved his own soul,*** was reluctant to believe that his father meant David harm. On this score he was rapidly disabused. When he told Saul at a feast that he had excused David from attending, his father became abusive, shouting ***Thou son of the perverse rebellious woman, do not I know that thou hast chosen the son of Jesse to thine own confusion, and unto the confusion of thy mother's nakedness? For as long as the son of Jesse liveth upon the ground, thou shalt not be established, nor thy kingdom. Wherefore now send and fetch him unto me, for he shall surely die.*** Jonathan tried to argue, but Saul threatened him with a spear. All rather uncomfortable for the guests, I'm sure.

Jonathan had devised a highly elaborate performance, involving shooting arrows and shouting to servants, to signal Saul's intentions to David. It seemed pointless, though, because no sooner had the drama been played out than they actually met, ***and they kissed one another, and wept one with another***, and spoke face to face.

The End of Saul

21 David was on the run once again. Pretending to be on a secret mission for Saul, he found a priest who gave him some consecrated bread – David assured him that it would be eaten by men who were pure, who had ***kept themselves at least from women*** – and a weapon. As it happened the only sword available was the very one he had captured from Goliath.

For some reason David journeyed straight on to Goliath's home town, which considering who he was and what he was carrying was the worst possible place to be. To escape ***he changed his behaviour before them, and feigned himself mad in their hands, and scrabbled on the doors of the gate, and let his spittle fall down upon his beard.*** It was convincing enough that he was sent away, finding refuge

22 in a cave where other rebels and malcontents came to join him. David arranged for his family to stay in a safe haven provided by the king of Moab.

When news of David's escape reached Saul, he summoned the priest who had provided assistance. The priest protested his innocence, very reasonably pointing out that as far as he knew David was an honoured member of the king's household.

Saul was implacable: the priest – no, the entire clan of priests – must die. After meeting some initial reluctance to carry out these orders, he found someone to execute ***both men and women, children and sucklings, and oxen, and asses,*** etc., etc.

23 David continued to move from place to place, with Saul never very far behind. At one point David's band was nearly surrounded when Saul's forces were suddenly called away. 24 They had an even closer brush a little later, after the pursuit was resumed. While David was concealed in a cave with some of his men, Saul came in to relieve himself. David refused to kill him, but surreptitiously crept up and cut off a piece of his cloak. As Saul went on his way David called out that he would do the king no harm: ***Wickedness proceedeth from the wicked: but mine hand shall not be upon thee. After whom is the king of Israel come out? after whom dost thou pursue? after a dead dog, after a flea.*** Saul was much moved, whether by David's mercy or his modesty I couldn't say, and confessed that he was in the wrong. He didn't invite his son-in-law to come back home, though.

25 It was at this time that ***Samuel died; and all the Israelites were gathered together, and lamented him, and buried him.*** David returned to the wilderness. Near his camp lived a prosperous shepherd, who was so ungrateful for the 'protection' of David's men that he refused to offer them any 'gifts'. His wife Abigail realised that this was a big mistake, and hurried up to the camp leading donkeys laden with food and drink.

David was, indeed, getting into a self-righteous lather, saying ***this fellow ... hath requited me evil for good. So and more also do God unto the enemies of David, if I leave of all that pertain to him by the morning light any that pisseth against the wall.*** Abigail managed to appease him before the vengeance was carried out, but her husband had a seizure when she described what had happened. David ended up with Abigail as his wife. He already had one extra wife to add to Saul's daughter, whom the king had meanwhile passed on to someone else.

26 The next meeting of Saul and David unfolded as a repeat of the previous episode. David and one of his captains crept into Saul's camp at night, where thanks to God's help in sending everyone fast asleep they were able to stand directly over the king. Again David refused to kill him, but took his spear and water jug. Once safely away, David stood on a hillside and shouted across to propose peace. ***Then said Saul, I have sinned: return, my son David: for I will no more do thee harm, because my soul was precious in thine eyes this day: behold, I have played the fool, and have erred exceedingly.*** His credibility wasn't high, though, and David didn't join him.

27 Instead, David decided to ***escape into the land of the Philistines***, where he was welcomed as an enemy of Israel. Telling his hosts that he was making raids on his former countrymen, he was in fact attacking the people round about, taking care to leave no one alive to tell tales. 28 The pretence was so convincing that he was even invited along as a bodyguard when the Philistines went to war against the Israelites.

Saul was at a low ebb; God would no longer speak to him. In desperation he sought advice from the dead. Here he had no easy task, having already ***put away those that had familiar spirits, and the wizards, out of the land.*** His servants did manage, however, to find a woman at Endor who could act as a spirit medium, and he asked her to get in touch with Samuel. The old prophet was not happy about being disturbed, but Saul was even less happy with what Samuel had to tell him: that ***to morrow shalt thou and thy sons be with me.***

Saul collapsed, ***and there was no strength in him; for he had eaten no bread all the day, nor all the night.*** Like a worried mother the medium offered to make him a little food; he refused, but she forced him to get up and eat. Luckily ***the woman had a fat calf in the house.*** You never know when the king might come to visit, talk to a dead prophet and need a good dinner.

29 As the Philistines mustered their forces, most were far from happy to see David among them. His protector was obliged to send him back home, though he ***said to David, I know that thou art good in my sight, as an angel of God*** – not a comparison I would encourage. His lack of suspicion was astonishing.

30 On returning to the place where they were settled, David and his men discovered that it had been raided by the Amalekites (the group Saul had not been sufficiently zealous in exterminating). The city was burnt, and all the women and children had been carried off, including David's two wives. He ***was greatly distressed; for the people spake of stoning him***, which is always an upsetting thought. Happily he was able to overtake the enemy, recovering everyone and everything that had been taken.

31 Meanwhile the Israelites suffered the predicted disaster at the hands of the Philistines. Jonathan and two of his brothers were killed in the battle, while Saul himself was badly wounded by enemy archers. Unwilling to be taken alive, he asked his armour-bearer to run him through with his sword. The man refused. ***Therefore Saul took a sword, and fell upon it.***

When they found him, the Philistines cut off his head and nailed his body to a wall. In the night men came and took down the corpses of Saul and his sons, giving them a proper burial. That was the least this man, chosen and abandoned by God, deserved.

10

The Second Book of Samuel

News of the death of Saul and Jonathan was brought to David by a survivor of the battle. Asked how he knew, the man claimed to have been passing when Saul, mortally wounded and close to capture, told him to administer the coup de grace. ***So I stood upon him, and slew him, because I was sure that he could not live after that he was fallen: and I took the crown that was upon his head, and the bracelet that was on his arm, and have brought them hither unto my lord.*** Far from thanking the man, David had him killed. It seems that there were, after all, some orders that you weren't supposed to follow. 1

David, in deep mourning, composed a majestic lament (which curiously makes no mention of God):

The beauty of Israel is slain upon thy high places:
how are the mighty fallen!

Tell it not in Gath,
publish it not in the streets of Askelon;
lest the daughters of the Philistines rejoice,
lest the daughters of the uncircumcised triumph.
...
Saul and Jonathan were lovely and pleasant in their lives;
and in their death they were not divided:
they were swifter than eagles,
they were stronger than lions.

Ye daughters of Israel, weep over Saul,
who clothed you in scarlet, with other delights,
who put on ornaments of gold upon your apparel.
How are the mighty fallen in the midst of the battle!
O Jonathan, thou wast slain in thine high places.
I am distressed for thee, my brother Jonathan:
very pleasant hast thou been unto me:
thy love to me was wonderful,
passing the love of women.

How are the mighty fallen,
and the weapons of war perished!

2 David took up residence in Hebron and was made king over the tribe of Judah. The other tribes were ruled by a surviving son of Saul, supported by Abner, his father's military commander. Inevitably, the two sides went to war.

In an early battle one of David's captains pursued Abner, who told the young upstart to tackle someone else before he got hurt. ***Howbeit he refused to turn aside: wherefore Abner with the hinder end of the spear smote him under the fifth rib, that the spear came out behind him; and he fell down there, and died in the same place.*** It was a blood feud in the making.

3 ***Now there was long war between the house of Saul and the house of David: but David waxed stronger and stronger, and the house of Saul waxed weaker and weaker.*** The position of Saul's son deteriorated further when Abner defected after a quarrel over a concubine. In addition, David was able to secure the return of Saul's daughter. He was not exactly short of female companionship; already in Hebron he had produced six sons by six different women. Still, his first wife was sent back to him, despite the fact that she had been remarried; ***And her husband went with her along weeping behind her***, until Abner told him to go away. I wondered which one the woman wanted, but it was just idle curiousity.

Hopes that Abner would bring easy success were short lived; he was assassinated by Joab, the brother of the man he hadn't wanted to kill. Appalled, David dissociated himself from this act of revenge. He led the burial ceremony, saying ***Know ye not that there is a prince and a great man fallen this day in Israel?***

4 Another murder changed the situation again. Two officers in the army of Saul's son crept up to where the king ***lay on his bed in his bedchamber, and they smote him, and slew him, and beheaded him, and took his head,*** and brought it to David. That was not a bright idea. David's men ***slew them, and cut off their hands and their feet, and hanged them up over the pool in Hebron.*** There was a brief fashion for mutilating dead bodies.

King David

5 ***So the elders of Israel came ... and they anointed David king over Israel. David was thirty years old when he began to reign, and he reigned forty years.*** Having finally come into his kingdom, he achieved his great triumph, the capture of Jerusalem, ***the strong hold of Zion: the same is the city of David.*** Victory was pleasant; he ***took him more concubines and wives out of Jerusalem, after he was come from Hebron: and there were yet sons and daughters born to David.***

6 It was decided to bring the ark to Jerusalem. Making a great procession, ***David and all the house of Israel played before the LORD on all manner of instruments made of fir wood, even on harps, and on psalteries, and on timbrels, and on***

cornets, and on cymbals. As ever, being near the ark could be dangerous; when a man steadied it on the ox cart with his hand, God struck him dead on the spot.

Eventually they carried on, ***And David danced before the LORD with all his might.*** I don't know that he was wearing more than a loin cloth, which perhaps is why in Jerusalem ***Saul's daughter looked through a window, and saw king David leaping and dancing before the LORD; and she despised him in her heart.*** Later she upbraided her husband sarcastically, ***How glorious was the king of Israel to day, who uncovered himself to day in the eyes of the handmaids of his servants ...!*** David replied that it was all for God. Presumably their conjugal relations were affected by this incident, because ***the daughter of Saul had no child unto the day of her death.***

7 David thought that he should build a temple; as he told the prophet Nathan, ***I dwell in an house of cedar, but the ark of God dwelleth within curtains.*** God let Nathan know, however, that he was quite happy to stay in his tent until David's son and successor became king: then ***He shall build an house for my name, and I will stablish the throne of his kingdom for ever.*** It sounded fair to me.

8 Life wasn't easy for the inhabitants of neighbouring areas; not even the people of Moab, who had protected his family during his outlaw years and to whom he was related (through Ruth, his great-grandmother), were spared. They were made to lie on the ground end to end; the human chain was marked off using a rope, with two lengths killed for every one length saved. On another occasion David captured a thousand or more chariot horses and had most of them hamstrung. But ***the LORD preserved David whithersoever he went.***

9 Joab remained in command of the army, despite his crime against Abner, while a man named Zadok became high priest. The one surviving son of Jonathan, lame in both legs, was brought into David's household. He was greatly moved when David restored to him all of Saul's property, saying ***What is thy servant, that thou shouldest look upon such a dead dog as I am?***

10 One conflict at least was not of David's making. He had sent ambassadors to a neighbouring group, offering condolences for the death of their king. Fearing that the men were really spies, the new ruler ***took David's servants, and shaved off the one half of their beards, and cut off their garments in the middle, even to their buttocks, and sent them away***; fortunately David told them to ***Tarry at Jericho until your beards be grown.*** The incident not being calculated to encourage good relations, war broke out. Although the enemy was strong, the Israelites prevailed, killing in excess of 40,000 men. Lapses in protocol can be costly.

BATHSHEBA TAKES A BATH

11 Up to this point David had managed to stay on the right side of God, but now things began to go wrong. It all started one evening when ***David arose from off his bed, and walked upon the roof of the king's house: and from the roof he saw a woman***

washing herself; and the woman was very beautiful to look upon. ... And David sent messengers, and took her; and she came in unto him, and he lay with her. Her name was Bathsheba, and she was married to Uriah, a soldier off on campaign. It might have been just another royal fling, except that she became pregnant.

David's first response was to bring Uriah back from the war, so that the child might seem to be his. Unfortunately Uriah was rigorous in abstaining from intercourse while on military service; not even getting him drunk worked. David sent the inconvenient husband back to the front lines with a letter to Joab, ***saying, Set ye Uriah in the forefront of the hottest battle, and retire ye from him, that he may be smitten, and die.*** His orders were carried out, with the desired result; as for Bathsheba, ***David sent and fetched her to his house, and she became his wife, and bare him a son. But the thing that David had done displeased the LORD.*** Had he known, Uriah wouldn't have been too happy, either.

12 Nathan was brave enough to tell David a parable about a rich man and a poor man. ***The rich man had exceeding many flocks and herds: But the poor man had nothing, save one little ewe lamb, which he had bought and nourished up: and it grew up together with him, and with his children; it did eat of his own meat, and drank of his own cup, and lay in his bosom, and was unto him as a daughter.*** One day the rich man had a visitor, and instead of providing the meal from his own flock he took the poor man's lamb. ***And Nathan said to David, Thou art the man.*** God gave you everything you could have wanted, but you had someone killed to take his wife.

As punishment, God declared that he would produce calamity from within David's own family, and that another man would take his wives in broad daylight. In the mean time his new son would die. ***And the LORD struck the child that Uriah's wife bare unto David, and it was very sick.*** Not the clearest case of divine justice I had seen, I must admit.

After a week the infant died. David's servants expressed surprise that ***thou didst fast and weep for the child, while it was alive; but when the child was dead, thou didst rise and eat bread. And he said, While the child was yet alive, I fasted and wept: for I said, Who can tell whether God will be gracious to me, that the child may live? But now he is dead, wherefore should I fast? can I bring him back again? I shall go to him, but he shall not return to me. And David comforted Bathsheba his wife, and went in unto her, and lay with her: and she bare a son, and he called his name Solomon: and the LORD loved him.***

13 Now the family problems began, and they were king-sized problems. David's eldest son Amnon was infatuated with his half-sister Tamar; but ***she was a virgin; and Amnon thought it hard for him to do any thing to her.*** To lure her into his room he pretended to be ill, asking that she be sent to prepare him cakes. ***And when she had brought them unto him to eat, he took hold of her, and said unto her, Come lie with me, my sister. And she answered him, Nay, my brother, do not force me; for no such thing ought to be done in Israel: do not thou this folly. ... Howbeit he would not hearken unto her voice: but, being stronger than she,***

forced her, and lay with her. Feeling the wrong-doer's disgust for his victim, Amnon told Tamar ***Arise, be gone***; she was in such distress that ***he called his servant that ministered unto him, and said, Put now this woman out from me, and bolt the door after her.*** The man was contemptible.

I wasn't greatly impressed by David's response, which was to do nothing, and it came as no surprise when Tamar's full brother Absalom took matters into his own hands. Two years later he had Amnon murdered at a sheep-shearing festival, and then went into exile.

ABSALOM REBELS

14 Seeing that the king was unhappy to have lost his son Absalom as well as Amnon, Joab concocted a story of fratricide and found a woman to appeal to David on behalf of her 'son'. When he granted that man protection, the woman asked why ***the king doth not fetch home again his banished. For we must needs die, and are as water spilt on the ground, which cannot be gathered up again.*** David realised that Joab had put her up to this performance (she fawningly said ***my lord is wise, according to the wisdom of an angel of God, to know all things that are in the earth***; luckily for her I'm tolerant of blasphemy) but he let Absalom return.

Absalom dwelt two full years in Jerusalem, and saw not the king's face. He couldn't even get Joab to visit him. Losing patience, ***he said unto his servants, See, Joab's field is near mine, and he hath barley there; go and set it on fire.*** When Joab came and asked him what he thought he was doing, Absalom replied that if no one was going to speak to him he would be better off in exile. The message was passed to David, who relented, and Absalom returned to court. The king might have been more careful not to encourage arson, in my view.

15 Absalom promptly began to plot against his father. Every day he would go out to the city gate and suggest to the litigants who came from far and wide that they would do better if he were king, and ***so Absalom stole the hearts of the men of Israel.*** When the day came to make his move, he went to Hebron and proclaimed himself king. David realised that he would have to evacuate Jerusalem, not having the forces to hold it against Absalom's growing strength.

The priests started to follow him out of the city with the ark, and I was glad to see that he sent them back. David recognised that the ark was a symbol, not a talisman: ***If I shall find favour in the eyes of the LORD, he will bring me again*** to see the ark; if not, ***here am I, let him do to me as seemeth good unto him.*** Near the summit of the Mount of Olives David was met by one of his counsellors; he, too, was sent back, with instructions to defect and act as a double agent. They were becoming more sophisticated all around.

16 David ignored a relative of Saul who threw stones and cursed him, ***thou bloody man.*** His captain said ***Why should this dead dog curse my lord the king? let me go over, I pray thee, and take off his head.*** David replied that with his own son

out to kill him, the resentful stranger hardly mattered: ***let him alone, and let him curse.*** This moral rationality made me feel quite cheerful.

Back in Jerusalem, Absalom was looking for ways of asserting his authority. His chief advisor recommended that he have intercourse with the concubines David left behind so that no one could doubt the seriousness of his rebellion. ***So they spread Absalom a tent upon the top of the house; and Absalom went in unto his father's concubines in the sight of all Israel.*** People complain about what children see these days; they don't know what they missed.

17 The advisor next urged him to send out a force immediately in hot pursuit, as David's death would end the conflict. To forestall this plan (which had every prospect of success) the double agent argued that David was too wily and would escape, that early losses to the enemy would demoralise Absalom's followers, and that he would do better to delay until he could command a larger army. Absalom foolishly agreed, giving David time to cross the Jordan to safety. When the unfortunate advisor ***saw that his counsel was not followed, he saddled his ass, and arose, and gat him home to his house, to his city, and put his household in order, and hanged himself, and died.*** He could see what was coming.

18 Briefing his troops as the confrontation approached, David said ***Deal gently for my sake with the young man, even with Absalom.*** In the course of the battle ***Absalom rode upon a mule, and the mule went under the thick boughs of a great oak, and his head caught hold of the oak, and he was taken up between the heaven and the earth; and the mule that was under him went away.*** When it was reported to Joab, the commander, that Absalom had been left hanging in a tree, he ignored David's orders and dispatched the usurper. (Perhaps he bore a grudge over the burnt field?)

The victory belonged to David, but at the news of his son's death he cried ***O my son Absalom, my son, my son Absalom! would God I had died for thee, O***
19 ***Absalom, my son, my son!*** David's grief was so great that his troops had to creep back into the city like beaten men. Joab remonstrated with him that apparently ***thou lovest thine enemies, and hatest thy friends. ... I perceive, that if Absalom had lived, and all we had died this day, then it had pleased thee well.*** For the sake of morale the king went out to see the army pass in review.

David remained beyond the river Jordan, however, until representatives of the people came to urge him to return. Those who had backed the wrong side arrived to offer their excuses, which David accepted. In seeking reconciliation, he even went to the extraordinary length of replacing Joab as commander with the former
20 chief of Absalom's army. As for his concubines who had been defiled, ***they were shut up unto the day of their death, living in widowhood.*** There's nothing sadder than a celibate concubine.

An uprising obliged David's army to set out under its new commander, but Joab wanted his old job back. He greeted his successor on the open road, grasped his beard as if to kiss him, and with his sword ***shed out his bowels to the ground***; the victim ***wallowed in blood in the midst of the highway.*** Joab had a knack for getting his way. Using his powers of persuasion, the insurrection was quickly ended. Following Abner and Absalom, Joab had now killed three leaders against the wishes of David; I don't know whether the king kept him in charge out of admiration for his effectiveness, or from fear of becoming number four.

Flashbacks

21 With David finally having carried the day, it's worth mentioning a few incidents earlier in his reign. There was a famine which God blamed on certain misdeeds of Saul; the people who had been wronged demanded the sacrifice of Saul's two surviving sons and five of his grandsons. The elimination of his predecessor's heirs was suspiciously convenient for David, I must say. Their bodies were left unburied in the open, but Rizpah, the mother of Saul's sons, camped beside the corpses for months ***and suffered neither the birds of the air to rest on them by day, nor the beasts of the field by night.*** Her staunchness was rewarded when David arranged an honourable burial.

The Philistines had a number of giants in their ranks, four of whom fell to Israelites at one time or another. The killing of Goliath was even credited to someone other than David, which just shows how careful you have to be about history.

22 David was a poet and musician as well as a fighter and ruler; he was able to celebrate his own victories, giving due credit to God: ***The LORD is my rock, and my fortress, and my deliverer.*** Some of it was distinctly triumphalist:

> ***I have pursued mine enemies, and destroyed them;***
> ***and turned not again until I had consumed them. ...***
> ***Then did I beat them as small as the dust of the earth,***
> ***I did stamp them as the mire of the street.***

23 Happily, ***David the son of Jesse ... the man who was raised up on high, the anointed of the God of Jacob, and the sweet psalmist of Israel,*** had another voice, and a lighter touch:

> ***He that ruleth over man must be just,***
> ***ruling in the fear of God.***
> ***And he shall be as the light of the morning,***
> ***when the sun riseth, even a morning without clouds;***
> ***as the tender grass springing out of the earth by***
> ***clear shining after rain.***

The man could write like an angel, if I may say so myself.

David's victories produced many heroes, but the exploits of three of them stand out. Once David expressed a great longing for water from a well in Bethlehem, then occupied by the Philistines. In a feat of audacity, the daredevils fought their way through and brought back some water, only to see David pour it on the ground, saying ***is not this the blood of the men that went in jeopardy of their lives?*** No one recorded their reply, but if it was polite they were even more heroic than people thought.

Another group of thirty heroes was also listed. For some reason the list contains thirty-one names, and ends by giving a total of ***thirty and seven in all.*** Hero inflation, perhaps?

24 They were strange times. Apparently following the divine will, David ordered Joab to take a census, saying ***Go now through all the tribes of Israel, from Dan even to Beer-sheba, and number ye the people.*** Close to ten months later he came back with the count: 1,300,000 fighting men. David was promptly stricken with guilt – I have no idea why – and offered to atone. God invited him to choose between years of famine, months of flight from the enemy, or days of pestilence. David went for the short, sharp shock, but it still cost 70,000 lives.

With considerable understatement God told the angel who was busy destroying the Israelites – not me, I hasten to say – ***It is enough, stay now thine hand.*** David purchased the threshing floor where the angel happened to be standing at the time to build an altar. God was placated by the sacrifices, ***and the plague was stayed from Israel.***

11

The First Book of Kings

1

Now king David was old and stricken in years; and they covered him with clothes, but he gat no heat. Wherefore his servants said unto him, Let there be sought for my lord the king a young virgin: and let her stand before the king, and let her cherish him, and let her lie in thy bosom, that my lord the king may get heat. So they sought for a fair damsel throughout all the coasts of Israel, until they found just the woman. She was attentive and lovely and kept the king warm, though he was past the point of requiring more personal services.

David continued to be plagued by his troublesome family. His son Adonijah decided, with the support of Joab, that he should be next in line to the throne. A rival faction led by Bathsheba was determined to forestall this claim; she reminded David of his promise that their son Solomon would succeed him.

When Nathan the prophet brought news that Adonijah was celebrating his coming power, David was spurred to act. He told them to take Solomon outside the city on the royal mule, ***And let Zadok the priest and Nathan the prophet anoint him there king over Israel: and blow ye with the trumpet, and say, God save king Solomon.*** He appeared to be a popular choice. Whether out of prudence or genuine enthusiasm, ***all the people came up after him, and the people piped with pipes, and rejoiced with great joy, so that the earth rent with the sound of them.*** Adonijah's banquet came to a hasty end, and he clung to the altar until Solomon declared that ***there shall not an hair of him fall to the earth***, so long as he behaved.

2

David, on his deathbed, gave Solomon a few final instructions, sacred and secular, lofty and lowly. In the first place he was to obey God, ***to walk in his ways, to keep his statutes, and his commandments, and his judgments,*** etc., etc. All that aside, he should eliminate the ruthless Joab. Also among the unfinished business was the relative of Saul who, I thought, had been so nobly forgiven his swearing and stone-throwing; David's last command was ***Now therefore hold him not guiltless: for thou art a wise man, and knowest what thou oughtest to do unto him; but his hoar head bring thou down to the grave with blood.*** And so he died like a gangster, leaving no score unsettled.

Solomon learnt the lesson well. One day Bathsheba sat next to him and said ***I desire one small petition of thee; I pray thee, say me not nay. And the king said unto her, Ask on, my mother: for I will not say thee nay.*** He hadn't yet heard what it was, though. Adonijah wanted to marry the young woman who had kept David's bed warm at the end of his life. Now I don't know whether Adonijah was attracted by her charms or by her symbolic importance as the king's concubine, but Solomon was furious. ***As the LORD liveth***, he declared, ***Adonijah shall be put to death this day***. His hit man, Benaiah, carried out the order.

Knowing that he was next, Joab fled to the tabernacle and clung to the altar, saying ***I will die here***. Even a trained killer like Benaiah felt obliged to report back for further orders. ***And the king said unto him, Do as he hath said, and fall upon him, and bury him***. If the man wanted to die by the altar, Solomon was happy to oblige.

Still, I don't think he was savage by nature. The man who had insulted David was allowed to live, but told that if he left Jerusalem ***thou shalt surely die: thy blood shall be upon thine own head***. Three years later the man foolishly pursued a couple of his runaway slaves out of the city, and even more foolishly came back. Solomon didn't like to be crossed, and Benaiah (now head of the army as well as chief assassin) was given another assignment.

THE WISDOM OF SOLOMON

3 Solomon did many extraordinary things, not least forming an alliance with Pharaoh, king of Egypt, and marrying his daughter. It was his wisdom, though, that made the biggest impression. This went back to a dream in which God allowed him to make a request, and he asked for ***an understanding heart to judge thy people, that I may discern between good and bad***. It was granted him, God declaring ***I have given thee a wise and an understanding heart***, better than any before or since, with riches and honour as a bonus.

Then came there two women, that were harlots, unto the king, and stood before him, and gave him a chance to display his wisdom. The two women shared a house, each had recently given birth, and one child had died; so much was agreed. The dispute was over whose child had survived, one woman saying that the babies had been switched in the middle of the night and the other denying it. Both claimed the living child.

And the king said, Bring me a sword. And they brought a sword before the king. And the king said, Divide the living child in two, and give half to the one, and half to the other. This solution was acceptable to one of the women, but the true mother said ***O my lord, give her the living child, and in no wise slay it***. Recognising her maternal feelings, Solomon awarded her the child. Very ingenious, though why the other woman was ready to accept half is a mystery to me.

4 Solomon ruled over the whole country, and all was well. ***Judah and Israel were many, as the sand which is by the sea in multitude, eating and drinking, and making merry*** – high time, too, I thought. Finally they ***dwelt safely, every man under his vine and under his fig tree, from Dan even to Beer-sheba***. Solomon acquired a great reputation; ***he spake three thousand proverbs: and his songs were a thousand and five***. People came from all over ***to hear the wisdom of Solomon***.

The temple

Solomon's glory also lay in more visible achievements, in particular the construction of the temple. His first step was to do a deal for timber with the king of Tyre, who ***rejoiced greatly, and said, Blessed be the LORD this day, which hath given unto David a wise son over this great people.*** He was happy thinking of what Solomon was going to pay, if you want my opinion. 5

To be more accurate, of course, it was the people who paid. Quite apart from all the food sent in exchange for the cedar and pine, ***Solomon raised a levy out of all Israel; and the levy was thirty thousand men. And he sent them to Lebanon, ten thousand a month by courses: a month they were in Lebanon, and two months at home.*** There were another 70,000 men drafted to carry loads, and 80,000 to work in the stone quarries. The popular resentment this created led directly, in my view, to the future revolt; in building the temple Solomon split the kingdom.

And it came to pass in the four hundred and eightieth year after the children of Israel were come out of the land of Egypt, in the fourth year of Solomon's reign ... that he began to build the house of the LORD. Among the tens of thousands of forced labourers I imagine that more than a few thought they might as well be back in Egypt; the fact that the king was married to Pharaoh's daughter must have seemed all too appropriate. 6

Essentially the temple was a rectangular stone box, panelled with wood, and overlaid with gold. The decoration was overwrought for my taste; ***he carved all the walls of the house round about with carved figures of cherubims and palm trees and open flowers, within and without***, and gilded to boot. It took seven years to complete.

The temple was not Solomon's only construction project. He also built palaces for himself and for Pharaoh's daughter, as well as a large hall for state purposes. Various touches were added in and around the temple, notably two large bronze pillars, an enormous basin, ten bronze supports for smaller bowls, and miscellaneous pots and pans. ***And Solomon left all the vessels unweighed, because they were exceeding many: neither was the weight of the brass found out.*** It's safe to say that he spared no expense. 7

When the time came to dedicate the temple, Solomon summoned all the leading citizens and sacrificed more sheep and oxen than anyone could count. The ark, which contained the two tablets of stone put there by Moses, was installed in the inner chamber, whereupon a ***cloud filled the house of the LORD***, forcing the priests to leave. 8

Solomon turned towards the altar, spread his arms, and launched into a long prayer. He seemed to recognise that God might be more universal and less tangible than they generally made out, asking ***But will God indeed dwell on the earth? behold, the heaven and heaven of heavens cannot contain thee; how much less this house that I have builded?***

Yet hear our prayers, he appealed to God, ***hear thou in heaven thy dwelling place: and when thou hearest, forgive.*** Be just but merciful, save us from drought, famine, plague and siege. ***Moreover concerning a stranger, that is not of thy people Israel, but cometh out of a far country for thy name's sake***: grant his prayers, so ***that all people of the earth may know thy name.*** Finally, let captives be treated with compassion by the enemy.

Solomon arose from his knees and blessed the congregation, asking that his prayer be granted ***That all the people of the earth may know that the LORD is God, and that there is none else.*** It was a wonderful moment. As in the days of Moses, the animals had a less happy time: 22,000 oxen and 120,000 sheep were sacrificed. The altar being too small for the offerings, Solomon was obliged to consecrate the courtyard, though it still didn't make sense: the entire city was hardly big enough to hold all those animals, much less slaughter them.

9 God appeared to Solomon in a dream and tempered the euphoria. If everyone is properly obedient, he declared, you will indeed be protected; but if you violate the laws and worship other gods, ***Then will I cut off Israel out of the land which I have given them; and this house, which I have hallowed for my name, will I cast out of my sight; and Israel shall be a proverb and a byword among all people.*** It sounded ominous.

The cost of the temple and other building projects had been heavy; Solomon had even had to hand over twenty cities in the land of Galilee to the king of Tyre in exchange for trees and gold. The original Canaanite peoples were enslaved, and even the Israelites were pressed into service. Solomon was wearing the country down.

THE WOMEN OF SOLOMON

10 Still, the reputation of the king spread to distant parts. ***When the queen of Sheba heard of the fame of Solomon concerning the name of the LORD, she came to prove him with hard questions.*** He had an answer to everything, and she admitted that before coming she hadn't believed what people had said; but ***behold, the half was not told me: thy wisdom and prosperity exceedeth the fame which I heard. Happy are thy men, happy are these thy servants.*** She gave him large quantities of gold, spice and precious stones, ***And king Solomon gave unto the queen of Sheba all her desire, whatsoever she asked.*** There's been some gossip about what she desired.

Solomon was trading by land and by sea. Despite the earlier strain on national resources, he was accumulating great wealth; ***once in three years came the navy of Tharshish, bringing gold, and silver, ivory, and apes, and peacocks. So king Solomon exceeded all the kings of the earth for riches and for wisdom.*** He had it all. Solomon even established a corps of 1,400 chariots; he was becoming more Egyptian than his wife.

But king Solomon loved many strange women; he just couldn't resist exotic females. As we know this tended to bring trouble; not that God was racist, of course, he simply explained that ***Ye shall not go in to them, neither shall they come in unto you: for surely they will turn away your heart after their gods.*** Foreigners just weren't brought up with the same values. Solomon took no notice, however; ***he had seven hundred wives, princesses, and three hundred concubines.*** He wasn't a man to do things by halves. 11

In his later years Solomon did, in fact, go too far in accommodating his wives, building shrines for one foreign god after another. ***And the LORD was angry with Solomon***, because Israel was supposed to be his exclusive territory. He declared that as punishment Solomon's son would have the larger part of the kingdom torn from his hands. Having parents was a heavy responsibility; you would be blamed if they went bad.

Internal opposition emerged in the figure of a certain Jeroboam. One day he met a prophet on the road, who tore his cloak into twelve strips and said, ***Take thee ten pieces: for thus saith the LORD, the God of Israel, Behold, I will rend the kingdom out of the hand of Solomon, and will give ten tribes to thee.*** Somehow this reached the ears of Solomon, and Jeroboam had to flee for his life.

For Solomon, though, it was too late. ***And the time that Solomon reigned in Jerusalem over all Israel was forty years. And Solomon slept with his fathers, and was buried in the city of David his father: and Rehoboam his son reigned in his stead.***

THE KINGDOM DIVIDES

The people were determined to escape from the burdens that Solomon had imposed. They told the new king ***Thy father made our yoke grievous:*** make it lighter, ***and we will serve thee.*** The elders advised conciliation, but the young men of the court urged Rehoboam to reply ***My little finger shall be thicker than my father's loins ... my father hath chastised you with whips, but I will chastise you with scorpions.*** That was the line he chose. Some people inherit power and think that they have it by divine right. 12

So when all Israel saw that the king hearkened not unto them, the people answered the king, saying, What portion have we in David? ... to your tents, O Israel. Rehoboam was deserted by everyone except the tribes of Judah and Benjamin. Jeroboam, who had returned from exile, was acclaimed king by the other ten tribes. From then on the country was divided into the northern kingdom of Israel and the southern kingdom of Judah.

The idea had been to punish the house of David, but the rival kingdom caused us just as much trouble. With Jerusalem in the hands of the old guard, Jeroboam set up golden calves for people to worship, at Dan and at Bethel. God sent a holy man to Bethel warning that the day would come when pagan priests would be burnt 13 there; before he left, the altar was miraculously destroyed.

A local prophet came and pressed his hospitality on the man, who had been forbidden by God to eat or drink in the sinful city. The would-be host insisted, asserting that ***an angel spake unto me by the word of the LORD, saying, Bring him back with thee into thine house, that he may eat bread and drink water. But he lied unto him.*** I would have liked to punish the so-called prophet who misrepresented me, but God was more concerned about the too-gullible holy man, and arranged for him to meet a lion on his way home.

14 Next it was the turn of Jeroboam. The prophet who had first announced his destiny now declared that his entire family would be destroyed, every man ***that pisseth against the wall***, all of them swept away by God ***as a man taketh away dung, till it be all gone. Him that dieth of Jeroboam in the city shall the dogs eat; and him that dieth in the field shall the fowls of the air eat.*** Even more ominously, he prophesied that God ***shall root up Israel out of this good land, which he gave to their fathers, and shall scatter them.*** All of this was announced to Jeroboam's unfortunate wife, who had merely come to ask the prophet about their sick child. I hardly need mention that the child died.

To the south, meanwhile, the picture was not much brighter. In the kingdom of Judah idolatry was on the rise, and ***there were also sodomites in the land: and they did according to all the abominations of the nations which the LORD cast out before the children of Israel.*** Even national security had deteriorated; the king of Egypt raided Jerusalem and carried off the temple treasures.

15 Rehoboam was succeeded by his son, and then by his grandson, Asa. He at least ***took away the sodomites out of the land, and removed all the idols that his fathers had made.*** Not even his grandmother escaped the new broom; being found in possession of an obscene fertility symbol, she lost her place at court. The wild parties had to stop.

War between Judah and Israel continued. Asa was forced at one stage to seek help from the king of Syria, sending him all the remaining gold and silver. Beyond that, there's little to tell. ***The rest of all the acts of Asa, and all his might, and all that he did, and the cities which he built, are they not written in the book of the chronicles of the kings of Judah? Nevertheless in the time of his old age he was diseased in his feet.*** Sorry, perhaps I should have mentioned the feet. When Asa died, ***Jehoshaphat his son reigned in his stead.***

Back in the kingdom of Israel, Jeroboam's son was deposed after just two years on the throne, his entire family being destroyed as predicted. God was no happier

16 with his successor, though, and again decreed that all the descendants would be eliminated, their bodies eaten by dogs in the city or by birds in the country as the case might be. As before the son of the sinner paid the price; two years into his reign he got drunk and was assassinated by one of his captains, who proceeded to exterminate his relatives: ***he left him not one that pisseth against a wall, neither of his kinsfolk, nor of his friends.*** Having a king in the family must have aroused mixed feelings.

The usurper lasted only seven days, and when surrounded burnt down the palace over his head. He was succeeded by Omri, founder of a new dynasty who built his capital at Samaria. ***But Omri wrought evil in the eyes of the LORD, and did worse than all that were before him.*** Israel was having a hard time of it, and there was more to come. Omri was followed by his son Ahab, who continued the tradition; he too ***did evil in the sight of the LORD above all that were before him.*** At some point the one-upmanship would have to stop.

I don't believe Ahab was really such a bad fellow, but his wife Jezebel did get him into trouble. The daughter of a neighbouring king, she was a staunch follower of nature gods. At her instigation Ahab built a shrine for Baal in Samaria. Ironically, in view of her reputation and interest in fertility, the name Jezebel means 'chaste'.

ELIJAH

Grave times demand great prophets, and this was the moment for Elijah to appear. He told Ahab that no rain would come unless he said so. At God's command he then went into hiding, ***and dwelt by the brook Cherith, that is before Jordan. And the ravens brought him bread and flesh in the morning, and bread and flesh in the evening; and he drank of the brook.*** He didn't ask what sort of meat they were bringing. 17

When the stream dried up Elijah went to stay with a widow and her son. She told him that there was just ***an handful of meal in a barrel, and a little oil in a cruse: and, behold, I am gathering two sticks, that I may go in and dress it for me and my son, that we may eat it, and die.*** Elijah insisted that God would provide, and indeed ***she, and he, and her house, did eat many days. And the barrel of meal wasted not, neither did the cruse of oil fail.*** I wish I knew, though, whether it was in hope, or faith, or despair that she first gave their remaining food to the stranger.

Elijah did have the opportunity to repay her hospitality with a second miracle. Her son fell ill, and stopped breathing. Elijah ***stretched himself upon the child three times, and cried unto the LORD, and said, O LORD my God, I pray thee, let this child's soul come into him again.*** When the boy revived ***the woman said to Elijah, Now by this I know that thou art a man of God***; the bottomless barrel wasn't enough, it seems.

In the third year of the drought God sent Elijah back to confront Ahab. Jezebel had ordered the massacre of God's prophets and Elijah's position was precarious; nevertheless Ahab agreed to a trial of divine strength on mount Carmel. God and Elijah would take on Baal and 450 of his prophets in front of all the children of Israel. 18

Elijah came unto all the people, and said, How long halt ye between two opinions? if the LORD be God, follow him: but if Baal, then follow him. He proposed that each side chop up a bull, placing the pieces on a pile of wood. Whichever god could light the fire, ***let him be God. And all the people answered***

and said, It is well spoken. Everyone enjoys a contest.

The opposition team went first, appealing to Baal all morning. ***And it came to pass at noon, that Elijah mocked them, and said, Cry aloud: for he is a god; either he is talking, or he is pursuing*** (urinating, to be less delicate), ***or he is in a journey, or peradventure he sleepeth, and must be awaked.*** Elijah played to the crowd when it was his turn, saying ***Fill four barrels with water, and pour it on the burnt sacrifice, and on the wood. And he said, Do it the second time. And they did it the second time. And he said, Do it the third time. And they did it the third time.*** When everything was well soaked he called out to God, and ***the fire of the LORD fell, and consumed the burnt sacrifice, and the wood, and the stones, and the dust, and licked up the water.*** The verdict was unanimous: God was God.

Elijah, it has to be said, was not a gracious winner. Ordering that all the prophets of Baal be rounded up, he took them down the mountain and killed them. With God now appeased, Elijah could at least report that ***there is a sound of abundance of rain.*** In fact at first there was neither sight nor sound of anything; again and again Elijah told his servant to look west, and finally the man announced ***there ariseth a little cloud out of the sea, like a man's hand.*** As the skies darkened Ahab set out for his summer palace by chariot, but Elijah ***girded up his loins, and ran before Ahab*** the whole way.

19 When she heard what had happened Jezebel vowed that Elijah would be dead by the following day. He fled to the opposite end of the country, where he wearily asked God to let him die. Instead, God sent me down. ***And as he lay and slept under a juniper tree, behold, then an angel touched him, and said unto him, Arise and eat.*** I made sure that he ate a couple of meals, because he was about to travel forty days and forty nights to mount Sinai.

Whether Elijah understood what happened there I couldn't say; I'm not even sure that I do. But it was wonderful: ***the LORD passed by, and a great and strong wind rent the mountains, and brake in pieces the rocks before the LORD; but the LORD was not in the wind: and after the wind an earthquake; but the LORD was not in the earthquake: And after the earthquake a fire; but the LORD was not in the fire: and after the fire a still small voice. And it was so, when Elijah heard it, that he wrapped his face in his mantle, and went out.***

Following God's new orders he found Elisha, the man who would succeed him as prophet, ploughing in a field. To signify the succession ***Elijah passed by him, and cast his mantle upon him.*** No one ever seemed surprised or sceptical when the holy summons came: all Elisha said was ***Let me, I pray thee, kiss my father and my mother, and then I will follow thee.*** Off they went to anoint new kings.

AHAB DOES WRONG

20 Israel, meanwhile, was with God's help having military success. The king of Syria had announced that he intended to come and take all of Ahab's gold, silver, wives

and children. Ahab replied ***Let not him that girdeth on his harness boast himself as he that putteth it off.*** The heavily outnumbered Israelites won the ensuing battle and then repeated the performance the following year, killing some 127,000 Syrians.

Despite the concessions won from the Syrians, at least one prophet thought that the enemy had been let off too lightly. He devised a complex drama to make his point – getting someone eaten by a lion in the process – which concluded with a message from God to Ahab: ***Because thou hast let go out of thy hand a man whom I appointed to utter destruction, therefore thy life shall go for his life, and thy people for his people. And the king of Israel went to his house heavy and displeased.*** I could hardly blame him.

21 There was worse to come for Ahab. He wished to buy a vineyard next to his summer palace in Jezreel, but the owner, Naboth, refused to sell. Ahab went to his room and sulked; ***he laid him down upon his bed, and turned away his face, and would eat no bread.*** Not believing that a king has to take 'no' for an answer, Jezebel arranged for Naboth to be liquidated. Ahab was able to claim his vineyard.

Who should be waiting for him there but Elijah. ***Hast thou found me, O mine enemy?*** asked Ahab, as the prophet pronounced the familiar curse on errant kings: ***I will bring evil upon thee, and will take away thy posterity, and will cut off from Ahab him that pisseth against the wall.*** For good measure, ***The dogs shall eat Jezebel by the wall of Jezreel.*** They would also eat Ahab's family, unless birds got to the bodies first. It was only to be expected: ***there was none like unto Ahab, which did sell himself to work wickedness in the sight of the LORD, whom Jezebel his wife stirred up.*** Naturally Ahab was very cut up about all this, and seemed so penitent that God decided ***I will not bring the evil in his days: but in his son's days will I bring the evil upon his house.*** I couldn't quite see the justice in that, to be honest.

22 By this time Jehoshaphat was the king of Judah, and he had formed an alliance with Ahab against Syria. Although four hundred court prophets predicted that their campaign would succeed, Jehoshaphat insisted on summoning another, one greatly disliked by Ahab for his pessimism. I could understand why; ***he said, I saw all Israel scattered upon the hills, as sheep that have not a shepherd.*** This not being what the king wanted to hear, he gave the order to ***Put this fellow in the prison, and feed him with bread of affliction and with water of affliction, until I come in peace.***

Ahab went into battle in disguise, but a random arrow killed him. When his chariot was brought back to Samaria dogs licked up the blood, and prostitutes washed themselves in it. Jehoshaphat survived, going on to reign twenty-five years in Jerusalem. He was a good man; idolatry was not eliminated, but ***the remnant of the sodomites, which remained in the days of his father Asa, he took out of the land.***

As for Israel, it was the same old story. Ahab's son Ahaziah ***did evil in the sight of the LORD, and walked in the way of his father, and in the way of his mother***

... For he served Baal, and worshipped him, and provoked to anger the LORD God of Israel. God had been angry a lot, and there was worse to come.

12

The Second Book of Kings

And Ahaziah fell down through a lattice in his upper chamber that was in Samaria, and was sick: and he sent messengers, and said unto them, Go, enquire of Baalzebub the god of Ekron whether I shall recover of this disease. When the king of Israel falls out of a window and then seeks a prognosis from a god whose name means 'lord of the flies', you start to wonder whether you chose the right people in the first place. In later days Baalzebub became famous as 'Beelzebub', but at this point he was a nobody. 1

I told Elijah to intercept the king's messengers, letting them know that with his attitude he woudn't be surviving much longer. Ahaziah sent an officer and fifty soldiers to bring the prophet to him. Elijah resisted arrest; to be precise, he ***said to the captain of fifty, If I be a man of God, then let fire come down from heaven, and consume thee and thy fifty.*** He was, so it did. Another posse was sent out, and met the same fate.

The third time around the officer in charge was highly respectful, which to me makes all the difference. ***And the angel of the LORD said unto Elijah, Go down with him: be not afraid of him.*** Face to face with the king Elijah merely repeated the death sentence: ***thou shalt not come down off that bed on which thou art gone up, but shalt surely die. So he died according to the word of the LORD which Elijah had spoken.*** He wouldn't be changing consultants again.

Elijah managed his own departure in a more spectacular fashion. Followed by Elisha, he struck the waters of the river Jordan with his mantle, whereupon they divided to allow the two prophets to cross. ***And it came to pass, as they still went on, and talked, that, behold, there appeared a chariot of fire, and horses of fire, and parted them both asunder; and Elijah went up by a whirlwind into heaven. And Elisha saw it, and he cried, My father, my father, the chariot of Israel, and the horsemen thereof. And he saw him no more.*** Elisha picked up Elijah's mantle, parted the waters again – it was becoming routine – and went back across the river. 2

Perhaps the other holy men were sceptical of this story, because they insisted on sending out a search party for Elijah. Elisha passed the time in Jericho, where he miraculously purified the polluted waters: a very useful skill. He should have paid more attention to his image, though.

As he was going up by the way, there came forth little children out of the city, and mocked him, and said unto him, Go up, thou bald head; go up, thou bald head. And he turned back, and looked on them, and cursed them in the name of the LORD. And there came forth two she bears out of the wood, and tare forty

and two children of them. I know that discipline is important, but summoning bears to maul 42 naughty children strikes me as heavy-handed. Mutilating one or two would have been sufficient.

Elisha's miracles

3 Elisha was never short of miracles. One military campaign against Moab by the allied forces of Israel and Judah had nearly come to an early end in the desert, when he saved them by providing water. Their subsequent victory was followed, on God's orders, by extensive vandalism, which lasted until the king of Moab ***took his eldest son that should have reigned in his stead, and offered him for a burnt offering upon the wall.*** The Israelites went home after that.

4 Often Elisha seemed to find himself in much the same situations as Elijah, needing the same miracles. A widow's sons, for example, were taken into slavery because she could not meet her debts. The only thing she had in the house was a pot of oil. Elisha told her to borrow every container she could, filling them from this pot; she ended up with enough to settle all the debts and still have a comfortable sum left over.

There was another woman whose hospitality to Elisha had been more than generous. Her only problem, he was told, was that ***she hath no child, and her husband is old.*** That was easily remedied, and the following year she bore a son. The child did well until one day in the fields he cried out ***My head, my head,*** collapsed, and died. The woman went off in search of Elisha. When he arrived, ***he went up, and lay upon the child, and put his mouth upon his mouth, and his eyes upon his eyes, and his hands upon his hands: and he stretched himself upon the child; and the flesh of the child waxed warm. ... the child sneezed seven times, and the child opened his eyes.*** Elisha really knew how to play doctor.

Once when he was eating with his fellow prophets someone noticed a poisonous vegetable in the stew, crying out ***O thou man of God, there is death in the pot.*** Elisha stirred in some meal and the problem was solved. On another occasion he had only twenty loaves and some corn to feed a multitude of people. When his servant objected that they could hardly put that in front of a hundred men, Elisha promised that there would even be leftovers. He was right, and I don't think that it was just his cooking.

5 Elisha soon acquired an international reputation. News of his exploits reached Naaman, the commander of the Syrian army, who was a leper. His own sovereign wrote to the king of Israel demanding that he be cured. ***And it came to pass, when the king of Israel had read the letter, that he rent his clothes, and said, Am I God, to kill and to make alive, that this man doth send unto me to recover a man of his leprosy?*** Luckily Elisha volunteered to take over.

Elisha didn't even bother to see the patient, just sending word that he should wash seven times in the Jordan. Naaman was not pleased; he had expected some serious praying and arm waving, not an instruction to go and jump in the river. As he put it, ***Are not Abana and Pharpar, rivers of Damascus, better than all the waters of Israel? may I not wash in them, and be clean? So he turned and went away in a rage. And his servants came near, and spake unto him, and said, My father, if the prophet had bid thee do some great thing, wouldest thou not have done it? how much rather then, when he saith to thee, Wash, and be clean?*** It was sound advice, and he came out of the river with ***the flesh of a little child.***

Elisha declined to accept any gratuity. Naaman, of course, became a great partisan of God, asking for two mule-loads of earth so that he could take a piece of Israel back home with him. It was thought that gods could only function on their own turf.

Elisha's servant couldn't resist the temptation to obtain by false pretences part of the rich reward his master had declined, but nothing escaped the knowledge of the prophet. Elisha casually listed for the fellow what money could buy, and then declared that leprosy ***shall cleave unto thee, and unto thy seed for ever. And he went out from his presence a leper as white as snow.*** These holy men really knew how to twist the knife.

Elisha made miracles into everyday events; no problem was too small. One day he was watching his followers chop wood on the banks of the Jordan when ***as one was felling a beam, the axe head fell into the water: and he cried, and said, Alas master! for it was borrowed.*** Elisha had the iron axe head float to the surface, and all was well. 6

The powers were also used on more critical occasions, of course. When the king of Syria sent out a force to capture Elisha, who had been operating as a psychic spy, the soldiers never had a chance. They were assailed by visions, blinded, led to Samaria, made to see again, entertained, and finally released. After that experience they were so befuddled that ***the bands of Syria came no more into the land of Israel.***

No more until the next time, that is. On that occasion the Syrians ***besieged Samaria. And there was a great famine in Samaria: and, behold, they besieged it, until an ass's head was sold for fourscore pieces of silver, and the fourth part of a cab of dove's dung for five pieces of silver.*** One day the king was out walking when a woman called for his help, saying ***This woman said unto me, Give thy son, that we may eat him to day, and we will eat my son to morrow. So we boiled my son, and did eat him: and I said unto her on the next day, Give thy son, that we may eat him: and she hath hid her son.*** The king seemed to think that it was all Elisha's fault, and I admit that if God was planning to intervene, the moment might have come sooner.

Still, better late than never. Elisha announced that ***To morrow about this time shall a measure of fine flour be sold for a shekel, and two measures of barley for a shekel, in the gate of Samaria.*** God chased away the besiegers, and so the surrounding countryside was littered with abandoned tents, animals, provisions, and so on. Elisha's price-cutting prophecy was confirmed. 7

ANNOINTING NEW KINGS

8 Wars notwithstanding, Elisha was welcome in Damascus, where he showed another side of his art: the self-fulfilling prophecy. Being ill, the Syrian king had sent Hazael, one of his commanders, to ask if he would recover. Elisha said ***Go, say unto him, Thou mayest certainly recover: howbeit the LORD hath shewed me that he shall surely die.*** Then Elisha began to weep, explaining ***I know the evil that thou wilt do unto the children of Israel: their strongholds wilt thou set on fire, and their young men wilt thou slay with the sword, and wilt dash their children, and rip up their women with child. And Hazael said, But what, is thy servant a dog, that he should do this great thing? And Elisha answered, The LORD hath shewed me that thou shalt be king over Syria.*** Apparently he had all the necessary qualities.

Hazael went back to see the king, and the next day smothered him. Prophets can put ideas in people's heads.

The kingdoms of Israel and Judah were carrying on as before. In Judah, Jehoshaphat was succeeded by his son, who ***did evil in the sight of the LORD***: no great surprise, as he was married to the daughter of Ahab and Jezebel. He had the same name as the king of Israel, which added greatly to the general confusion; fortunately his reign lasted only eight years.

9 Elisha delegated his next important task to a young prophet. His instructions went as follows: find the comander named Jehu in the army mess, lead him to a private spot, ***Then take the box of oil, and pour it on his head, and say, Thus saith the LORD, I have anointed thee king over Israel. Then open the door, and flee.*** Having just poured oil over the head of an armed man, running was advisable.

In fact Jehu was more than receptive. He set out immediately in his chariot for Jezreel, the summer palace. ***There went one on horseback to meet him, and said, Thus saith the king, Is it peace? And Jehu said, What hast thou to do with peace? turn thee behind me.*** A second messenger got the same treatment. The watchman recognised the visitor, though, observing that ***the driving is like the driving of Jehu the son of Nimshi, for he driveth furiously.*** The king himself came out, calling the greeting ***Is it peace, Jehu? And he answered, What peace, so long as the whoredoms of thy mother Jezebel and her witchcrafts are so many?*** Not a tactful man, Jehu. The king tried to escape, but fell with an arrow through his heart; his ally the king of Judah was also mortally wounded.

And when Jehu was come to Jezreel, Jezebel heard of it; and she painted her face, and tired her head, and looked out at a window. Every inch the queen, she noted his arrival with disdain. ***And he lifted up his face to the window, and said, Who is on my side? who? And there looked out to him two or three eunuchs. And he said, Throw her down. So they threw her down: and some of her blood was sprinkled on the wall, and on the horses: and he trode her under foot.*** After having a meal Jehu decided to do the decent thing, ***And they went to bury her: but***

they found no more of her than the skull, and the feet, and the palms of her hands. It was as God had ordered: dogs had eaten her.

From that point it was one long bloodbath. Ahab's 70 sons were killed, and their heads put on display in two heaps. Then ***Jehu slew all that remained of the house of Ahab in Jezreel, and all his great men, and his kinfolks, and his priests, until he left him none remaining.*** Next came a massacre of 42 relatives of the king of Judah, I suppose because their sympathies might have been in the wrong place. ***And when he came to Samaria, he slew all that remained unto Ahab,*** which can't have been much. Finally he gathered all the priests and prophets of Baal for a great ceremony, surrounded their temple, and butchered them. The building was torn down and, for good measure, turned into a latrine. 10

And the LORD said unto Jehu, Because thou hast done well in executing that which is right in mine eyes, and hast done unto the house of Ahab according to all that was in mine heart, thy children of the fourth generation shall sit on the throne of Israel. Nice job, Jehu. How satisfying to see good deeds rewarded.

KINGS AND COUPS

The house of Ahab wasn't quite finished, though. When the king of Judah died as a result of Jehu's coup in Israel, his mother Athaliah seized power in Jerusalem. She was the daughter of Ahab and Jezebel, and proceeded to exterminate the royal line in Judah with the same thoroughness that Jehu was showing in eliminating her father's dynasty in Israel – and she was killing her own family. Unluckily for Athaliah one of her young grandsons escaped. Some six years later the boy was brought out of hiding to be crowned king by the priests, and the queen was put to death. 11

The new king faced an uphill struggle; even the priests were corrupt. He directed that all contributions received by the temple should be used for its repair, but by the twenty-third year of his reign no repairs had yet been made. The king was obliged to take over the responsibility himself, putting a chest beside the altar with a hole bored in the top for donations. Even worse, Hazael of Syria threatened to conquer the kingdom and only the accumulated wealth of Jerusalem bought him off. Forty years after coming to power the king was assassinated by his own men. 12

In Israel, meanwhile, Jehu had died, to be succeeded by his son, and then by his son's son. ***Now Elisha was fallen sick of his sickness whereof he died.*** The king came to visit him on his deathbed and performed various tricks with arrows, on which basis Elisha foretold the partial defeat of the Syrians. ***And Elisha died, and they buried him.*** Considering the way Elijah had made his exit, this was notably low key. 13

The great magician still had one miracle left in him, though. Some time later there was a commotion during a man's burial, and as the mourners scattered ***they cast the man into the sepulchre of Elisha: and when the man was let down, and***

touched the bones of Elisha, he revived, and stood up on his feet. From then on, I don't imagine a day went by without a hopeful corpse being launched into his grave.

14 Back in Judah there was a new king, Amaziah. ***And it came to pass, as soon as the kingdom was confirmed in his hand, that he slew his servants which had slain the king his father. But the children of the murderers he slew not: according unto that which is written in the book of the law of Moses,*** to the effect that children shouldn't die for the sins of their fathers. Too bad no one had thought of that earlier. Being merciful didn't save him from being killed, unfortunately. His 15 16-year-old son succeeded him, but ***the LORD smote the king, so that he was a leper unto the day of his death.*** It was a high-risk occupation.

Jehu's great-grandson, a new Jeroboam, had come and gone in Israel. Next in line was Zachariah, who only lasted six months before the whole dynasty was overthrown. Still, it was enough to confirm God's promise to Jehu that ***Thy sons shall sit on the throne of Israel unto the fourth generation.*** The usurper was king for a month before being overthrown himself. It appeared to me that the situation was getting out of hand.

The new ruler attacked towns in which there was opposition, ***and all the women therein that were with child he ripped up.*** He managed to keep the throne for his son, but then there was a coup, and then another. The disintegration of Israel was well under way; the forces of Assyria off to the north east captured large areas of the country and deported the people.

Jotham, son of the leper, was now king of Judah. God was content until his son, 16 Ahaz, took over. This man was bad; ***he made his son to pass through the fire, according to the abominations of the heathen, whom the LORD cast out from before the children of Israel. And he sacrificed and burnt incense in the high places, and on the hills, and under every green tree.*** He even replaced the temple altar with one of foreign design.

ASSYRIA WINS AND LOSES

17 The impending disaster in Israel should have served as a warning. Hoshea, who had emerged as king, was by no means the worst the country had known. But it was too late: Israel was overwhelmed, Samaria captured, and the people carried off into Assyria. Having been unfaithful to God, they had only themselves to blame. Apart from ordinary idolatry, ***they caused their sons and their daughters to pass through the fire, and used divination and enchantments, and sold themselves to do evil in the sight of the LORD, to provoke him to anger. Therefore the LORD was very angry with Israel, and removed them out of his sight: there was none left but the tribe of Judah only.***

The king of Assyria replaced the deported Israelites with people from his own part of the world. They did not worship God; ***therefore the LORD sent lions among***

them, which slew some of them. Being a practical man, the king sent back a priest, saying ***let him teach them the manner of the God of the land.*** Thus there grew up among the Samaritans – the new inhabitants of Samaria and the surrounding country – a curious mixture of religious practice, recognising both the gods they had brought with them and the God of Israel.

Judah continued its oscillation between virtue and vice with a devout king, Hezekiah. Not only did he destroy the pagan shrines, he even chopped up the bronze serpent that Moses had used for curing snake bite in the desert, because people had started to treat it as an idol. (Religious promiscuity was rampant: anything that stood still was liable to be worshipped.) After the fall of Israel, however, the future looked grim. 18

Three emissaries from the king of Assyria came to Jerusalem and publicly demanded its surrender. Hezekiah's aides asked them to ***talk not with us in the Jews' language in the ears of the people that are on the wall***, but this was precisely what the ambassador intended. The king of Assyria's warning about the consequences of resistance wasn't just for the royal court, he replied; ***hath he not sent me to the men which sit on the wall, that they may eat their own dung, and drink their own piss with you?*** So far he was only vulgar, but then he went too far, mocking the idea that God would save them. ***Hath any of the gods of the nations delivered at all his land out of the hand of the king of Assyria?*** If anything made God furious it was being compared to the competition.

The prophet Isaiah told Hezekiah not to worry; God had sent him a message about the king of Assyria: 19

By the way he came, by the same shall he return,
and shall not come into this city.

God saw to it that 185,000 men in the Assyrian army died overnight; ***when they arose early in the morning, behold, they were all dead corpses.*** There's nothing worse than waking up dead. The king of Assyria withdrew, and Judah, for the moment, was spared.

I was delighted for the people, though to be honest king Hezekiah struck me as selfish and egotistical. Once when he was ill Isaiah warned him that death was imminent, and that God instructed him to ***Set thine house in order.*** Hezekiah made such a fuss praying and weeping that God granted him another 15 years. He then demanded a sign as guarantee, and Isaiah had to make the shadows on a sun-clock go backwards to satisfy him. 20

On another occasion Isaiah told the king that the entire assets of the royal family would be taken to Babylon; even his sons would be carried off, ***and they shall be eunuchs in the palace of the king of Babylon. Then said Hezekiah unto Isaiah, Good is the word of the LORD which thou hast spoken. And he said, Is it not good, if peace and truth be in my days?*** In other words, so long as I'm all right, who cares.

THE END OF JUDAH

21 Hezekiah was just a spoiled brat, but his son was genuinely wicked. ***Therefore thus saith the LORD God of Israel, Behold, I am bringing such evil upon Jerusalem and Judah, that whosoever heareth of it, both his ears shall tingle. ... I will wipe Jerusalem as a man wipeth a dish, wiping it, and turning it upside down.*** The downhill slide continued under the next king, but following his assassination a new ruler, Josiah, led a religious revival.

22 Josiah ordered that the temple be repaired. During this work the high priest declared ***I have found the book of the law in the house of the LORD***; the story seemed fishy, but the king apparently didn't object. What he read was alarming, though; he hadn't realised just how many transgressions they had committed. His belief that God would punish them was confirmed by a prophetess, but she did pass on the word that ***thou shalt be gathered into thy grave in peace; and thine eyes shall not see all the evil which I will bring upon this place.*** I wondered who would be unlucky enough to be king when the bill finally fell due.

23 The king threw himself into the task of national purification. Gathering all the people together, ***he read in their ears all the words of the book of the covenant which was found***; he formally promised to obey the commandments. Symbols of idolatry were destroyed, ground to powder and scattered over a graveyard, and in addition ***the houses of the sodomites, that were by the house of the LORD***, were torn down: an aggressive instance of urban renewal. More dramatically, when the king spotted graves near a suspect shrine, he ***took the bones out of the sepulchres, and burned them upon the altar, and polluted it***, as had been prophesied. This grand tour was quite a spectacle, sacrificing heathen priests and burning bones on their altars, but a shade too fanatical, I thought.

Despite all the king's efforts, including the revival of passover, ***the LORD turned not from the fierceness of his great wrath, wherewith his anger was kindled against Judah.*** And so in the shadow of the hills by Megiddo, the har megiddon - or as people came to say, Armageddon – Josiah met the Egyptians in battle and was killed. The victors extorted tribute from his successors, as a result of which the children of Israel in the promised land suffered the irony and indignity of being taxed at Pharaoh's command.

24 Judah's subjection to Egypt had not lasted long, however, when a much more powerful empire asserted its authority: that of Nebuchadnezzar, king of Babylon. After acting as overlord for a few years, he captured Jerusalem and deported the entire royal household to Babylon, stripping the palace and the temple of their treasures. ***And he carried away all Jerusalem, and all the princes, and all the mighty men of valour, even ten thousand captives, and all the craftsmen and smiths: none remained, save the poorest sort of the people of the land.*** Lack of status has its privileges.

A puppet king was installed in Jerusalem. Some nine years later he was unwise enough to rebel, and Nebuchadnezzar laid siege to the city. After 18 months, famine forced it to surrender; the king failed in his attempt to escape. Before being taken in chains to Babylon his eyes were put out, though only after he had witnessed the execution of his sons. 25

The fate of Jerusalem itself was just as unpleasant. The temple, the palace, and all the houses were destroyed by fire. The city walls were torn down. All the remaining objects of any value in the temple were removed. The priests and various public officials were carried off, beaten and then killed. Most of the people who had previously been allowed to stay were deported.

The promised land was lost; the people were captive in Babylon. After 37 years in prison, the king of Judah who had been among the first of those taken into exile was released, and accorded a place of respect in the Babylonian court. It was a small thing, but not a minor one: for a time, survival would be their highest aspiration. Everyone waited to see if God would give them another chance.

13

The First Book of Chronicles

1 When things are going badly, go back and try to see what happened: that was the approach taken by a compiler of chronicles. He went back to the beginning, and I do mean the beginning: ***Adam, Seth, Enosh ...***

Genealogies are rarely absorbing except to the families concerned, and even 2 then only if you know who did what. But out of hundreds of names, merely the occasional detail slips out: for example, ***Sheshan had no sons, but daughters. And Sheshan had a servant, an Egyptian, whose name was Jarha. And Sheshan gave his daughter to Jarha his servant to wife.*** There's one I wish I knew more about.

3 Thirteen sons of David are named, and that doesn't even include those he had by concubines. The only daughter to get a mention is Tamar; apparently women had to be raped by their brothers to get noticed.

4 When it came to dispossessing the natives, people certainly didn't suffer from liberal guilt. One group wanting to expand, for example, ***found fat pasture and good, and the land was wide, and quiet, and peaceable; for they of Ham had dwelt there of old. And these written by name came in the days of Hezekiah king of Judah, and smote their tents, and the habitations that were found there, and destroyed them utterly unto this day, and dwelt in their rooms: because there was pasture there for their flocks.*** At least the sheep were happy. In another conquest 5 the enemy was crushed, and ***there fell down many slain, because the war was of God.*** How thoughtful to give us the credit.

6 They weren't all warlike; there were, for instance, those ***whom David set over the service of song in the house of the LORD.*** On the whole, though, men with 7 alarming names like Uzzi are listed as ***valiant men of might***, or (equivalently?) ***mighty men of valour***, not as good baritones.

8 Every so often domestic dramas emerge. A man about whom we know nothing else discarded two of his wives, but he ***begat children in the country of Moab, after he had sent them away***. Mostly, though, they are just names, names, and 9 more names. ***So all Israel were reckoned by genealogies; and, behold, they were written in the book of the kings of Israel and Judah, who were carried away to Babylon for their transgression.*** The people might be in exile, but they knew where they came from.

THE KINGDOM

The lists suddenly end, and the pace slows, when the chronicler reaches the death of Saul. He tells the story as I remember it, except that Saul's head rather than his torso ends up nailed to a wall. Perhaps he was more interested in the mind than the body. 10

David became king, and conquered Jerusalem. He was assisted by groups of audacious followers, especially the three, and the thirty. These heroes, like the one who ***went down and slew a lion in a pit in a snowy day***, proved their mettle by feats that generally struck me as slightly useless. 11

My recollection is that David was the leader of an outlaw band before he became king, but generations later every family and clan had jumped on the bandwagon, conveniently discovering that their ancestors had been with him all along. The result is a long list of partisans and a revision of history: ***All these men of war, that could keep rank, came with a perfect heart to Hebron, to make David king over all Israel: and all the rest also of Israel were of one heart to make David king.*** And I'm a cabbage. 12

The first attempt to bring the ark to Jerusalem foundered, you might recall, when a man accidentally touched it and died. There was a three-month delay while the problems of hazardous material transport were resolved. The king took the opportunity to defeat the Philistines a couple of times, ***And the fame of David went out into all lands; and the LORD brought the fear of him upon all nations.*** He knew how to look after his reputation: any harp playing was done behind closed doors. 13 14

In making another attempt to move the ark, David supposedly decided that they had failed the first time around because the Levites weren't running the show. I imagine that that's what the Levites themselves decided years later, if only as an excuse to list several dozen names of their forefathers as close associates of the great king. This time, anyway, the ark was successfully installed. David led a prayer, proclaiming ***O give thanks unto the LORD; for he is good; for his mercy endureth for ever***, and at the end ***all the people said, Amen, and praised the LORD.*** 15 16

David's offer to build a temple was turned down by God, who promised however that ***I will ordain a place for my people Israel, and will plant them, and they shall dwell in their place, and shall be moved no more*** – that's what we hoped at the time, anyway. David returned to making war on his enemies. There's nothing to add to what we already know, except that with the passage of time seven hundred captured horsemen have turned into seven thousand. The same inflationary tendency affects the claim that ***David slew of the Syrians seven thousand men which fought in chariots.*** 17 18 19

I was entertained by the notion that after sacking one city David ***brought out the people that were in it, and cut them with saws, and with harrows of iron, and with axes.*** Gory but mistaken, I think: he obliged them to cut and chop, not to be cut and chopped. The variation on the Goliath story, though, is a blatant attempt 20 to cover up the suggestion that the giant had been killed by someone other than David. Instead of repeating that Elhanan the Beth-lahmi slew Goliath, the chronicler says that Elhanan ***slew Lahmi the brother of Goliath***. Nice try, but no cigar.

21 Even God gets his image touched up. He had incited David to take a census, and then sent a plague which shaved some seventy thousand off its total. The revised version is that Satan stood up against Israel, and provoked David to number Israel. That's the first appearance of this great adversary, and to be frank I'd rather he had been blamed for the plague than the head count. Maybe taking a census was presumptuous – though that was never made clear – but demography doesn't seem like Satan's work, somehow.

With retelling the number of fighting men in Israel swelled from 800,000 to 1,100,000, though in Judah the 500,000 figure was cut to 470,000. Naturally it's the money, though, that's most affected by retroactive inflation: David pays ***six hundred shekels of gold by weight*** for the threshing floor, up from fifty shekels of

22 silver. But then it was prime real estate since, as the chronicles reveal, that threshing floor would be the site of the future temple.

THE TEMPLE

Building the temple was to be Solomon's job, but David decided to make everything ready for him. The fact that it would be the house of God didn't stop David from conscripting non-Israelites to hew the stones. All the raw materials were gathered, and the king showed Solomon what he had assembled: ***Now, behold, in my trouble I have prepared for the house of the LORD an hundred thousand talents of gold, and a thousand thousand talents of silver; and of brass and iron without weight***. Trouble would be an understatement, if we took him at his word. Being conservative, these amounts exceed 3,000 tons of gold and 30,000 tons of silver. Solomon would have needed to build a temple just to store it all, never mind use it.

23 His problems wouldn't have stopped there. David designated 24,000 Levites just to supervise operations in the temple: over-manning on a gargantuan scale. That didn't include the 4,000 guardians, 4,000 musicians, etc. Of course it helped

24 that the priests were divided into 24 groups, each to serve two weeks of the year.

25 The singers likewise cast lots for their places; remarkably, every one of the two

26 dozen clans had exactly a dozen members. Porters, clerks, and administrators of

27 various sorts also found jobs. The army was divided into twelve units of 24,000 each.

28 Finally, David was ready to hand over responsibility in a public ceremony. ***Solomon my son, know thou the God of thy father, and serve him with a perfect heart and with a willing mind: for the LORD searcheth all hearts, and understandeth all the imaginations of the thoughts: if thou seek him, he will be found of thee; but if thou forsake him, he will cast thee off for ever***. At that he delivered

all the plans, showing everything in detail down to the weight of the last fork.

29 From his personal funds he offered yet more mountains of gold and silver, and invited the leaders of the tribes to do the same. They responded with equally enormous contributions in gold, silver, bronze, iron, and, supposedly, darics, these being Persian coins no more current in David's day than pieces of eight. But we get the idea: everyone was happy about the temple.

Wherefore David blessed the LORD before all the congregation: and David said, Blessed be thou, LORD God of Israel our father, for ever and ever. Thine, O LORD, is the greatness, and the power, and the glory, and the victory, and the majesty: for all that is in the heaven and in the earth is thine; thine is the kingdom, O LORD, and thou art exalted as head above all. ...

But who am I, and what is my people, that we should be able to offer so willingly after this sort? for all things come of thee, and of thine own have we given thee. For we are strangers before thee, and sojourners, as were all our fathers: our days on the earth are as a shadow, and there is none abiding.

This paean to God the august became a prototype of ceremonial prayers to come. And so with his task accomplished, after forty years as king, David ***died in a good old age, full of days, riches and honour: and Solomon his son reigned in his stead.*** If there are lessons to be learnt about why Israel was forsaken by God, the recapitulation of history has yet to reveal them: but there are chronicles still to come.

14

The Second Book of Chronicles

1 ***And Solomon the son of David was strengthened in his kingdom, and the LORD his God was with him, and magnified him exceedingly.*** God granted him wisdom and knowledge, and threw in wealth and honour for good measure. No transformation, even ecological, was too great for Solomon: ***the king made silver and gold at Jerusalem as plenteous as stones, and cedar trees made he as the sycomore trees that are in the vale for abundance.***

2 Having acquired the materials, Solomon then found the slave labour needed to build the temple: all 153,600 foreigners resident in the country – though of course 3 the aliens were, in fact, natives. ***Then Solomon began to build the house of the LORD at Jerusalem in mount Moriah.*** Apart from being where God's post-enumeration plague had stopped – the threshing floor purchased by David – it just might have been the hill top on which Abraham had prepared to sacrifice Isaac.

Most of the temple's interior decoration I've already described, though the stories were improving with retelling. The quantities of gold were such that stone would hardly seem necessary in the construction. ***Also he made before the house two pillars of thirty and five cubits high***, nearly double their first-reported height 4 of 18 cubits. The giant basin, however, increased its capacity by a mere fifty per cent.

5 ***Thus all the work that Solomon made for the house of the LORD was finished.*** The ark was brought up, and God moved into his new home. Solomon delivered 6 his prayer of dedication, concluding ***Now therefore arise, O LORD God, into thy resting place, thou, and the ark of thy strength: let thy priests, O LORD God, be clothed with salvation, and let thy saints rejoice in goodness.***

7 God accepted the invitation, ***And the priests could not enter into the house of the LORD, because the glory of the LORD had filled the LORD's house.*** Fortunately everything went on outside. For a couple of weeks everyone feasted, and then the king ***sent the people away into their tents, glad and merry in heart for the goodness that the LORD had shewed unto David, and to Solomon, and to Israel his people.*** I'm not so sure it was God's goodness that made them merry, but there's nothing wrong with celebrating.

8 Solomon said that ***My wife shall not dwell in the house of David king of Israel, because the places are holy, whereunto the ark of the LORD hath come.*** I imagine he gave his wife a more flattering explanation for building a new house.

9 Riches flowed into the kingdom from all over. Of that there seems little doubt, though the idea that ***the king's ships went to Tarshish***, which from their base in

the Red Sea would have required the circumnavigation of Africa, is based on a misunderstanding: ships of Tarshish were a certain kind of vessel, not ones from a particular place.

THE DIVIDED KINGDOM

Solomon was succeeded by his son Rehoboam, the foolish young man whose lack of political skill precipitated the division of the kingdom. ***And Israel rebelled against the house of David unto this day***, with Jeroboam becoming king in the northern half of the country. 10

I think the chronicler was beginning to see an explanation: perhaps it was secular as much as religious disobedience that caused the catastrophe. If David was God's agent, then breaking away from one was mutiny against the other. 11

Rehoboam ***took eighteen wives, and threescore concubines; and begat twenty and eight sons, and threescore daughters.*** I'm not sure whether to be impressed that for once the daughters outnumbered the sons, or surprised that the ratio of children to partners barely exceeded one to one. They say that ***he desired many wives***, but perhaps he was more of a collector than a practitioner.

Politically he was a larger failure, forsaking God and suffering in consequence an Egyptian invasion. His son was more successful, at least against the errant cousins of Israel. If we believe the reports, he went to war to preserve orthodoxy: while in Judah the priests had to be descendants of Aaron, in Israel, it is claimed, anyone with a few spare animals would qualify: ***whosoever cometh to consecrate himself with a young bullock and seven rams, the same may be a priest of them that are no gods.*** In the battle ***there fell down slain of Israel five hundred thousand chosen men***, i.e. roughly half the adult male population, which shows how excited people become about ordination. 12 13

Next up as king was Asa, who ***did that which was good and right in the eyes of the LORD his God, For he took away the altars of the strange gods, and the high places,*** etc. It was just as well, because he needed God on his side when one of his enemies fielded an army of a million men. Asa won, naturally. 14

In keeping with the religious revival everyone agreed ***That whosoever would not seek the LORD God of Israel should be put to death, whether small or great, whether man or woman.*** I'm not sure just how hard you were expected to seek. The campaign continued, ***But the high places were not taken away*** – had he put them all back, or what? 15

Asa's downfall – and by extension, the downfall of the whole people – is said to have resulted from a failure to put absolute faith in God. When hard pressed by Israel he asked the Syrians for help, instead of relying on divine intervention. Stay in bed, trust in God, seemed to be the advice. 16

The king didn't learn his lesson, though. ***Asa in the thirty and ninth year of his reign was diseased in his feet, until his disease was exceedingly great: yet in his***

disease he sought not to the LORD, but to the physicians. With God wanting to do everything, he had condemned himself to death.

17 His son Jehoshaphat was another who ***took away the high places***, maybe. He built up the army so successfully that he apparently had more soldiers than there were people: 1,160,000 based in Jerusalem alone. Perhaps it was to reduce the

18 numbers that he joined king Ahab of Israel in making war on Syria.

That was the occasion on which Ahab grudgingly sought an opinion from the prophet Micaiah, ***And he said, Go ye up, and prosper, and they shall be delivered into your hand. And the king said to him, How many times shall I adjure thee that thou say nothing but the truth to me in the name of the LORD?*** He wasn't one to take 'yes' for an answer. Micaiah duly obliged by prophesying disaster, at which Ahab, never satisfied, had him put in prison ***until I return in peace***. Since the king never returned at all Micaiah must have finished his days on bread and water – that was the last anyone heard of him, at least.

19 Jehoshaphat appointed judges in Judah, telling them ***Deal courageously, and the LORD shall be with the good.*** This motto, as usual, was established most clearly

20 in battle. In the last conflict of his reign there was not even any need to fight, as the enemy soldiers very obligingly killed each other; ***when Jehoshaphat and his people came to take away the spoil of them, they found among them in abundance both riches with the dead bodies, and precious jewels, which they stripped off for themselves, more than they could carry away: and they were three days in gathering of the spoil, it was so much.*** Not only had the enemy saved the people the trouble of fighting, they had gone into battle wearing all their jewellery: they were really most considerate.

The king did ***that which was right in the sight of the LORD. Howbeit the high places were not taken away***. Some things remain a mystery.

THE DECLINE OF JUDAH

21 The next king, Jehoram, was a less complex character. On coming to the throne he killed all his brothers and various other potential competitors, and married the daughter of Ahab and Jezebel. ***He made high places in the mountains of Judah, and caused the inhabitants of Jerusalem to commit fornication, and compelled Judah thereto.*** (By my observation very little arm twisting is required, but it's useful to have someone else to blame.) His record of dastardly achievement was so striking that ***there came a writing to him from Elijah the prophet***, who wasn't even supposed to be around at this point.

The letter passed on a message from God: ***Behold, with a great plague will the LORD smite thy people, and thy children, and thy wives, and all thy goods: And thou shalt have great sickness by disease of thy bowels, until thy bowels fall out by reason of the sickness day by day.*** This was not going to do anything for the popularity of the royal family.

So God instigated an invasion of Judah in which Jehoram's possessions, his wives and all but his youngest son were carried off. ***And after all this the LORD smote him in his bowels with an incurable disease. And it came to pass, that in process of time, after the end of two years, his bowels fell out by reason of his sickness: so he died of sore diseases.*** Sore isn't the word for it; losing God's approval could really turn you inside out.

22

His son took over at the age of 42, according to the chronicler, though at the time we made him 22. ***He also walked in the ways of the house of Ahab: for his mother was his counsellor to do wickedly.*** With the father he had, I'm amazed that his mother got the blame. At any rate he was unlucky enough to be in Israel when Jehu launched his coup, and was killed – though exactly where, when and by whom is again not quite as I remember it.

23 24

Athaliah, the wicked mother, took over, killed more members of the family, and in due course came to a bloody end; ***And all the people of the land rejoiced.*** The new king was only seven years old, but had as advisor the high priest responsible for his coronation, a man who ***waxed old, and was full of days when he died; an hundred and thirty years old was he when he died.*** Having made a good start, the king rapidly deteriorated after the old man's death; he even had the priest's son stoned for remonstrating with him. With a record like that he was unlikely to die in bed. In fact that's just where he did die, but only because his servants murdered him there.

25

His son, the amazing Amaziah, succeeded him. Amaziah's principal achievement was a victory over Edom, in the course of which his army killed 10,000 people. ***And the other ten thousand left alive did the children of Judah carry away captive, and brought them unto the top of the rock, and cast them down from the top of the rock, that they all were broken in pieces.*** Very messy.

God didn't object to imaginative ways of handling a prisoner-of-war problem, but there were some things he couldn't tolerate. The king took the Edomite idols, ***and set them up to be his gods, and bowed down himself before them, and burned incense unto them. Wherefore the anger of the LORD was kindled against Amaziah.*** Why he wanted to worship the gods of people he had just pushed over a cliff was a mystery to me, but God made certain that he paid the price: defeat and violent death.

26

Foolishness seemed to run in the family. His son insisted on burning incense in the temple, despite a warning from the priest that he was exceeding his authority. Being stubborn, he stayed, whereupon he was struck by leprosy in front of the altar. He couldn't get out fast enough, but there's no escape from God; ***the king was a leper unto the day of his death*** – and beyond, because his disease excluded him from the kings' burial ground. The dead can't be too careful about their neighbours.

27 28

His son Jotham provided a respite in the line of royal misfortune, but it was only temporary. Next on the throne was Ahaz, who managed to lose wars to everyone. Israel took 200,000 women and children captive, but then made a remarkable gesture: they ***took the captives, and with the spoil clothed all that were naked***

among them, and arrayed them, and shod them, and gave them to eat and to drink, and anointed them, and carried all the feeble of them upon asses, and brought them to Jericho, the city of palm trees, to their brethren: then they returned to Samaria. War crimes were not inevitable.

THE FALL OF JUDAH

29 Judah was in danger of being overrun, but God's favour was restored by the piety of king Hezekiah. First he ordered the purification of the temple, telling the Levites to ***carry forth the filthiness out of the holy place.*** That being accomplished, 30 ***Hezekiah sent to all Israel and Judah ... that they should come to the house of the LORD at Jerusalem, to keep the passover unto the LORD God of Israel.*** The northern kingdom had already fallen, with most of its people deported. His messengers were not warmly received by those remaining – ***they laughed them to scorn, and mocked them*** – but a number did come south for the celebration, which 31 was a great success. In a further demonstration of Hezekiah's virtue, tithes to support the priests and other Levites were reintroduced.

32 All of this was enough to ensure that God took action against the Assyrians, and Judah endured. As sometimes happens to children of excessively devout parents, 33 however, Hezekiah's son went bad in spectacular fashion, promoting all the usual forms of heathen worship, making his children pass through the fire, using witchcraft, and so on. Although he repented later, his successor continued in the bad old ways, lasting only two years before being murdered by members of his own court.

34 ***Josiah was eight years old when he began to reign, and he reigned in Jerusalem one and thirty years.*** He was another reformer, cleaning up the temple 35 and observing passover; indeed, ***there was no passover like to that kept in Israel from the days of Samuel the prophet,*** which makes me wonder what was wrong with Hezekiah's great celebration. The king died in a futile attack on the Egyptian army, ***And Jeremiah lamented for Josiah: and all the singing men and the singing women spake of Josiah in their lamentations to this day.*** We shall hear more from Jeremiah in due course.

36 Lamentations were called for, because the kingdom was now on its last legs. Jehoiachin (described as being eight, though surely he was eighteen) was taken into captivity. By this time Nebuchadnezzar, king of Babylon, was pulling the strings; it only needed one more tug and the kingdom would collapse. The people were warned repeatedly, ***But they mocked the messengers of God, and despised his words, and misused his prophets, until the wrath of the LORD arose against his people, till there was no remedy.*** And so Jerusalem was burnt, and the population of Judah exiled to Babylon.

The day would come, however, when the king of Persia would announce that ***All the kingdoms of the earth hath the LORD God of heaven given me; and he***

hath charged me to build him an house in Jerusalem, which is in Judah. The people would return to the promised land.

15

Ezra

1 Nearly fifty years after the fall of Jerusalem, Babylon – where the people had been resettled – and its empire were overrun by the Persians. Having taken control, the new king ***made a proclamation throughout all his kingdom, and put it also in writing, saying, Thus saith Cyrus king of Persia, The LORD God of heaven hath given me all the kingdoms of the earth; and he hath charged me to build him an house at Jerusalem, which is in Judah. Who is there among you of all his people? his God be with him, and let him go up to Jerusalem, which is in Judah, and build the house of the LORD God of Israel.*** They had it in writing: the exile had ended.

Cyrus even offered them a going-home present: 5,400 gold and silver vessels taken from the temple by Nebuchadnezzar. Not everyone, of course, was in a hurry

2 to leave; only a minority could have had any recollection of the promised land. None the less, many did go back. Adding up the numbers returning family by family and group by group I counted 29,818, but perhaps I made a mistake, because ***The whole congregation together was forty and two thousand three hundred and threescore, Beside their servants and their maids, of whom there were seven thousand three hundred thirty and seven: and there were among them two hundred singing men and singing women.*** They had a walking sound system.

3 Work on the new temple did not get under way until the second year of their return. When finally the foundations were laid it aroused mixed emotions, those old enough to remember the first temple being reminded of their loss. In fact ***the people could not discern the noise of the shout of joy from the noise of the weeping of the people: for the people shouted with a loud shout, and the noise was heard afar off.***

4 Rebuilding the temple was obviously going to be a major event, and the people of mixed heritage already in the area (who would become the Samaritans) wanted to participate. They said ***Let us build with you: for we seek your God, as ye do.*** But the returned exiles were haughty, not to say foolish and bigoted: ***Ye have nothing to do with us to build an house unto our God.*** This rejection created such animosity that during the following years the local leaders sent letters to each new king of Persia, complaining about the newcomers.

Years later, for example, they wrote a letter saying ***Be it known unto the king, that the Jews which came up from thee to us are come unto Jerusalem, building the rebellious and the bad city, and have set up the walls thereof, and joined the foundations. Be it known now unto the king, that, if this city be builded, and the***

walls set up again, then will they not pay toll, tribute, and custom, and so thou shalt endamage the revenue of the kings. Tittle-tattle in bureaucratese, was my verdict.

After a 16-year delay – whether because of political problems, lack of funds, or loss of energy, I can't now recall – construction was resumed. The prophets Haggai and Zechariah had been lobbying for the project, and the leaders of the people decided to act. The provincial ruler asked king Darius what to do, and the answer came back ***Let the work of this house of God alone; let the governor of the Jews and the elders of the Jews build this house of God in his place.*** He even ordered that their expenses be paid, and food provided for sacrifices, concluding ***Also I have made a decree, that whosoever shall alter this word, let timber be pulled down from his house, and being set up, let him be hanged thereon; and let his house be made a dunghill for this.*** I wonder where Darius had learnt to be so persuasive. 5 6

The temple took another four and a half years to finish. It was dedicated with the traditional slaughter of bulls, rams and lambs, though numbered only in hundreds rather than thousands. Passover was celebrated once again by the returned exiles, and by everyone who kept themselves apart ***from the filthiness of the heathen of the land.*** It was just like the good old days, I thought.

The new wave

A further migration from Babylon was made nearly sixty years later, in the reign of Artaxerxes. It was led by a religious leader named Ezra, who traced his ancestry back to Aaron – though since the genealogy offered only 16 generations to cover some 800 years, it seemed, like most pedigrees, to be more concerned with flattery than accuracy. In a letter to Ezra the king decreed ***that all they of the people of Israel, and of his priests and Levites, in my realm, which are minded of their own freewill to go up to Jerusalem, go with thee.*** 7

The king also granted him broad authority to appoint judges, ***And whosoever will not do the law of thy God, and the law of the king, let judgment be executed speedily upon him, whether it be unto death, or to banishment, or to confiscation of goods, or to imprisonment.*** Giving that sort of power to religious leaders, even our own, has not in my experience been a good idea.

Ezra gathered together the migrants, recruited some Levites to perform the sacred duties, and set out. I found him somewhat lacking in common sense. He admits in his memoirs that ***I was ashamed to require of the king a band of soldiers and horsemen to help us against the enemy in the way: because we had spoken unto the king, saying, The hand of our God is upon all them for good that seek him; but his power and his wrath is against all them that forsake him.*** Expecting God to protect you when you don't take proper precautions is like expecting him to feed you when you don't bother to work: it has happened, but you shouldn't 8 push your luck. The fact that they were carrying a huge quantity of gold and silver makes the failure to secure an escort seem all the more foolhardy. None the less they reached Jerusalem unmolested.

9 Once there, Ezra discovered just how prevalent mixed marriages had become. He was horrified that ***the holy seed have mingled themselves with the people of those lands: yea, the hand of the princes and rulers hath been chief in this trespass. And when I heard this thing, I rent my garment and my mantle, and plucked off the hair of my head and of my beard, and sat down astonied.*** You'd almost think his daughter had married one. Admittedly, he was simply responding to God's warning: ***The land, unto which ye go to possess it, is an unclean land with the filthiness of the people of the lands, with their abominations, which have filled it from one end to another with their uncleanness.*** The original intention, though, had been to prevent idolatry, not to denigrate all foreigners as unfit partners.

10 Faced with the wrath of Ezra, someone suggested that all the foreign wives and their children be sent away. The returned exiles were summoned from across Judah to appear in Jerusalem within three days, on pain of exposing their property to confiscation. It was a winter day when they gathered, ***and all the people sat in the street of the house of God, trembling because of this matter, and for the great rain.***

Ezra harangued them, saying ***Now therefore make confession unto the LORD God of your fathers, and do his pleasure: and separate yourselves from the people of the land, and from the strange wives.*** There was little choice. The congregation did, however, point out that ***it is a time of much rain ... neither is this a work of one day or two***. Suddenly throwing the wife and children out into the winter rain was too much, even if it was a religious duty. Within three months, though, everyone had complied. I could have wished for a happier homecoming.

16

Nehemiah

1

Thirteen years after Ezra introduced his puritanical decrees the country was as wretched as ever. The people desperately needed leadership, and the man to provide it was at that moment the king's cupbearer in the Persian court. His name was Nehemiah.

In the ninth month of the year, one of his relatives visited the winter palace with news from Judah. The returned exiles, he reported, ***are in great affliction and reproach: the wall of Jerusalem also is broken down, and the gates thereof are burned with fire.*** Nehemiah was greatly distressed, and asked God to remember his promise to bring the penitent sinners back home. Granted, the people – or some of them – were back, but it wasn't yet much of a home.

2

According to Nehemiah the sequel occurred in the first month of the same year, but he must have confused the dates. He brought wine to the king, who enquired ***Why is thy countenance sad, seeing thou art not sick? this is nothing else but sorrow of heart.*** Nehemiah asked how he could not be sad when his native land lay in ruins. His journal continues: ***Then the king said unto me, For what dost thou make request? So I prayed to the God of heaven. And I said unto the king, If it please the king, and if thy servant have found favour in thy sight, that thou wouldest send me unto Judah, unto the city of my fathers' sepulchres, that I may build it. And the king said unto me, (the queen also sitting by him,) For how long shall thy journey be? and when wilt thou return? So it pleased the king to send me; and I set him a time.*** He refrains from saying what length of time they agreed, but I'm sure that the king would have fallen off his throne had he known what it would turn out to be.

When he arrived in Jerusalem, Nehemiah made a moonlight tour of the city walls. I found it a strikingly romantic scene: he rode alone, going ***out by night by the gate of the valley, even before the dragon well, and to the dung port, and viewed the walls of Jerusalem, which were broken down, and the gates thereof were consumed with fire.*** The survey complete, he told the local leaders of the returned exiles what he proposed to do. They threw themselves into the rebuilding with enthusiasm, but some of the other groups were antagonistic. For them, Nehemiah had a sectarian response: ***The God of heaven, he will prosper us; therefore we his servants will arise and build: but ye have no portion, nor right, nor memorial, in Jerusalem.***

3

Different families were assigned different portions of the wall to repair. The key points had picturesque names: the sheep gate, the fish gate, the valley gate, the

dung gate, the gate of the fountain, the water gate, and the horse gate, not to mention
4 the tower of the furnaces. There was much jeering from the hostile leaders: ***What do these feeble Jews? ... will they revive the stones out of the heaps of rubbish which are burned? ... Even that which they build, if a fox go up, he shall even break down their stone wall.*** Nehemiah, who didn't find these remarks humorous, asked God to remember the villains.

The rebuilding went well, ***for the people had a mind to work***, but at the first signs of progress their enemies turned to violence. Nehemiah kept up morale, saying ***Be not ye afraid of them: remember the Lord, which is great and terrible, and fight for your brethren, your sons, and your daughters, your wives, and your houses.*** (In that order, no doubt: at least he put wives before houses.) He was obliged, though, to split the work force, with one half standing guard while the other half laboured, and even then ***every one with one of his hands wrought in the work, and with the other hand held a weapon.***

They stayed dressed all night to be in a state of constant readiness, Nehemiah wrote: ***neither I, nor my brethren, nor my servants, nor the men of the guard which followed me, none of us put off our clothes, saving that every one put them off for washing.*** Fortunately they always seemed to be wearing nightgowns anyway.

5 The fact that everyone pulled together to rebuild the walls didn't rule out economic exploitation within the community. Just to buy food pressed the poor to desperation; they cried out ***We have mortgaged our lands, vineyards, and houses ... and some of our daughters are brought unto bondage already.*** Nehemiah chastised the prominent citizens for profiting from the misery of their neighbours, and extracted a promise that the property would be restored and usury ended.

Nehemiah spent large sums entertaining, without once drawing on his expense account during his first twelve years as governor. This generosity was the cause of considerable self-satisfaction: ***Think upon me, my God, for good, according to all that I have done for this people.*** Perhaps he was a bit too pleased with himself, but I can't deny his qualities.

6 The rebuilding continued, as did the campaign to stop it. Nehemiah fended off threats of all kinds, including intimidation, blackmail and trickery, saying ***Should such a man as I flee?*** At last ***the wall was finished ... in fifty and two days***, which is remarkable, to say the least.

7 Nehemiah set out a register of the first group to return to Judah. These numbers add up to 31,089, still falling a long way short of the total of 42,360. I was glad to see, though, that this time ***they had two hundred forty and five singing men and singing women***, up from 200. The more the merrier.

REDISCOVERING THE LAW

8 ***And all the people gathered themselves together as one man into the street***, to

hear Ezra read from the book of the law of Moses. Showing an unexpected concern for equal opportunity, he ***brought the law before the congregation both of men and women, and all that could hear with understanding***. Everyone wept at what they heard, though whether this was because of what they had done, or what they would have to do in the future, wasn't clear. I was even more perplexed when they went on ***to make great mirth, because they had understood the words that were declared unto them***. Perhaps hysteria had set in.

When they found the feast of tabernacles described, everyone ***made booths, and sat under the booths: for since the days of Jeshua the son of Nun unto that day had not the children of Israel done so***. They did like to exaggerate: since the time of Joshua the feast had been celebrated not only by Solomon, but even by the first group of returned exiles.

9 The people, wearing sackcloth and covered in dust, assembled to hear a prayer of confession and entreaty. Their leaders expressed the hopeful, not to say rosy, view that ***thou art a God ready to pardon, gracious and merciful, slow to anger, and of great kindness***. All the disasters in the whole history of the children of Israel had occurred only after the greatest provocation; the theme was that ***thou art just in all that is brought upon us; for thou hast done right, but we have done wickedly***. A bit of servile flattery combined with self-flagellation never went amiss.

10 Everybody swore to uphold the law as given to Moses. Frankly it read like a priests' charter, with the emphasis less on moral virtue than on religious purity and – more to the point – financing. The agreement was entirely devoted to tithes, offerings, and other maintenance payments, apart from confirming that ***we would not give our daughters unto the people of the land, nor take their daughters for our sons: And if the people of the land bring ware or any victuals on the sabbath day to sell, that we would not buy it of them***.

11 Jerusalem was such an unpopular place to live – housing was a problem, and the presence of the temple didn't help to make it a fun town – that they were obliged to ***cast lots, to bring one of ten to dwell in Jerusalem the holy city***. Priests made up a large proportion of the population, though the numbers varied by nearly fifty per cent depending on which list you consulted. But now that the walls were built, the city was due for a revival.

12 At the ceremony to dedicate the completed wall Nehemiah divided everyone into two groups, each led by musicians. One company marched around the circuit in one direction and the other in the opposite direction, combining forces again at the temple. ***That day they offered great sacrifices, and rejoiced: for God had made them rejoice with great joy: the wives also and the children rejoiced: so that the joy of Jerusalem was heard even afar off***. Letting the women and children join in was appreciated, I'm sure.

13 Twelve years after arriving Nehemiah left to see the king, but before long he was back in Jerusalem. He wasn't happy with what he found. A non-Israelite named Tobiah had been given a room in the temple, and Nehemiah remarked that ***it grieved me sore: therefore I cast forth all the household stuff of Tobiah out of***

the chamber. Tenants could be evicted without notice, it seems. In addition, he saw people pressing wine and selling food of all kinds on the sabbath. He did his best to suppress these activities; when a few traders continued outside the walls he told them ***if ye do so again, I will lay hands on you.***

For people in mixed marriages, the violence was more than just a threat. Nehemiah wrote that ***I contended with them, and cursed them, and smote certain of them, and plucked off their hair, and made them swear by God, saying, Ye shall not give your daughters unto their sons, nor take their daughters unto your sons, or for yourselves. Did not Solomon king of Israel sin by these things? ... God made him king over all Israel: nevertheless even him did outlandish women cause to sin.*** Everyone should be so lucky.

The people had a home once again. Were they better, and better led, than before? Personally I wasn't impressed, but only one opinion really mattered, of course. Nehemiah's final words were appropriate: ***Remember me, O my God, for good.***

17

Esther

1

The people in exile had stories of their own. Turning back the clock a few decades, ***it came to pass in the days of Ahasuerus*** – better known as Xerxes, who had a small problem with the Greeks at Thermopylae – that the king gave a banquet for all the men in the palace.

Being a week-long feast, there was ***royal wine in abundance*** (though to be fair ***the drinking was according to the law; none did compel***, and everyone had as much or as little as he chose). ***On the seventh day, when the heart of the king was merry with wine,*** he ordered his eunuchs ***To bring Vashti the queen before the king with the crown royal, to shew the people and the princes her beauty: for she was fair to look on. But the queen Vashti refused to come at the king's commandment***, having a good idea, no doubt, as to the sort of reception she would get at a drunken stag party.

This glimmer of feminism did not sit well with Ahasuerus, who was advised that the insubordination would set a bad example to other women. A royal edict was therefore issued, and put ***among the laws of the Persians and the Medes, that it be not altered***, removing Vashti as queen. A counsellor claimed that on hearing this proclamation ***all the wives shall give to their husbands honour***, but I imagine that some had other reactions.

2

As a divorcee, Ahasuerus faced the problem of finding a new partner. His advisors suggested that to streamline the matchmaking process, ***let the king appoint officers in all the provinces of his kingdom, that they may gather together all the fair young virgins ... And let the maiden which pleaseth the king be queen instead of Vashti.*** Rank certainly has its privileges.

Now in Shushan the palace there was a certain Jew, whose name was Mordecai ... Who had been carried away from Jerusalem with the captivity. (Spiritually rather than physically, I imagine, over 115 years having passed since the deportation.) Mordecai had a cousin named Esther, and as ***the maid was fair and beautiful*** she was a candidate for the royal sweepstakes. That he should put his adoptive daughter – which Esther had become when her parents died – into the harem seemed to me poor form, but might simply have reflected his confidence in her ability to win the grand prize.

The try-out in the king's bedroom demanded rigorous preparation, ***to wit, six months with oil of myrrh, and six months with sweet odours, and with other things for the purifying of the women.*** Considering the trouble involved, each virgin had only a brief moment of glory. When finally one would get her turn with

Ahasuerus, ***In the evening she went, and on the morrow she returned into the second house of the women ... which kept the concubines: she came in unto the king no more, except the king delighted in her, and that she were called by name.*** Assuming he could remember.

Some four years after the fateful banquet, Esther had her chance at last. How she won Ahasuerus, what talents she revealed, should not concern us; perhaps he was simply worn out, and she let him sleep. In any event ***the king loved Esther above all the women, and she obtained grace and favour in his sight more than all the virgins; so that he set the royal crown upon her head, and made her queen instead of Vashti.***

No doubt Mordecai was well pleased, though he had instructed Esther to keep her background a secret. Ahasuerus had reason to be grateful to him for more than just procuring a replacement wife; Mordecai discovered two eunuchs plotting against the king, ***And when inquisition was made of the matter, it was found out; therefore they were both hanged on a tree*** – unlucky in life as in love.

3 The trouble started when the king appointed a man named Haman as his chief minister. Everyone bowed down to him; everyone, that is, except Mordecai, which made Haman furious. Not content to take action against Mordecai alone, ***Haman sought to destroy all the Jews that were throughout the whole kingdom of Ahasuerus***. Fortunately when he ***cast Pur, that is, the lot***, to discover the most auspicious time for this pogrom, the date chosen was eleven months away.

And Haman said unto king Ahasuerus, There is a certain people scattered abroad and dispersed among the people in all the provinces of thy kingdom; and their laws are diverse from all people; neither keep they the king's laws: therefore it is not for the king's profit to suffer them. If it please the king, let it be written that they may be destroyed. Ahasuerus saw nothing wrong with this proposal, and so ***letters were sent by posts into all the king's provinces, to destroy, to kill, and to cause to perish, all Jews, both young and old, little children and women, in one day, even upon the thirteenth day of the twelfth month***. It wouldn't be easy to find a loophole in that.

4 When he heard the news ***Mordecai rent his clothes, and put on sackcloth with ashes, and went out into the midst of the city, and cried with a loud and a bitter cry***; indeed, there was much weeping and wailing everywhere among the people. Mordecai asked Esther to intervene with the king, but at first she was hesitant. She hadn't seen the king for a month, and anyone entering his inner court uninvited risked death. When Mordecai pressed her, though, she agreed to try, saying ***if I perish, I perish***. A quick note asking for an audience would have spoiled the drama, I suppose.

5 ***Esther put on her royal apparel, and stood in the inner court of the king's house ... And it was so, when the king saw Esther the queen standing in the court, that she obtained favour in his sight***. He offered to grant any wish, up to half of his kingdom. All she asked, though, was that he and Haman come to dinner that evening. There the offer was repeated, and again she delayed, inviting them

back the following day.

Haman went home and boasted to his friends and family about ***the glory of his riches, and the multitude of his children, and all the things wherein the king had promoted him***, and how he dined privately with the king and queen. ***Yet all this availeth me nothing,*** he said, ***so long as I see Mordecai the Jew sitting at the king's gate.*** His friends advised him to build a gallows on which, with the king's permission, to hang Mordecai the very next day: ***then go thou merrily with the king unto the banquet.***

6 Meanwhile the king, who was having trouble sleeping, had the court chronicles read to him. It was a sure cure for insomnia, no doubt. He was reminded, however, of Mordecai's good deed, which had so far gone unrewarded. And so when Haman came in Ahasuerus asked ***What shall be done unto the man whom the king delighteth to honour? Now Haman thought in his heart, To whom would the king delight to do honour more than to myself?*** Jumping to conclusions can be very foolish.

Haman suggested that the lucky man be dressed in royal robes, mounted on the king's horse, and led through the streets by an important official. ***Then the king said to Haman, Make haste, and take the apparel and the horse, as thou hast said, and do even so to Mordecai the Jew.*** Thus we had the delightful spectacle of Haman lionising a man he had expected to hang. Even his wife and friends thought that it was a bad omen.

7 ***So the king and Haman came to banquet with Esther the queen.*** When Ahasuerus again offered to grant her wish, she declared ***let my life be given me at my petition, and my people at my request: For we are sold, I and my people, to be destroyed, to be slain, and to perish.*** Had it only been a question of slavery, she said, ***I had held my tongue***, but the king might find annihilation excessive. Ahasuerus exclaimed ***Who is he, and where is he, that durst presume in his heart to do so?***, as if he would never contemplate such a thing. But Esther was tactful enough to lay the blame elsewhere, declaring ***The adversary and enemy is this wicked Haman.***

When the king stepped outside to calm down, Haman threw himself, rather too enthusiastically, on the mercy of the queen. ***Then the king returned out of the palace garden into the place of the banquet of wine; and Haman was fallen upon the bed whereon Esther was. Then said the king, Will he force the queen also before me in the house?*** To finish him off, it only needed one of the eunuchs to mention the newly built gallows, 75 feet high, intended for the king's man of the day. ***So they hanged Haman on the gallows that he had prepared for Mordecai.*** If only justice were always so neat.

8 Mordecai took over Haman's position, undoubtedly helped by the fact that Esther revealed their kinship. They still faced the problem of preventing the scheduled massacre, ***for the writing which is written in the king's name, and sealed with the king's ring, may no man reverse.*** Their solution was to allow ***Jews which were in every city to gather themselves together, and to stand for their life,***

to destroy, to slay, and to cause to perish, all the power of the people and province that would assault them, both little ones and women, and to take the spoil of them for a prey. I could see that it was going to be quite a civil war.

With their comrades now in positions of such power, the tide had turned for the people; ***the Jews had joy and gladness, a feast and a good day. And many of the people of the land became Jews; for the fear of the Jews fell upon them.*** It was almost like the good old days under Joshua.

9 And so when the day came, ***the Jews smote all their enemies with the stroke of the sword, and slaughter, and destruction, and did what they would unto those that hated them.*** Five hundred men were killed in the palace alone, including the ten sons of Haman. When the king granted Esther a further request, she didn't bother with pious wishes for peace or reconciliation; she simply asked that the free-for-all be extended a day in the capital, and that the bodies of Haman's sons be suspended from the gallows. Presumably they didn't need an extra day in the provinces, where 75,000 people had already been killed.

When the fighting had stopped, and the excitement was over, the people celebrated. So the holiday was established ***As the days wherein the Jews rested from their enemies, and the month which was turned unto them from sorrow to joy, and from mourning into a good day: that they should make them days of feasting and joy, and of sending portions one to another, and gifts to the poor.*** Since Haman had originally fixed the date by casting lots, or Pur, ***they called these days Purim.***

10 Everything the wicked Haman had attempted was turned against him, and Ahasuerus made Mordecai the second ranking man in the kingdom. The poetic justice was highly satisfying. I say poetic and not divine justice because God was never even mentioned. Was he directing events from behind the scenes? I can't be sure, but events did seem to bear his imprint.

18

Job

There was a man in the land of Uz, whose name was Job; and that man was perfect and upright, and one that feared God, and eschewed evil. If he had been a little less good he might not have suffered the calamities that followed, but I'm not making any recommendations. 1

Job was blessed with seven sons, three daughters, and a very large number of sheep, camels, oxen, donkeys and slaves. He was so pious that he even made sacrifices to atone for any sins that his children might have committed unintentionally.

Now there was a day – I remember it quite clearly – ***when the sons of God came to present themselves before the LORD, and Satan came also among them. And the LORD said unto Satan, Whence comest thou? Then Satan answered the LORD, and said, From going to and fro in the earth, and from walking up and down in it. And the LORD said unto Satan, Hast thou considered my servant Job, that there is none like him in the earth, a perfect and an upright man, one that feareth God, and escheweth evil? The Satan answered the LORD, and said, Doth Job fear God for nought?***

His point was that God had made it easy for Job to be faithful and virtuous; the man had everything he could want. ***But put forth thine hand now, and touch all that he hath, and he will curse thee to thy face.*** For my taste God was a little too ready to make experiments of this kind, but Satan's wager aroused his interest.

And so one day Job was visited by four messengers in succession, the first announcing that his oxen and donkeys had been captured and the herdsmen killed, the second that his sheep and shepherds had died in a fire storm, the third that his camels had been seized and their drivers murdered, and the fourth that all his children had died when a house collapsed on top of them in a storm. With a death toll like that, Job wasn't the only one I felt sorry for. At any rate ***Job arose, and rent his mantle, and shaved his head, and fell down upon the ground, and worshipped, And said,***

> ***Naked came I out of my mother's womb,***
> ***and naked shall I return thither;***
> ***the LORD gave, and the LORD hath taken away;***
> ***blessed be the name of the LORD.***

It was round one to God.

2 At the next celestial gathering God pointedly asked Satan what he thought of Job: ***still he holdeth fast his integrity, although thou movedst me against him, to destroy him without cause. And Satan answered the LORD, and said, Skin for skin, yea, all that a man hath will he give for his life. But put forth thine hand now, and touch his bone and his flesh, and he will curse thee to thy face.*** No one was going to leave the table while Job was supplying the stakes.

With God's permission Satan went straight out and caused Job to be covered in boils from head to toe. Job was in a sorry state, sitting in ashes and scratching his sores with a broken piece of pottery. ***Then said his wife unto him, Dost thou still retain thine integrity? curse God, and die. But he said unto her, Thou speakest as one of the foolish women speaketh. What? shall we receive good at the hand of God, and shall we not receive evil? In all this did not Job sin with his lips,*** although he wasn't very polite to his wife. This willingness to take the bad with the good gave Job a reputation for patience – one I'm surprised he kept, in view of some of his later remarks.

THE DISCUSSION

Three of Job's friends came to offer their sympathy. For a whole week nobody said
3 a word, and then Job spoke.

Let the day perish wherein I was born,
and the night in which it was said,
There is a man child conceived.

Being born, ***why did I not give up the ghost when I came out of the belly?*** Death would have been a blessing,

For now should I have lain still and been quiet,
I should have slept: then had I been at rest,
With kings and counsellors of the earth,
which built desolate palaces for themselves;
...
There the wicked cease from troubling;
and there the weary be at rest.

So far, Job merely wished he were dead; it took his friends to make him really unhappy.

4 They tried at first to be reassuring. As a good man, he should get what he deserved; ***who ever perished, being innocent? or where were the righteous cut off?*** – I thought of Job's children, for a start – whereas ***they that plow iniquity, and sow wickedness, reap the same.*** The friend then recounted a dream, a revelation

that no one – not even an angel, I'm sorry to say – is worthy of God's confidence.

Fear came upon me, and trembling,
  which made all my bones to shake.
Then a spirit passed before my face;
  the hair of my flesh stood up: …
  there was silence, and I heard a voice, saying
Shall mortal man be more just than God?
  shall a man be more pure than his maker?
Behold, he put no trust in his servants;
  and his angels he charged with folly:
How much less in them that dwell in houses of clay …?

People are prone to bring trouble on themselves: ***wrath killeth the foolish man, and envy slayeth the silly one.*** Harm doesn't descend out of thin air, for ***man is born unto trouble, as the sparks fly upwards.*** The only answer is to submit yourself to God, for better or worse. He brings the mighty down, ***he taketh the wise in their own craftiness***, he looks after the poor. God may knock you down, but he will pick you up: 5

Behold, happy is the man whom God correcteth:
therefore despise not thou the chastening of the Almighty:
For he maketh sore, and bindeth up:
he woundeth, and his hands make whole.

I think Job would happily have forgone both the wounding and the healing.

The friend was becoming carried away, claiming that ***At destruction and famine thou shalt laugh***: he should try it, I thought. With God's grace there was nothing to fear,

For thou shalt be in league with the stones of the field:
and the beasts of the field shall be at peace with thee.
…
Thou shalt come to thy grave in a full age,
like as a shock of corn cometh in in his season.

Job replied that he only wanted to die, ***For the arrows of the Almighty are within me, the poison whereof drinketh up my spirit***. What reason was there to wait and be patient? ***Is my strength the strength of stones? or is my flesh of brass?*** He was still waiting for someone to show him where he had gone wrong. ***How forcible are right words! but what doth your arguing reprove?*** 6

Life is a futile struggle, Job continued. At night 7

I am full of tossings to and fro unto the dawning of the day.
My flesh is clothed with worms and clods of dust;
my skin is broken, and become loathsome.
My days are swifter than a weaver's shuttle,
and are spent without hope.

There is only death, when a man vanishes; ***He shall return no more to his house, neither shall his place know him any more.***

Job implored God to stop toying with him, so that his life could end.

I loathe it; I would not live alway:
let me alone; for my days are vanity.

ROUND ONE CONTINUES

8 A different friend took up the argument. ***Doth the Almighty pervert justice?*** Your children were punished for their sins. If you are virtuous, then God will look after you; I wonder how much worldly experience he had had. He maintained that God would yet ***fill thy mouth with laughing, and thy lips with rejoicing.***

9 Job was ready for justice, ***but how should man be just with God?*** There's no court of appeal. He knocks over mountains, shakes the earth, controls the heavens, and acts as judge and jury in his own case. No one can challenge him, or force him to listen even though he ***multiplieth my wounds without cause.*** I'm afraid Job was singled out precisely because there was no cause.

It seemed clear that God's eyes were closed to the suffering of the innocent and the success of the villainous; ***if not, where, and who is he?*** If justice is to be done, it will need an impartial judge ***that might lay his hand upon us both.*** The day that becomes possible, I predict, God will spend his entire time in court.

10 Job imagined that God had made and watched him just so that ***If I be wicked, woe unto me***. In any event he had been struck down, and now had only a last request: ***let me alone, that I may take comfort a little, Before I go whence I shall not return, even to the land of darkness and the shadow of death ... where the light is as darkness.*** It needed a hard heart not to be moved.

11 None the less the third friend showed no sympathy at all. ***Should thy lies make men hold their peace? ... Know therefore that God exacteth of thee less than thine iniquity deserveth. Canst thou by searching find out God?*** From the fact that God is unfathomable, I don't see how he could infer that Job was getting his deserts. Maybe God just had a wager on whether he'd crack, for example.

Anyway, Job was advised to repent. If he could offer himself sinless to God, ***thou shalt forget thy misery, and remember it as waters that pass away: And thine age shall be clearer than the noonday; thou shalt shine forth, thou shalt be as the morning.*** Taking every disaster as evidence of sin is a recipe for insanity, in my view; you can't blame God for everything, but you can't always blame yourself either.

12 The sanctimonious arguments of his friends finally provoked bitter sarcasm from Job: ***No doubt but ye are the people, and wisdom shall die with you.*** The condescension of the fortunate is insufferable. Once ruined ***the just upright man is laughed to scorn***, however respected he might have been before.

Perhaps you wonder who is responsible for the calamity?

But ask now the beasts, and they shall teach thee:
and the fowls of the air, and they shall tell thee:
Or speak to the earth, and it shall teach thee:
and the fishes of the sea shall declare unto thee.

They will all recognise the hand of God.

With the ancient is wisdom; and in length of days understanding. There's no doubt that God is powerful. What he destroys cannot be rebuilt; he can create drought or flood, make rulers weak and the old foolish; he will obliterate entire nations, and leave people to wander without help; truly, ***He discovereth deep things out of darkness, and bringeth out to light the shadow of death.***

13 Momentarily exhilarated, Job asked nothing more than to speak to God. He wondered how his friends would fare under divine interrogation; they would do better to stay silent. As for himself, why shouldn't he be ready to ***put my life in mine hand? Though he slay me, yet will I trust in him: but I will maintain mine own ways before him.*** Confident of his innocence, Job was prepared to run any risk to get a hearing.

14 His mood changed, though, and he became melancholy.

Man that is born of a woman is of few days, and full of trouble.
He cometh forth like a flower, and is cut down:
he fleeth also as a shadow, and continueth not.

Surely it would be best, he told God, to leave everyone alone, to allow a little privacy in the daily struggle.

For there is hope of a tree, if it be cut down,
that it will sprout again,
and that the tender branch thereof will not cease.
...
But man dieth, and wasteth away:
yea, man giveth up the ghost, and where is he?

Though knowing that the dead ***shall not awake, nor be raised out of their sleep,*** Job dreamt of lying hidden somewhere until God had returned to his senses. It was an idle notion: ***If a man die, shall he live again?*** As thoroughly as the rain washes away the earth, ***thou destroyest the hope of man.***

THE SECOND ROUND

15 The first friend re-entered the argument with a sharp retort. ***Should a wise man utter vain knowledge, and fill his belly with the east wind?*** Apart from being a windbag, Job was claiming a monopoly on wisdom. ***Art thou the first man that was born? or wast thou made before the hills?*** He repeated that no man is innocent, and that the wicked are continually in torment. If he were right I'd expect everyone to be wretched all the time.

16 ***Miserable comforters are ye all***, Job replied; ***I also could speak as you do: if your soul were in my soul's stead.*** God had destroyed him for no reason, he 17 repeated, and now he was forced to endure the taunts of the ignorant. Declaring that ***My days are passed***, Job could see nothing left but the grave:

I have made my bed in the darkness.
I have said to corruption, Thou art my father:
to the worm, Thou art my mother, and my sister.
And where is now my hope?

18 The second friend returned to the fray, describing in lurid detail the fate of the wicked, the none-too-subtle implication being that Job belonged to their number. The villain will be caught in a trap, made to piss on his feet with fear. His skin will be devoured – another gibe at Job, with his running sores – his sin will drive him from home, ***and it shall bring him to the king of terrors.*** His name will be expunged from the earth.

19 You should be ashamed of yourselves, Job answered: the insults are undeserved. With sublime eloquence he exclaimed that not only God but everyone, all

    they whom I loved are turned against me.
My bone cleaveth to my skin and to my flesh,
    and I am escaped with the skin of my teeth.
Have pity upon me, have pity upon me, O ye my friends;
    for the hand of God hath touched me.
Why do ye persecute me as God,
    and are not satisfied with my flesh?
Oh that my words were now written!
    oh that they were printed in a book!
That they were graven with an iron pen
    and lead in the rock forever!
For I know that my redeemer liveth,

and that he shall stand at the latter day upon the earth:
And though after my skin worms destroy this body,
yet in my flesh shall I see God.

I should mention that no one is quite sure whether he said that he expected to see God 'in my flesh' or 'without my flesh', but in any case it was a dramatic expression of confidence in his ultimate vindication. To claim that his persecution was justified, Job said, ***seeing the root of the matter is found in me***, was false and sinful.

20 The third friend dutifully took his turn to offer more platitudes and dire warnings: didn't Job realise ***That the triumphing of the wicked is short, and the joy of the hypocrite but for a moment?*** However powerful, the bad man leaves as little trace as his own excrement. ***Though wickedness be sweet in his mouth, though he hide it under his tongue***, he will not be able to digest his gains: ***he shall vomit them up again***. God will attack him, an arrow will pierce him: the glittering point will come out through his gall-bladder.

21 ***Suffer that I may speak***, Job said, ***and after that I have spoken, mock on.*** The fate of the wicked is nothing like that: they prosper, live long, and die quietly, asking

What is the Almighty, that we should serve him?
and what profit should we have, if we pray unto him?

That's a question everyone should be trying to answer, in my view, instead of assuming that God's function is to contrive happy endings. If there are rewards in piety, they can't be defined so simply as some people appear to believe.

Experience, Job maintained, gives us no reason to suppose that the wicked are punished, and the claim that their children will suffer can hardly give us any satisfaction. Job wasn't trying to give lessons – ***Shall any teach God knowledge?*** – he was simply describing reality. Rich and poor, good and bad, ***They shall lie down alike in the dust, and the worms shall cover them.*** The powerful, though, are respected, remembered, watched over even in the grave.

ONE LAST CIRCUIT

22 As the debate entered its third round, the first speaker told Job that he was a miserable sinner: ***Is not thy wickedness great? and thine iniquities infinite?*** I'm always amazed at people who borrow God's authority in order to insult everyone in sight. Job was even presented with a list of sins to which he should confess: he had ***stripped the naked of their clothing … withholden bread from the hungry … sent widows away empty, and the arms of the fatherless have been broken.*** Talking like that, his friend was liable to end up with something broken himself.

23 Job merely said that he wanted nothing more than to present his case to God, if
24 only he knew where to find him. Others were in the same position; the poor and the oppressed groan like wounded men, and God ignores them. As for the criminals, ***They are of those that rebel against the light***: the murderer, the thief, the adulterer, slink about under cover of darkness. ***The womb shall forget him; the worm shall feed sweetly on him; he shall be no more remembered*** – but isn't this everyone's fate?

25 The second friend had little more to add. He could only repeat that God was lofty,

yea, the stars are not pure in his sight.
How much less man, that is a worm?
and the son of man, which is a worm?

Perhaps no one deserves any more than a mouthful of dirt, but I didn't notice him
26 volunteering to join Job on the manure pile. His comments were of no help, and
27 Job told him so. He swore that he would plead 'not guilty' to his dying day.

28 There is something hidden from every creature on earth, Job declared. We can mine for metal and precious stones,

But where shall wisdom be found?
and where is the place of understanding?
Man knoweth not the price thereof;
neither is it found in the land of the living.

It cannot be bought, ***for the price of wisdom is above rubies.*** God alone knows how to find it, ***For he looketh to the ends of the earth, and seeth under the whole heaven.*** He found it, comprehended it, ***And unto man he said, Behold, the fear of the Lord, that is wisdom; and to depart from evil is understanding.***

29 Job looked back nostalgically on the days when he enjoyed the respect of all. His good works were everywhere to be seen; ***I caused the widow's heart to sing for joy … I was eyes to the blind, and feet was I to the lame. I was a father to the poor.*** A little self-satisfied, too, but let that pass. Previously everyone would look
30 to him for advice, ***But now they that are younger than I have me in derision, whose fathers I would have disdained to have set with the dogs of my flock.*** He was bitter, and who can blame him: ***They abhor me, they flee far from me, and spare not to spit in my face.*** People clearly thought that Job had been cursed, which in a way was true; his very virtue had made him God's guinea pig.

Addressing God directly, Job said ***I know that thou wilt bring me to death, and to the house appointed for all living.*** To that he seemed resigned, though it still rankled that

When I looked for good, then evil came unto me:
and when I waited for light, there came darkness.
My bowels boiled, and rested not: ...
I am a brother to dragons,
and a companion to owls.

He had received neither divine justice nor human solace.

Job made one last attempt to clear himself of suspicion. If I have so much as looked at young women, he swore, ***Then let my wife grind unto another, and let others bow down upon her.*** If I have ever been unfair to slaves, unkind to widows and orphans, or ungenerous to the poor, ***Then let mine arm fall from my shoulder blade, and mine arm be broken from the bone.*** Condemn me, too, if I was obsessed with wealth, or tempted to worship the sun and moon; ***If I rejoiced at the destruction of him that hated me, or lifted up myself when evil found him.*** It was an impressive roster; the mere fact that Job counted delight in vengeance a vice put him in advance of most people. 31

My desire is, he said, ***that the Almighty would answer me, and that mine adversary had written a book***; he would happily use it in his own defence. And so he let his case rest: ***The words of Job are ended.***

ADDITIONAL ADVICE

At this point a completely new speaker entered the debate. Thus far he had deferred to his elders, but ***Great men are not always wise***. He couldn't wait to offer his opinion: 32

For I am full of matter,
the spirit within me constraineth me.
Behold, my belly is as wine which hath no vent;
it is ready to burst like new bottles.

Unfortunately the people who have most to say are not always right, or even very interesting.

Suffering is a motive for approaching God, he asserted. You find an angel, ***one among a thousand***, to plead your case, you repent, and God saves you from the pit. I'd have to say that finding an angel with that kind of influence isn't easy, but this man was as big-headed as they come; just listen, he told Job, ***hold thy peace, and I shall teach thee wisdom.*** You think yourself innocent, but ***far be it from God, that he should do wickedness; and from the Almighty, that he should commit iniquity.*** It seemed, though, that his only reason for thinking God perfectly just was that he holds absolute power, which is hardly much of an argument. 33 34

He then claimed, amazingly, that God takes no notice of what anyone does, 35 good or bad. Being above it all, God ignores the self-centred cries from down below. ***Therefore doth Job open his mouth in vain; he multiplieth words without knowledge.*** It sounded to me like what Job had been saying all along.

36 Reverting to the argument that the wicked suffer, he suggested that kings die as wretchedly as temple prostitutes if they don't obey God. He had to admit that others suffer too, but then declared that suffering is good for you. ***Behold, God exalteth by his power: who teacheth like him?*** Fortunately no one, Job might have said under his breath.

37 On divine power, he said ***Hearken unto this, O Job: stand still, and consider the wondrous works of God.*** His examples, though, were not especially to the point, being concerned with thunder and lightning, snow and rain. It was not the might but the right that Job doubted. Still, if ***Fair weather cometh out of the north***, then perhaps there was yet hope.

GOD'S TURN

38 It was at this moment that ***the LORD answered Job out of the whirlwind, and said, Who is this that darkeneth counsel by words without knowledge? Gird up now thy loins like a man.*** He offered not so much an answer as a challenge: ***Where wast thou when I laid the foundations of the earth? declare, if thou hast understanding. ... who laid the corner stone thereof; When the morning stars sang together, and all the sons of God shouted for joy?*** He sounded a little defensive to me, like someone who might have difficulty justifying what he had done.

God's lecture continued. Were you around when I set limits for the sea, commanding ***Hitherto shalt thou come, but no further: and here shall thy proud waves be stayed?*** Have you ever grasped the horizon and shaken out the stars at dawn?

Hast thou entered into the springs of the sea?
or hast thou walked in the search of the depth?
Have the gates of death been opened unto thee?
or hast thou seen the doors of the shadow of death?
Hast thou perceived the breadth of the earth?
declare if thou knowest it all.

Job had no chance to reply. God asked if he knew where snow and hail were stored, and which paths the wind and storm followed. ***Hath the rain a father? or who hath begotten the drops of dew?*** And then there would still be the sky to understand:

Canst thou bind the sweet influences of Pleiades,

or loose the bands of Orion?
Canst thou bring forth Mazzaroth in his season?
or canst thou guide Arcturus with his sons?

If you summon bolts of lightning, will they answer ***Here we are?*** And when the earth needs rain, ***who can number the clouds in wisdom? or who can stay the bottles of heaven ...?***

Job was being thoroughly browbeaten. What do you know of lions, mountain goats, wild donkeys, ostriches? 39

Hast thou given the horse strength?
hast thou clothed his neck with thunder? ...
He paweth in the valley, and rejoiceth in his strength:
he goeth on to meet the armed men. ...
He swalloweth the ground with fierceness and rage:
neither believeth he that it is the sound of the trumpet.
He saith among the trumpets, Ha, ha;
and he smelleth the battle afar off,
the thunder of the captains, and the shouting.

I hadn't realised that God was so interested in horses. But by pointing out that the lives of other creatures are beyond human comprehension, he was letting Job know that his species isn't quite so special as it likes to think.

Having hectored Job for long enough, God asked him what he had to say. ***Then Job answered the LORD, and said, Behold, I am vile; what shall I answer thee? I will lay mine hand upon my mouth.*** God was barely mollified, grumbling that perhaps Job wanted to put the wicked in their place himself. He was still sounding touchy. 40

Job had to sit through more examples of how little power people have over creation. ***Behold now behemoth, which I made with thee; he eateth grass as an ox. ... he drinketh up a river, and hasteth not.*** (God was probably thinking of the hippopotamus, but that's just a guess.) Or for that matter, ***Canst thou draw out leviathan with an hook?*** (Here he might have had the crocodile in mind, though the whale is another possibility.) 41

Will he make many supplications unto thee?
will he speak soft words unto thee?
Will he make a covenant with thee?
wilt thou take him for a servant for ever?

If this was a parody of the relationship between God and mankind, it was in poor taste.

God was so pleased with leviathan that he lovingly described its invincibility at length. ***His heart is as firm as a stone; yea, as hard as a piece of the nether millstone.*** No weapon can harm him, and the lashings of his tail are fearsome: ***He maketh the deep to boil like a pot.*** Indeed,

Upon earth there is not his like,
who is made without fear.
He beholdeth all high things:
he is a king over all the children of pride.

People being such a problem, I wondered if perhaps God would have preferred raising animals – especially ones with lots of teeth.

Not a word had been offered to explain Job's calamity. No doubt God was embarrassed to admit that it had all been an experiment. Still, he avoided the central issue – that he had the power to prevent suffering, and didn't use it – while stressing the insignificance of human beings, and how foolish they are to ask questions. It was highly unsatisfactory. That people shouldn't look for reasons may be right, but if God is going to be unpredictable, intervening here and there as it suits him, he shouldn't sound so self-righteous about it. Though if God can't act holier-than-thou, who can?

42 Job knew better than to argue. He affirmed that God could do anything he wanted. Previously he had known him only by repute;

I have heard of thee by the hearing of the ear:
  but now mine eye seeth thee.
Wherefore I abhor myself,
  and repent in dust and ashes.

I would have liked God to reciprocate with an apology, which of course was unrealistic. He did oblige the three friends to atone for their disrespect, though.

And then, to send everyone away happy, ***the LORD gave Job twice as much as he had before***: thousands of sheep, camels, oxen and donkeys. ***So the LORD blessed the latter end of Job more than his beginning.*** If only everyone could be so fortunate. Moreover, ***He had also seven sons and three daughters. And he called the name of the first, Jemima ... And in all the land were no women found so fair as the daughters of Job: and their father gave them inheritance among their brethren***, which was a radical thing to do. He lived for another 140 years, seeing his family grow through four generations. ***So Job died, being old and full of days.***

19

Psalms

Life in the promised land was not all smiting, sinning, sacrificing and supplicating. There was time for singing as well. Of course most of the songs dealt with smiting, etc., but then what can you expect? Despite the tedium of hearing God compared to a rock for the umpteenth time, I used to enjoy the performances. And if the lyrics weren't always very original, just occasionally someone managed to come up with a show stopper.

Book I

First in the song book was a standard story about the two ways of living: 1

Blessed is the man
that walketh not in the counsel of the ungodly,
nor standeth in the way of sinners,
nor sitteth in the seat of the scornful.
But his delight is in the law of the LORD;
and in his law doth he meditate day and night.
And he shall be like a tree planted by the rivers of water,
that bringeth forth his fruit in his season;
his leaf also shall not wither;
and whatsoever he doeth shall prosper.
The ungodly are not so:
but are like the chaff which the wind driveth away.
Therefore the ungodly shall not stand in judgment,
nor sinners in the congregation of the righteous.
For the LORD knoweth the way of the righteous:
but the way of the ungodly shall perish.

I shouldn't be in a hurry to call the undertaker, though.

Political enemies don't stand a chance, according to the singer. ***Why do the heathen rage, and the people imagine a vain thing?*** They want to overthrow the anointed ruler, but God laughs in their face. He tells the king ***Thou shalt break them with a rod of iron; thou shalt dash them in pieces like a potter's vessel.*** By contrast, of course, ***Blessed are all they that put their trust in him.*** They'll know 2

3 to be thankful, ***for thou hast smitten all mine enemies upon the cheek bone; thou hast broken the teeth of the ungodly.***

4 It's not all violence, thank heavens. We had some easy listening:

LORD, lift thou up the light of thy countenance upon us.
Thou hast put gladness in my heart,
more than in the time that their corn and their wine increased.
I will both lay me down in peace, and sleep:
for thou, LORD, only makest me dwell in safety.

5 I'd have to say, though, that the general taste was for heavy metal.

For there is no faithfulness in their mouth;
their inward part is very wickedness;
their throat is an open sepulchre;
they flatter with their tongue.
Destroy thou them, O God.

Crash, bang, scream, cheers.

6 At least the protest songs showed a bit of ingenuity. For example, there was the fellow who came up with a wonderful reason for God to spare his life:

For in death there is no remembrance of thee:
in the grave who shall give thee thanks?
I am weary with my groaning;
all the night make I my bed to swim;
I water my couch with my tears.

7 And if you try you can even find a hint that vice is its own punishment, because the wicked person, ***He made a pit, and digged it, and is fallen into the ditch which he made.***

8 I was quite fond of the jolly sing-along, praise-God-and-all-creation numbers. Of course sometimes they got carried away about the place of people in the scheme of things.

Out of the mouth of babes and sucklings
hast thou ordained strength because of thine enemies,
that thou mightest still the enemy and the avenger.
When I consider thy heavens, the work of thy fingers,
the moon and the stars, which thou hast ordained;
What is man, that thou art mindful of him?
and the son of man, that thou visitest him?

For thou hast made him a little lower than the angels,
and hast crowned him with glory and honour.

A little lower! There's wishful thinking for you. That one ends, by the way, with a rousing chorus of ***O LORD our Lord, how excellent is thy name in all the earth!***

Lyricists got bored writing that sort of thing, and occasionally one would play a game such as making the first letter of every line form the alphabet. The technique came in handy with an otherwise boring ditty about the wicked man: ***as for all his enemies, he puffeth at them. He hath said in his heart, I shall not be moved.*** There's a good song there somewhere, though. 9 10

Don't worry if you are being plagued by evil-doers, ran another popular message. ***In the LORD put I my trust: how say ye to my soul, Flee as a bird to your mountain?*** God will deal with your pursuers, because anyone ***that loveth violence his soul hateth. Upon the wicked he shall rain snares, fire and brimstone, and an horrible tempest.*** Violence just made him murderous. 11

He viewed insincerity in a similar light, and hence ***The LORD shall cut off all flattering lips, and the tongue that speaketh proud things.*** Some people started to wonder, though, when the promised justice and redistribution of fortune might arrive. ***How long wilt thou forget me, O LORD? for ever?*** Naturally too much questioning didn't go down well with the faithful, who grumbled that ***The fool hath said in his heart, There is no God.*** In fact they were quite grouchy about humanity in general; ***they are all together become filthy: there is none that doeth good, no, not one.*** 12 13 14

After listening to those complainers, it was almost a relief to hear suggestions for the virtuous – a new set of ten commandments, in fact. 15

LORD, who shall abide in thy tabernacle?
who shall dwell in thy holy hill?
He that walketh uprightly, and worketh righteousness,
and speaketh the truth in his heart.
He that backbiteth not with his tongue,
nor doeth evil to his neighbour,
nor taketh up a reproach against his neighbour.
In whose eyes a vile person is contemned;
but he honoureth them that fear the LORD.
He that sweareth to his own hurt, and changeth not.
He that putteth not out his money to usury,
nor taketh reward against the innocent.
He that doeth these things shall never be moved.

If you do all that, you can look forward to a generously marked-out inheritance: ***The lines are fallen unto me in pleasant places; yea, I have a goodly heritage.*** This estate is not necessarily material, but all the better for that. 16

Thou wilt shew me the path of life:
in thy presence is fulness of joy;
at thy right hand there are pleasures for evermore.

I was glad to hear someone suggest that the good prosper in some way other than acquiring more and more property.

17 Too many of the songsters were stuck-up and self-righteous, telling God ***Keep me as the apple of the eye, hide me under the shadow of thy wings***. Their enemies are dangerous ***men of the world***, not to be trusted. But God would come to the
18 rescue, ***And he rode upon a cherub, and did fly: yea, he did fly upon the wings of the wind.*** That much I loved.

19 For the less egocentric, God is both a physical and a moral force: both god of nature and god of the law.

The heavens declare the glory of God;
and the firmament sheweth his handywork.
Day unto day uttereth speech,
and night unto night sheweth knowledge.
There is no speech nor language,
where their voice is not heard.
Their line is gone out through all the earth,
and their words to the end of the world.
In them hath he set a tabernacle for the sun,
Which is as a bridegroom coming out of his chamber,
and rejoiceth as a strong man to run a race.
His going forth is from the end of the heaven,
and his circuit unto the ends of it:
and there is nothing hid from the heat thereof.

The law of the LORD is perfect, converting the soul:
the testimony of the LORD is sure, making wise the simple.
The statutes of the LORD are right, rejoicing the heart:
the commandment of the LORD is pure, enlightening the eyes.
The fear of the LORD is clean, enduring for ever:
the judgments of the LORD are true and righteous altogether.
More to be desired are they than gold,
yea, than much fine gold:
sweeter also than honey and the honeycomb.
Moreover by them is thy servant warned:
and in keeping of them there is great reward.

Who can understand his errors?
cleanse thou me from secret faults.

Keep back thy servant also from presumptuous sins;
let them not have dominion over me:
then shall I be upright,
and I shall be innocent from the great transgression.
Let the words of my mouth, and the meditation of my heart,
be acceptable in thy sight, O LORD,
my strength, and my redeemer.

A song like that was enough to make me forgive the next, in which the warriors say that ***in the name of our God we will set up our banners***, or even more pointedly, ***Some trust in chariots, and some in horses: but we will remember the name of the LORD our God.*** I could never get them to stop using God as a mascot. It's one thing to look at the king and say ***Thou hast given him his heart's desire, and hast not withholden the request of his lips***, but quite another to assume that divine power would be available on demand. Knowing the fate of God's enemies – ***Thou shalt make them as a fiery oven in the time of thine anger ... Their fruit shalt thou destroy from the earth, and their seed from among the children of men*** – people always wanted to suggest that their foes were God's foes. 20 21

For anyone with eyes to see, though, the hope that God is on your side is in constant tension with the fear that he takes no notice. Despair being common to all, the following lends itself to quotation. 22

My God, my God, why hast thou forsaken me?
why art thou so far from helping me,
and from the words of my roaring? ...
But I am a worm, and no man;
a reproach of men, and despised of the people.
All they that see me laugh me to scorn:
they shoot out the lip, they shake the head, saying,
He trusted on the LORD that he would deliver him:
let him deliver him, seeing he delighted in him.

Even I found the appeal poignant. ***Be not far from me; for trouble is near; for there is none to help.*** And combined with physical affliction is human callousness: ***They part my garments among them, and cast lots upon my vesture.*** Still, the faith remains that in the end ***The meek shall eat and be satisfied: they shall praise the LORD that seek him.***

We like to give David the credit for what became the most popular song of all. 23

The LORD is my shepherd; I shall not want.
He maketh me to lie down in green pastures:
he leadeth me beside the still waters.
He restoreth my soul:

he leadeth me in the paths of righteousness for his name's sake.
Yea, though I walk through the valley of the shadow of death,
I will fear no evil: for thou art with me;
thy rod and thy staff they comfort me.

Thou preparest a table before me in the presence of mine enemies:
thou anointest my head with oil; my cup runneth over.
Surely goodness and mercy shall follow me all the days of my life:
and I will dwell in the house of the LORD for ever.

Later interpretations notwithstanding, what he said in the last line was that he would spend all his time in the temple – which would have been a fearful waste of talent.

24 Another song gave advice on reaching God:

The earth is the LORD's, and the fulness thereof;
the world, and they that dwell therein.
For he hath founded it upon the seas,
and established it upon the floods.
Who shall ascend into the hill of the LORD?
or who shall stand in his holy place?
He that hath clean hands, and a pure heart;
who hath not lifted up his soul unto vanity,
nor sworn deceitfully.

Now by tradition the song was used when the ark was brought into Jerusalem. To appreciate its impact you have to imagine a priest asking each of the questions, and the congregation bellowing the response.

Lift up your heads, O ye gates;
and be ye lift up, ye everlasting doors;
and the King of glory shall come in.
Who is this King of glory?
The LORD strong and mighty,
the LORD mighty in battle.
Lift up your heads, O ye gates;
even lift them up, ye everlasting doors;
and the King of glory shall come in.
Who is this King of glory?
The LORD of hosts, he is the King of glory.

25 After a couple of great tunes, it was back to boredom and a dull acrostic (the first letter of each line making the alphabet), with guilty sentiments such as ***Remember not the sins of my youth, nor my transgressions***. Then the self-right-

eous got an encore. ***I have hated the congregation of evil doers; and will not sit with the wicked. I will wash mine hands in innocency***, and so on, and so forth. 26

Things brightened up when they returned to praising God. 27

The LORD is my light and my salvation;
whom shall I fear?
the LORD is the strength of my life;
of whom shall I be afraid?
When the wicked, even mine enemies and my foes,
came upon me to eat up my flesh, they stumbled and fell.
Though an host should encamp against me,
my heart shall not fear:
though war should rise against me,
in this will I be confident.

To return to supplication: ***Unto thee will I cry, O LORD my rock***, and to pile up the muscular metaphors, ***The LORD is my strength and my shield***. There's a softer side, of course – ***worship the LORD in the beauty of holiness*** – but the more popular view was that ***the God of glory thundereth***. 28 29

In times of trouble God may come to the rescue, and 30

in his favour is life:
weeping may endure for a night,
but joy cometh in the morning.

Or so we can hope, anyway. Thus the declaration (again, one famous for being quoted at a later date) that 31

Into thine hand I commit my spirit:
thou hast redeemed me, O LORD God of truth.

Their great problem was the tendency to see misfortune as a sign of divine displeasure. The consequences were awful; everyone avoided the sufferer.

I am forgotten as a dead man out of mind:
I am like a broken vessel.

There was only one place to turn. ***Thou art my God. My times are in thy hand.*** The righteous, fortunately, have a refuge: thou shalt keep them secretly in a pavilion from the strife of tongues.

For a change of pace, the relief of confession merits a song; ***Blessed is he whose transgression is forgiven***. Then it was back to victory celebrations. At least someone tried to explain why there were so many of these: God deserved some- 32 33 thing different each time. ***Rejoice in the LORD ... Sing unto him a new song; play skilfully with a loud noise.***

34 Next on the song list was a hymn of praise, of no great interest except in mentioning my role in protecting the godly. ***The angel of the LORD encampeth round about them that fear him, and delivereth them. O taste and see that the LORD is good.*** It also offered some succinct advice.

Come, ye children, hearken unto me:
I will teach you the fear of the LORD. ...
Keep thy tongue from evil, and thy lips from speaking guile.
Depart from evil, and do good; seek peace, and pursue it.

35 That was much more agreeable than the songs of paranoia. I was surprised not so much by their vindictiveness – everyone has fantasies of revenge – as by the suppposed number and hostility of the adversaries. How did they get so many enemies? They tended to act aggrieved if God didn't do his bit. ***Lord, how long wilt thou look on? rescue my soul from their destructions, my darling from the lions*** – the darling in question being his own life.

36 As for the praise, not all of it sounded sincere to me – but maybe I had just become jaded.

Thy righteousness is like the great mountains;
thy judgments are a great deep:
O LORD, thou preservest man and beast.
How excellent is thy lovingkindness, O God! ...
For with thee is the fountain of life:
in thy light shall we see light.

Very nice, if a bit extravagant.

37 One songwriter managed to produce an acrostic that said something, even if it did sound like Job's friends. Don't worry about evildoers,

For they shall soon be cut down like the grass,
and wither as the green herb.

But – wait for it –

But the meek shall inherit the earth;
and shall delight themselves in the abundance of peace.

The evidence, I have to say, was wholly unbelievable:

I have been young, and now am old;
yet have I not seen the righteous forsaken,
nor his seed begging bread.

The idea that the good are never deserted leads naturally to the notion that the bad are always punished.

I have seen the wicked in great power,
and spreading himself like a green bay tree.
Yet he passed away, and, lo, he was not:
yea, I sought him, but he could not be found.
Mark the perfect man, and behold the upright:
for the end of that man is peace.

The trouble with accepting these ideas came out in the lamentation that followed. The poor fellow begs for mercy, ***For thine arrows stick fast in me, and thy hand presseth me sore.*** Presumably accepting the principle that God ensures complete justice, the victim blames himself; ***My wounds stink and are corrupt because of my foolishness ... my loins are filled with a loathsome disease.*** Unsurprisingly, ***My lovers and my friends stand aloof.*** Only divine intervention can save him – or a more sensible point of view. 38

A more sophisticated sufferer has no illusions about life. In his melancholy he overcomes a reluctance to speak. 39

I said, I will take heed to my ways,
that I sin not with my tongue ...
My heart was hot within me,
while I was musing the fire burned:
then spake I with my tongue,
LORD, make me to know mine end,
and the measure of my days, what it is;
that I may know how frail I am.
Behold, thou hast made my days as an handbreadth;
and mine age is as nothing before thee:
verily every man at his best state is altogether vanity.
Surely every man walketh in a vain shew:
surely they are disquieted in vain:
he heapeth up riches, and knoweth not who shall gather them. ...
Hear my prayer, O LORD, and give ear unto my cry;
hold not thy peace at my tears:
for I am a stranger with thee, and a sojourner,
as all my fathers were.
O spare me, that I may recover strength,
before I go hence, and be no more.

40 After that, it's always a disappointment to go back to such bromides as ***I am poor and needy; yet the Lord thinketh upon me***. Even songs that started promis-
41 ingly – for example ***Blessed is he that considereth the poor: the LORD will deliver him in time of trouble*** – turned into conventional laments about the treacherous behaviour of enemies and the need to pay them back.

BOOK II

42 The poetry was never absent for long:

As the hart panteth after the water brooks,
so panteth my soul after thee, O God.
My soul thirsteth for God, for the living God:
when shall I come and appear before God? …
Deep calleth unto deep at the noise of thy waterspouts:
all thy waves and thy billows are gone over me.
Yet the LORD will command his lovingkindness in the daytime,
and in the night his song shall be with me,
and my prayer unto the God of my life. …
Why art thou cast down, O my soul?
and why art thou disquieted within me?
hope thou in God: for I shall yet praise him,
who is the help of my countenance, and my God.

43 The self-querying refrain gets repeated after a further appeal: ***O send out thy light and thy truth: let them lead me; let them bring me unto thy holy hill, and to thy tabernacles.***
44 I can take only so much personal angst, so complaints on behalf of the whole nation came almost as a relief. In the absence of any obvious sin deserving punishment, defeat was blamed on God: ***Thou sellest thy people for nought***. He was reminded of the faithfulness of Israel, and accused of letting his attention wander:

Yea, for thy sake are we killed all the day long;
we are counted as sheep for the slaughter.
Awake, why sleepest thou, O Lord?
arise, cast us not off for ever.
Wherefore hidest thou thy face,
and forgettest our affliction and our oppression?

That's the question, all right.
45 A wedding anthem provided a welcome change of pace. One story has it that

the couple described is Ahab and Jezebel; in any case, it concerns a king and his foreign bride. The singer declares that ***my tongue is the pen of a ready writer***, and his flattery is as extravagant as you might expect. The tinge of eroticism is rather spoilt by his notion of a woman's place:

Hearken, O daughter, and consider, and incline thine ear;
forget also thine own people, and thy father's house;
So shall the king greatly desire thy beauty:
for he is thy Lord; and worship thou him. ...
The king's daughter is all glorious within:
her clothing is of wrought gold.
She shall be brought unto the king in raiment of needlework:
the virgins her companions that follow her shall be brought unto thee.

I felt sorry for some of these lyricists; they should have made a fortune in royalties. Take the one, for example, who cranked out a few verses about divine victory; a couple of thousand years later someone else turned it into the chart-buster 'A mighty fortress is our God', and the cash never got near the Hebrew people, never mind the writer's family. 46

God is our refuge and strength,
a very present help in trouble.
Therefore will not we fear,
though the earth be removed,
and though the mountains be carried into the midst of the sea.

God will hold the city, and put an end to war; so

Be still, and know that I am God:
I will be exalted among the heathen,
I will be exalted in the earth.

If we're going to celebrate, I'd like to see more exuberance. ***O clap your hands, all ye people; shout unto God with the voice of triumph***. For that matter, why not ***Walk about Zion, and go round about her: tell the towers thereof.*** 47 48

Quieter songs need more philosophical lyrics, like those by the musician who announces that ***I will open my dark saying upon the harp.*** No one can buy his way out of death; ***wise men die, likewise the fool and the brutish person perish, and leave their wealth to others.*** Once gone, riches are of no use, ***But God will redeem my soul from the power of the grave***. There is no point in envy. ***Man that is in honour, and understandeth not, is like the beasts that perish.*** 49

On the subject of beasts that perish, God seems to have changed his mind about sacrifices. At any rate a singer quoted him as remarking that he needs no burnt 50 offerings, ***For every beast of the forest is mine, and the cattle upon a thousand hills. ... Will I eat the flesh of bulls, or drink the blood of goats?*** A lot of animals might wish he had seen their point of view earlier.

51 Humans, at least, know how to be penitent. We used to like to think that in the next number David is regretting how he won Bathsheba, but to be honest it might be anyone – which is why it could be turned into the general-purpose *Miserere*.

Have mercy upon me, O God, according to thy lovingkindness:
according unto the multitude of thy tender mercies
blot out my transgressions. ...

Behold, I was shapen in iniquity;
and in sin did my mother conceive me. ...
Purge me with hyssop, and I shall be clean:
wash me, and I shall be whiter than snow.
Make me to hear joy and gladness;
that the bones which thou hast broken may rejoice.
Hide thy face from my sins,
and blot out all mine iniquities.

Create in me a clean heart, O God;
and renew a right spirit within me.
Cast me not away from thy presence;
and take not thy holy spirit from me. ...

O Lord, open thou my lips;
and my mouth shall shew forth thy praise.
For thou desirest not sacrifice;
else would I give it: thou delightest not in burnt offering.
The sacrifices of God are a broken spirit:
a broken and a contrite heart, O God, thou wilt not despise.

52 That sort of breast-beating may be a bit extreme, but at least it doesn't try to blame anyone and everyone else, warning that ***God shall likewise destroy thee for***
53 ***ever***. Nor does it repeat an earlier song verbatim, which has happened. And it's a
54 great deal more attractive than the gloating that comes out in lyrics such as ***mine eyes hath seen his desire upon mine enemies***.

55 Still, my experience was that if you could sit through a few flops, a poet would come to the rescue.

Fearfulness and trembling are come upon me,
and horror hath overwhelmed me.
And I said, Oh that I had wings like a dove!

for then would I fly away, and be at rest.
Lo, then would I wander far off,
and remain in the wilderness.

The cause of the anguish was the treachery of a close friend.

For it was not an enemy that reproached me;
then I could have borne it:
neither was it he that hated me that did magnify himself against me;
then I would have hid myself from him:
But it was thou, a man mine equal, my guide, and mine acquaintance.
We took sweet counsel together,
and walked unto the house of God in company.

Nothing is more dangerous than a traitor.

The words of his mouth were smoother than butter,
but war was in his heart:
his words were softer than oil,
yet were they drawn swords.

Perhaps he suffered from persecution mania, but how pleasant to hear it so beautifully expressed. It can be jarring after that to meet such pedestrian thoughts as ***When I cry unto thee, then shall mine enemies turn back: this I know; for God is for me.*** As bad as wishful thinking is the practice of making opponents into demons: ***My soul is among lions: and I lie even among them that are set on fire, even the sons of men, whose teeth are spears and arrows, and their tongue a sharp sword.*** 56 57

It was the bloodcurdling vindictiveness, though, that dismayed me most. The wicked are as poisonous as snakes: 58

they are like the deaf adder that stoppeth her ear;
Which will not hearken to the voice of charmers,
charming never so wisely.
Break their teeth, O God, in their mouth:
break out the great teeth of the young lions, O LORD. ...
As a snail which melteth, let every one of them pass away:
like the untimely birth of a woman
that they may not see the sun. ...
The righteous shall rejoice when he seeth the vengeance:
he shall wash his feet in the blood of the wicked.
So that a man shall say, Verily there is a reward for the righteous:
verily he is a God that judgeth in the earth.

Verily the man should be locked up, if you ask me.

59 A companion piece suggested that ***thou, O LORD, shalt laugh at them; thou shalt have all the heathen in derision.*** The vision was not of God laughing at their foolishness, but of God laughing scornfully as he destroyed them. Getting down
60 to cases, the same idea was rendered more graphically as ***Moab is my washpot; over Edom will I cast out my shoe: Philistia, triumph thou because of me.***
61 At least they sometimes just asked for protection rather than triumph.

From the end of the earth will I cry unto thee, when my heart is overwhelmed:
lead me to the rock that is higher than I.
For thou hast been a shelter for me,
and a strong tower from the enemy.

62 And in more confident mood:

He only is my rock and my salvation:
he is my defence; I shall not be moved.

There was even some good advice: ***if riches increase, set not your heart upon them***, as well as the dubious dogma that ***thou renderest to every man according to his work.***

63 Just occasionally someone would show a longing for God, instead of taking him for granted; any novel idea gave me hope.

my soul thirsteth for thee,
my flesh longeth for thee in a dry and thirsty land,
where no water is;
To see thy power and thy glory …
When I remember thee upon my bed,
and meditate on thee in the night watches.

64 I know I've been complaining that all those songs of the persecuted – in which the embattled rail against those who ***shoot in secret at the perfect*** – were distasteful.
65 I do wonder, though, if the cloying songs of thanksgiving weren't just as bad.

Thou visitest the earth, and waterest it …
thou makest it soft with showers:
thou blessest the springing thereof.
Thou crownest the year with thy goodness …
and the little hills rejoice on every side.
The pastures are clothed with flocks;
the valleys also are covered over with corn;
they shout for joy, they also sing.

That's one for the under-eights.

Fortunately they weren't all like that. 66

Make a joyful noise unto God, all ye lands:
Sing forth the honour of his name:
make his praise glorious. ...
Come and see the works of God:
he is terrible in his doing toward the children of men. ...
Thou hast caused men to ride over our heads;
we went through fire and through water:
but thou broughtest us out into a wealthy place.

I rather liked, too, the innocent sense of wonder some had in the contemplation of their very own god: ***Then shall the earth yield her increase; and God, even our own God, shall bless us.*** It wasn't just a matter of blessing; ***God setteth the solitary in families: he bringeth out those which are bound with chains.*** Giving him credit for everything from social services to penal reform might be going too far, though. Once you start getting carried away, it's hard to resist the temptation to celebrate divine retribution, ***That thy foot may be dipped in the blood of thine enemies, and the tongue of thy dogs in the same.*** The final stage is when you actually tell God how to deal with the villains. ***Let their eyes be darkened, that they see not; and make their loins continually to shake. ... Let them be blotted out of the book of the living.*** 67 68 69

The next song was merely an encore, followed by the lament of an old man asking that God ***Cast me not off in the time of old age; forsake me not when my strength faileth.*** But then we pass on to a splendid description of the ideal king: 70 71 72

He shall come down like rain upon the mown grass:
as showers that water the earth.
In his days shall the righteous flourish;
and abundance of peace so long as the moon endureth.
He shall have dominion also from sea to sea,
and from the river unto the ends of the earth.
They that dwell in the wilderness shall bow before him;
and his enemies shall lick the dust.

If there's no escape from the glorying in conquest, at least some justification is offered; ***For he shall deliver the needy when he crieth; the poor also, and him that hath no helper.*** With achievements like these, ***His name shall endure for ever: his name shall be continued as long as the sun.***

Book III

73 I couldn't help thinking that all the songs of praise and glory were just a little over-wrought, that the sheer hyperbole was a sign of insecurity. Someone did at least admit the possibility of a loss of faith, saying ***my steps had well nigh slipped … when I saw the prosperity of the wicked***, who are arrogant and don't seem to suffer. But then, ***Surely thou didst set them in slippery places: thou castedst them down into destruction.*** Having persuaded himself, the singer apologised to God for being an ignorant brute. ***Whom have I in heaven but thee? and there is none upon earth that I desire beside thee.*** He couldn't press his doubts very far, but I give him some credit for frankness.

74 A lament for the destruction of the temple included the touching plea ***O deliver not the soul of thy turtledove unto the multitude of the wicked: forget not the*** 75 ***congregation of thy poor for ever.*** No fear, sang another, ***God is the judge: he putteth down one, and setteth up another.*** Indeed, how could we forget that ***At*** 76 ***thy rebuke, O God of Jacob, both the chariot and horse are cast into a dead sleep*** – more often dead than asleep, in fact. But the doubters remain, responding to 77 hardship by asking

Is his mercy clean gone for ever?
doth his promise fail for evermore?
Hath God forgotten to be gracious?
hath he in anger shut up his tender mercies?

78 A ballad reviewing the history of the people from Egypt onwards was intended as a cautionary tale, so that people ***might not be as their fathers, a stubborn and rebellious generation***. That lot didn't even appreciate it when God ***rained down manna upon them to eat, and … Man did eat angels' food***. Through it all God forgave them, ***For he remembered that they were but flesh; a wind that passeth away, and cometh not again.*** He did abandon them to disaster eventually, but the desertion was only temporary. ***Then the Lord awaked as one out of sleep, and like a mighty man that shouteth by reason of wine. And he smote his enemies in the hinder parts*** – with the divine boot, no doubt.

79 Not all the battles were won, though.

thy holy temple have they defiled;
they have laid Jerusalem on heaps.
The dead bodies of thy servants have they given to be meat unto the fowls of the heaven,
the flesh of thy saints unto the beasts of the earth.

Singers asked God to ***Pour out thy wrath upon the heathen that have not***

known thee, and upon the kingdoms that have not called upon thy name; that will teach them to be born in the right place. Israel was likened to a vine that has 80 taken root, but now needs to be defended from boars and beasts.

God thought he should offer a few words in his own defence. The people didn't 81 listen, he said, ***So I gave them up unto their own hearts' lust.*** He was occupied with other things:

> ***God standeth in the congregation of the mighty;*** 82
> ***he judgeth among the gods.***

There's a court where the litigation never stops. He did hand down some good rulings for terrestrial tribunals, such as ***Defend the poor and fatherless: do justice to the afflicted and needy.*** Human judges did not impress him:

> ***I have said, Ye are gods;***
> ***and all of you are children of the most High.***
> ***But ye shall die like men,***
> ***and fall like one of the princes.***

A few words of reproach from God were enough to make the song writers praise 83 him for everything from turning fallen enemies into ***dung for the earth***, to providing a home for sparrows. One of them even claimed to like nothing better 84 than to spend time in the house of God – as much time as possible, in fact. ***How amiable are thy tabernacles, O LORD of hosts!*** As for those who come to worship,

> ***They go from strength to strength,***
> ***every one of them in Zion appeareth before God ...***
> ***For a day in thy courts is better than a thousand.***
> ***I had rather be a doorkeeper in the house of my God,***
> ***than to dwell in the tents of wickedness.***

Following that buttering up, the moment seemed right to ask for forgiveness. 85 ***Shew us thy mercy, O LORD, and grant us thy salvation.*** The poet had a fine vision of what co-operation might bring:

> ***Mercy and truth are met together;***
> ***righteousness and peace have kissed each other.***
> ***Truth shall spring out of the earth;***
> ***and righteousness shall look down from heaven.***

Note that truth falls in the human sphere; God is in charge of morality, not of facts.

Disappointingly, after that, the next singer simply grovelled. But then ego- and 86 ethnocentrism vanished for once, in a picture of one universal nation – admittedly 87 with headquarters on Zion. Former enemies would be reconciled under God.

88 Just to restore the balance, the song that followed was the gloomiest of them all, one long lament from start to finish with no hint of relief. The author believed that, for all God cared, he might as well be dead:

I am as a man that hath no strength:
Free among the dead, like the slain that lie in the grave,
whom thou rememberest no more:
and they are cut off from thy hand.
Thou hast laid me in the lowest pit, in darkness, in the deeps. ...
LORD, why castest thou off my soul?
why hidest thou thy face from me?

As he said, it was definitely the pits.

89 They were complainers, all right. One song, though wrapped around in praise, protested God's breach of promise. Despite saying ***I have sworn unto David my servant, Thy seed will I establish for ever, and build up thy throne to all generations***, it appears that ***Thou hast made void the covenant of thy servant: thou hast profaned his crown by casting it to the ground.*** A bit tactless, maybe, but I'd have to admit that they had a grievance.

BOOK IV

90 Later on people became better at looking on the bright side; they even took what was essentially a funeral hymn, and used it to declare 'O God our help in ages past'.

Lord, thou hast been our dwelling place in all generations.
Before the mountains were brought forth,
or ever thou hadst formed the earth and the world,
even from everlasting to everlasting, thou art God.
Thou turnest man to destruction;
and sayest, Return, ye children of men.
For a thousand years in thy sight are but as yesterday when it is past,
and as a watch in the night.
Thou carriest them away as with a flood;
they are as a sleep:
in the morning they are like grass which groweth up.
In the morning it flourisheth, and groweth up;
in the evening it is cut down, and withereth.
For we are consumed by thine anger,
and by thy wrath are we troubled.
Thou hast set our iniquities before thee,

our secret sins in the light of thy countenance.
For all our days are passed away in thy wrath:
we spend our years as a tale that is told.
The days of our years are threescore years and ten;
and if by reason of strength they be fourscore years,
yet is their strength labour and sorrow;
for it is soon cut off, and we fly away.
Who knoweth the power of thine anger?
even according to thy fear, so is thy wrath.
So teach us to number our days,
that we may apply our hearts unto wisdom. ...
And let the beauty of the LORD our God be upon us:
and establish thou the work of our hands upon us;
yea, the work of our hands establish thou it.

As an antidote to all that, a subsequent singer provided a more cheerful view: 91

He that dwelleth in the secret place of the most High
shall abide under the shadow of the Almighty.
I will say of the LORD, He is my refuge and my fortress:
my God; in him will I trust.
Surely he shall deliver thee from the snare of the fowler,
and from the noisome pestilence.
He shall cover thee with his feathers,
and under his wings shalt thou trust:
his truth shall be thy shield and buckler.
Thou shalt not be afraid for the terror by night;
nor for the arrow that flieth by day;
Nor for the pestilence that walketh in darkness;
nor for the destruction that wasteth at noonday.
A thousand shall fall at thy side,
and ten thousand at thy right hand;
but it shall not come nigh thee. ...
There shall no evil befall thee,
neither shall any plague come nigh thy dwelling.
For he shall give his angels charge over thee,
to keep thee in all thy ways.
They shall bear thee up in their hands,
lest thou dash thy foot against a stone.
Thou shalt tread upon the lion and adder:
the young lion and the dragon shalt thou trample under feet.

Apart from the poetry, I was especially interested whenever anyone grappled 92 with ideas. To the problem of evil, the response was that appearances can be deceptive. If the evil flourish, it is because ***thy thoughts are very deep***; no one knows what the plan – the very secret plan – is, but it will certainly succeed, and justice will be done. ***The righteous shall flourish like the palm tree: he shall grow like a cedar in Lebanon.*** Certainly God has the power to do whatever he pleases.

93 ***The LORD on high is mightier than the noise of many waters, yea, than the mighty***

94 ***waves of the sea.*** This being the case, ***how long shall the wicked triumph? ... They slay the widow and the stranger, and murder the fatherless.*** So they do; it's a mystery.

95 I can't deny that songs lend themselves better to celebration than cerebration. Certainly the so-called Royal Psalms, applauding the rule of God, had more popular success. First the *Venite*:

O come, let us sing unto the LORD:
let us make a joyful noise to the rock of our salvation. ...
For the LORD is a great God,
and a great King above all gods.
In his hand are the deep places of the earth:
the strength of the hills is his also.
The sea is his, and he made it:
and his hands formed the dry land.
O come, let us worship and bow down:
let us kneel before the LORD our maker.
For he is our God;
and we are the people of his pasture,
and the sheep of his hand.

96 Then came the suggestion ***O sing unto the LORD a new song***, which unfortunately turned into one that sounded old. At least it introduced a note of universal-

97 ism, though, calling on people everywhere to worship him. Not only people, but nature too: ***The LORD reigneth; let the earth rejoice*** – and, of course, rival deities:

98 ***worship him, all ye gods.*** All in all, it was quite a celebration. ***Let the floods clap***

99 ***their hands: let the hills be joyful together***. Let everyone take note, ***The LORD is great in Zion.***

100 To complete the cycle, there's the good old *Old Hundred*:

Make a joyful noise unto the LORD, all ye lands.
Serve the LORD with gladness:
come before his presence with singing.
Know ye that the LORD he is God:
it is he that hath made us, and not we ourselves;
we are his people, and the sheep of his pasture.
Enter into his gates with thanksgiving,

and into his courts with praise:
be thankful unto him, and bless his name.
For the LORD is good; his mercy is everlasting;
and his truth endureth to all generations.

That might have been a good note on which to finish, in my view. Leave them wanting more, though, wasn't a principle they recognised. And so someone got up and sang about his good intentions, with the optimistic promise that ***I will behave myself wisely in a perfect way***. The mournful continued to hold sway, however. ***Hear my prayer, O LORD, and let my cry come unto thee. Hide not thy face from me … For my days are consumed like smoke … I watch, and am as a sparrow alone upon the house top.*** Heartier souls offered reassurance. 101 102

He hath not dealt with us after our sins; 103
nor rewarded us according to our iniquities.
For as the heaven is high above the earth,
so great is his mercy toward them that fear him. …
he remembereth that we are dust.
As for man, his days are as grass:
as a flower of the field, so he flourisheth.
For the wind passeth over it, and it is gone;
and the place thereof shall know it no more.

It was in singing of the glories of creation that the poets could really take flight, extolling God 104

Who layeth the beams of his chambers in the waters:
who maketh the clouds his chariot:
who walketh upon the wings of the wind.

Not forgetting, of course, his role in providing

wine that maketh glad the heart of man,
and oil to make his face to shine,
and bread which strengtheneth man's heart.

And to give shade to the picnic

The trees of the LORD are full of sap;
the cedars of Lebanon, which he hath planted;
Where the birds make their nests.

Naturally it's not all fun.

He appointed the moon for seasons:
the sun knoweth his going down.
Thou makest darkness, and it is night:
wherein all the beasts of the forest do creep forth.
The young lions roar after their prey,
and seek their meat from God.
The sun ariseth, they gather themselves together,
and lay them down in their dens.
Man goeth forth unto his work
and to his labour until the evening.
O LORD, how manifold are thy works!
in wisdom hast thou made them all:
the earth is full of thy riches.
So is this great and wide sea,
wherein are things creeping innumerable,
both great and small beasts.
There go the ships: there is that leviathan,
whom thou hast made to play therein.
These wait all upon thee;
that thou mayest give them their meat in due season.

The bad news is that ***thou takest away their breath, they die, and return to dust.*** The good news is that there are always more where those came from. So blast the sinners, and ***Praise ye the LORD*** – or to use the Hebrew, Hallelujah.

105 Another ballad followed, recounting events from the original covenant with Abraham through the exodus from Egypt. When Joseph was sold into slavery he was set in chains, or as the singer put it, 'his soul entered into the iron'. This came to be translated – incorrectly, though more beautifully – as 'the iron entered into his soul'.

106 I sometimes suspect that the more extravagant the crimes people can claim, the more gratified they feel. ***Yea, they sacrificed their sons and their daughters unto devils ... and the land was polluted with blood. Thus were they defiled with their own works, and went a whoring with their own inventions.*** God exacted retribution – on the descendants, of course – but now has forgiven his people. Hallelujah.

BOOK V

107 ***O give thanks unto the LORD, for he is good: for his mercy endureth for ever*** – even if it is a little erratic at times. God looks after everyone from the traveller, those wandering in empty wastes, to the prisoner, ***Such as sit in darkness and in the shadow of death, being bound in affliction and iron; Because they rebelled against the words of God*** (or more likely the laws of the land, I imagine). He

excuses those who have sinned and been punished by illness, and protects

They that go down to the sea in ships,
that do business in great waters;
These see the works of the LORD,
and his wonders in the deep.
For he commandeth, and raiseth the stormy wind,
which lifteth up the waves thereof.
They mount up to the heaven,
they go down again to the depths:
their soul is melted because of trouble.
They reel to and fro, and stagger like a drunken man,
and are at their wit's end.
Then they cry unto the LORD in their trouble,
and he bringeth them out of their distresses.
He maketh the storm a calm,
so that the waves thereof are still.
Then are they glad because they be quiet;
so he bringeth them unto their desired haven.

After a reprise of that popular favourite, ***Moab is my washpot***, the audience would be in the mood for blood-curdling vindictiveness. The curses that rained down on the adversary, not to mention his poor family, were astounding: 108 109

Let his days be few; and let another take his office.
Let his children be fatherless, and his wife a widow.
Let his children be continually vagabonds, and beg:
Let them seek their bread also out of their desolate places.
Let the extortioner catch all that he hath;
and let the strangers spoil his labour.
Let there be none to extend mercy unto him:
neither let there be any to favour his fatherless children.
Let his posterity be cut off;
and in the generation following let their name be blotted out.

That's what I call settling matters. The writer claimed that he deserved this carnage as a favour from God,

For I am poor and needy, and my heart is wounded within me.
I am gone like the shadow when it declineth:
I am tossed up and down as the locust.

An unusual reason to play executioner, I must say.

110 God was, of course, willing to help his friends with some muscle. One singer reports him saying to the priest-king, ***Sit thou at my right hand, until I make thine enemies thy footstool.*** The king was vigorous – ***thou hast the dew of thy youth*** – and with God on his side there were no worries; ***he shall judge among the heathen, he shall fill the places with the dead bodies.*** What more could anyone ask?

111 The next several songs began with a Hallelujah. ***The fear of the LORD is the beginning of wisdom: a good understanding have all they that do his command-*** 112 ***ments.*** For the God-fearing man, piety pays: ***Wealth and riches shall be in his house.*** As for the wicked man, envy is his lot; ***he shall gnash with his teeth, and*** 113 ***melt away.*** If only things were so well arranged. Hallelujah, anyway; ***From the rising of the sun unto the going down of the same the LORD's name is to be*** 114 ***praised.*** There's always cause for celebration. The escape from slavery, for example:

When Israel went out of Egypt,
the house of Jacob from a people of strange language;
Judah was his sanctuary,
and Israel his dominion.
The sea saw it, and fled:
Jordan was driven back.
The mountains skipped like rams,
and the little hills like lambs.
What ailed thee, O thou sea, that thou fleddest?
thou Jordan, that thou wast driven back?
Ye mountains, that ye skipped like rams;
and ye little hills, like lambs?
Tremble, thou earth, at the presence of the Lord,
at the presence of the God of Jacob;
Which turned the rock into a standing water,
the flint into a fountain of waters.

115 None of this stops the heathen from posing the question ***Where is now their God? But our God is in the heavens***, and if others want a slanging match, so be it.

Their idols are silver and gold, the work of men's hands.
They have mouths, but they speak not:
eyes have they, but they see not:
They have ears, but they hear not:
noses have they, but they smell not:
They have hands, but they handle not:
feet have they, but they walk not.

So praise the LORD and pass up the opposition. And do it while you can, because ***The dead praise not the LORD, neither any that go down into silence.***

Too narrow a focus on God, however, appeared to make people impervious to paradox. 116

I said in my haste, All men are liars.
What shall I render unto the LORD for all his benefits toward me?
I will take the cup of salvation, and call upon the name of the LORD.
I will pay my vows unto the LORD now in the presence of all his people.
Precious in the sight of the LORD is the death of his saints.

Let me emphasise that there's no hurry to become precious.

At this point they would sing the shortest song of all. 117

O praise the LORD, all ye nations:
praise him, all ye people.
For his merciful kindness is great toward us:
and the truth of the LORD endureth for ever.
Praise ye the LORD.

Some of the others might have been better at this length.

The next song but one was the longest, and making the connection was an exultant completion of the Hallelujah set. It contained a little of everything – violence: ***All nations compassed me about: but in the name of the LORD will I destroy them***; praise: ***The LORD is my strength and song, and is become my salvation***; thanks: ***The LORD hath chastened me sore: but he hath not given me over unto death.*** It also included an intriguing metaphor to encourage the unfortunate: 118

The stone which the builders refused is become the head stone of the corner.
This is the LORD's doing; it is marvellous in our eyes.
This is the day which the LORD hath made;
we will rejoice and be glad in it. ...
Blessed be he that cometh in the name of the LORD.

The longest song was another alphabet game in which each of the 22 stanzas was identified by a Hebrew letter, that letter being used to start each of the eight lines in the stanza. The content of the poem was just as obsessive as its form: the delight in keeping God's commandments. The author went so far as to proclaim ***It is good for me that I have been afflicted; that I might learn thy statutes.*** He wasn't a gloomy masochist, though, even if he was a bit touched. ***O how love I thy law! it is my meditation all the day.*** Having a rule for everything made him feel secure. ***Thy word is a lamp unto my feet, and a light unto my path.*** But to finish with a 119 confession, ***I have gone astray like a lost sheep; seek thy servant; for I do not forget thy commandments.*** That much was certainly clear.

120 The next 15 songs on the play-list were known as the songs of ascent, the ascent being that of pilgrims as they approached Jerusalem for the great annual festivals. The first is one more for the persecution-of-the-self-righteous collection: ***I am for***
121 ***peace: but when I speak, they are for war.*** The second, however, expressed the comfort of faith.

I will lift up mine eyes unto the hills,
from whence cometh my help.
My help cometh from the LORD,
which made heaven and earth.
He will not suffer thy foot to be moved:
he that keepeth thee will not slumber.
Behold, he that keepeth Israel
shall neither slumber nor sleep.
The LORD is thy keeper:
The LORD is thy shade upon thy right hand.
The sun shall not smite thee by day,
nor the moon by night.
The LORD shall preserve thee from all evil:
he shall preserve thy soul.
The LORD shall preserve thy going out and thy coming in
from this time forth, and even for evermore.

122 The pilgrims' songs were for the most part simple and to the point. ***I was glad when they said unto me, Let us go into the house of the LORD.*** Having reached the city, ***Pray for the peace of Jerusalem: they shall prosper that love thee. Peace***
123 ***be within thy walls, and prosperity within thy palaces.*** After a few more grumbles about bad treatment at the hands of the rich and powerful, they acknowledged that
124 ***If it had not been the LORD who was on our side ... Then the proud waters had***
125 ***gone over our soul.*** Still, if it's not too much to ask, ***Do good, O LORD, unto those that be good.***

126 Their thanks at being brought back to the promised land were heartfelt. ***Then was our mouth filled with laughter, and our tongue with singing ... The LORD hath done great things for us.*** With God's help ***they that sow in tears shall reap in joy. He that goeth forth and weepeth, bearing precious seed, shall doubtless come again with rejoicing, bringing his sheaves with him.***

127 In the view of the singers, God's protection was more than just desirable: it was essential.

Except the LORD build the house, they labour in vain that build it:
except the LORD keep the city, the watchman waketh but in vain.

They came out with the cryptic comment that

It is vain for you to rise up early, to sit up late, to eat the bread of sorrows: for so he giveth his beloved sleep.

It sounds like a recommendation to stay in bed all day. Thinking of which,

Lo, children are an heritage of the LORD:
and the fruit of the womb is his reward.
As arrows are in the hand of a mighty man;
so are children of the youth.
Happy is the man that hath his quiver full of them.

It amused me that while the man may be like an archer, his family is more nearly vegetable: ***Thy wife shall be as a fruitful vine by the sides of thine house: thy children like olive plants round about thy table.*** The action of enemies was also expressed in agricultural terms: ***The plowers plowed upon my back: they made long their furrows.*** Any such problem, of course, was put to God. ***Out of the depths have I cried unto thee, O LORD. ... My soul waiteth for the Lord more than they that watch for the morning.*** Even in the absence of trouble people looked for approval; ***Surely I have behaved and quieted myself, as a child that is weaned of his mother.*** 128 129 130 131

The pilgrims recalled the devotion of David, how he swore 132

I will not give sleep to mine eyes,
or slumber to mine eyelids,
Until I find out a place for the LORD,
an habitation for the mighty God of Jacob.

The temple, when it was built, served – briefly – to bring all the people together. ***Behold, how good and how pleasant it is for brethren to dwell together in unity!*** The last of the set rounded out the observance: ***Lift up your hands in the sanctuary, and bless the LORD.*** 133 134

Naturally there was a good deal more praise to come, along the lines of ***I know that the LORD is great, and that our Lord is above all gods.*** While it makes sense to ***give thanks unto the God of gods: for his mercy endureth for ever***, reciting all his works with the same refrain produced some odd effects; he ***smote Egypt in their firstborn: for his mercy endureth for ever***, or again he ***slew famous kings: for his mercy endureth for ever***. Mercy killings, I called them. 135 136

For me the next song was always the climax of the show, sorrow turning to anger, poignant with a vindictive twist: 137

By the rivers of Babylon, there we sat down, yea, we wept,
when we remembered Zion.
We hanged our harps upon the willows
in the midst thereof.
For there they that carried us away captive
required of us a song;
and they that wasted us required of us mirth, saying,
Sing us one of the songs of Zion.
How shall we sing the LORD's song
in a strange land?
If I forget thee, O Jerusalem,
let my right hand forget her cunning.
If I do not remember thee,
let my tongue cleave to the roof of my mouth;
if I prefer not Jerusalem
above my chief joy.
Remember, O LORD, the children of Edom
in the day of Jerusalem;
who said, Rase it, rase it,
even to the foundation thereof.
O daughter of Babylon, who art to be destroyed;
happy shall he be,
that rewardeth thee as thou hast served us.
Happy shall he be,
that taketh and dasheth thy little ones against the stones.

When it came to revenge, they didn't hold themselves back.

138 While promising that ***before the gods will I sing praise unto thee***, the singer entreated God to ***forsake not the works of thine own hands***. This led to something 139 more sophisticated altogether: the full-blown conception of God as all-knowing, everywhere present.

O LORD, thou hast searched me, and known me.
Thou knowest my downsitting and mine uprising,
thou understandest my thought afar off.
Thou compassest my path and my lying down,
and art acquainted with all my ways.
For there is not a word in my tongue,
but lo, O LORD, thou knowest it altogether.
Thou hast beset me behind and before,
and laid thine hand upon me.
Such knowledge is too wonderful for me;
it is high, I cannot attain unto it.

Whither shall I go from thy spirit?
or whither shall I flee from thy presence?
If I ascend up into heaven, thou art there:
if I make my bed in hell, behold, thou art there.
If I take the wings of the morning,
and dwell in the uttermost parts of the sea;
Even there shall thy hand lead me,
and thy right hand shall hold me.
If I say, Surely the darkness shall cover me;
even the night shall be light about me.
Yea, the darkness hideth not from thee;
but the night shineth as the day:
the darkness and the light are both alike to thee.

As God is reponsible for what happens in the womb, ***I will praise thee; for I am fearfully and wonderfully made.*** We aim to please. But by the same token, his agitation at the thought of those ***bloody men***, God's enemies, seemed unnecessary to me; an omnipresent God can look after himself.

140 I was enchanted by how oblivious to irony some of them appeared. To say of evil men that ***They have sharpened their tongues like a serpent*** is perhaps only slightly sharp-tongued, but to pray ***preserve me from the violent man***, and then demand ***Let burning coals fall upon them: let them be cast into the fire; into deep pits, that they rise not up again***, reveals an enviable lack of self-consciousness.

141 Though rarely showing an ascetic temperament, they occasionally offered a masochistic response to temptation. Thus one asks to be kept from sinners, ***and let me not eat of their dainties. Let the righteous smite me; it shall be a kindness.*** No doubt. Otherwise it was the usual cycle of complaint and recrimination, with only an occasional reference to self-improvement, such as ***Teach me to do thy will; for thou art my God.*** Unless, that is, you count exclamations such as ***Blessed be the LORD my strength, which teacheth my hands to war, and my fingers to fight.*** Life is just a breath of air, soon dispersed; and man, ***his days are as a shadow that passeth away.*** 142 143 144

145 The last set of songs contained – what else? – praise. First came an acrostic, arguably the most successful of these alphabet poems.

Thou openest thine hand,
and satisfiest the desire of every living thing.
The LORD is righteous in all his ways,
and holy in all his works.
The LORD is nigh unto all them that call upon him,
to all that call upon him in truth.

Next, human and divine support were contrasted. 146

Put not your trust in princes,
nor in the son of man, in whom there is no help.
His breath goeth forth, he returneth to his earth;
in that very day his thoughts perish.

147 Needless to say God is much more impressive. ***He telleth the number of the stars; he calleth them all by their names.*** When it came to cosmology, though,
148 they weren't very reliable. ***Praise him, ye heavens of heavens, and ye waters that be above the heavens.*** According to them, rain was the result of a leaky roof.
149 The penultimate psalm conjured up images of a pyjama-clad warrior lopping off heads in his bedroom.

Let the saints be joyful in glory:
let them sing aloud upon their beds.
Let the high praises of God be in their mouth,
and a twoedged sword in their hand;
To execute vengeance upon the heathen,
and punishments upon the people.

150 So then to the last hurrah, the final Hallelujah.

Praise ye the LORD.
Praise God in his sanctuary:
praise him in the firmament of his power.
Praise him for his mighty acts:
praise him according to his excellent greatness.
Praise him with the sound of the trumpet:
praise him with the psaltery and harp.
Praise him with the timbrel and dance:
praise him with stringed instruments and organs.
Praise him upon the loud cymbals:
praise him upon the high sounding cymbals.
Let every thing that hath breath praise the LORD.
Praise ye the LORD.

Which, having heard them all, I'd gladly echo. Hallelujah!

20

Proverbs

The people didn't just compile a songbook. They kept a suggestion book on God's behalf, and anyone who thought of good advice offered it for inclusion. There were a lot of sensible ideas, I thought; God would have done well to let them write his speeches.

Of course pithy sayings are like pills: healthy in small doses, fatal in large ones. 1 Wisdom isn't about proverbs any more than morality is about rules. The point of the whole exercise is ***To give subtilty to the simple, to the young man knowledge and discretion*** – and it doesn't just apply to the simple, the young and the male, either.

It's not exactly enlightening to say ***My son, if sinners entice thee, consent thou not***; the lad has to recognise that he's being seduced. Once he sees the trap he can avoid it, for ***Surely in vain the net is spread in the sight of any bird.*** I still notice a lot of birds walking straight into it, though.

Someone claimed that ***Wisdom crieth without; she uttereth her voice in the streets***, haranguing and threatening the foolish. If Wisdom were that vocal, people wouldn't find her so easy to ignore. For most of them, in fact, being wise meant 2 being dull. No doubt ***Discretion shall preserve thee***, but when the purpose is ***To deliver thee from the strange woman ... Which forsaketh the guide of her youth***, it's likely to come second best.

They were right that those ***whom the LORD loveth he correcteth***, but I suspect 3 that some of them hoped that more punishment implied more love. Wisdom offers a refuge: ***Length of days is in her right hand; and in her left hand riches and honour. Her ways are ways of pleasantness, and all her paths are peace.*** (Not even paradoxes were a threat, hence ***Be not afraid of sudden fear.***)

All in all, she appeared to be the ideal partner. ***Forsake her not, and she shall*** 4 ***preserve thee: love her, and she shall keep thee. Wisdom is the principal thing; therefore get wisdom: and with all thy getting get understanding.***

Following the ways of the wicked will make you lose sleep (with any luck, the sinner might say), ***But the path of the just is as the shining light, that shineth more and more unto the perfect day.*** So be good, and ***Keep thy heart with all diligence; for out of it are the issues of life.***

This was all too soggy for some tastes, and the moralising became more 5 muscular. 'Bad' women came in for some heavy fire: ***For the lips of a strange woman drop as an honeycomb, and her mouth is smoother than oil; But her end is bitter as wormwood, sharp as a twoedged sword. Her feet go down to death;***

her steps take hold on hell. I wonder why lust is blamed on its object.

6 The lazy person was also scourged, though it seemed to me that the lash tickled rather than stung – the unfavourable comparison to an ant notwithstanding.

Go to the ant, thou sluggard;
consider her ways, and be wise:
Which having no guide, overseer, or ruler,
Provideth her meat in the summer,
and gathereth her food in the harvest.
How long wilt thou sleep, O sluggard?
when wilt thou arise out of thy sleep?
Yet a little sleep, a little slumber,
a little folding of the hands to sleep:
So shall thy poverty come as one that travelleth,
and thy want as an armed man.

This was a mere aside, however, a pause for breath before the next tirade against ***the evil woman***:

Lust not after her beauty in thine heart;
neither let her take thee with her eyelids.
For by means of a whorish woman a man is brought to a piece of bread:
and the adulteress will hunt for the precious life.
Can a man take fire in his bosom,
and his clothes not be burned?
Can one go upon hot coals,
and his feet not be burned?
So he that goeth in to his neighbour's wife;
whosoever toucheth her shall not be innocent.

If these slurs on the woman's character don't put you off, you might bear in mind the possible reaction of her husband, ***For jealousy is the rage of a man: therefore he will not spare in the day of vengeance.***

7 Just to illustrate what the defenceless chaps were up against, someone offered a seduction fantasy, a shameless married woman saying

I have perfumed my bed with myrrh, aloes, and cinnamon.
Come, let us take our fill of love until the morning:
let us solace ourselves with loves.
For the goodman is not at home,
he is gone a long journey:
He hath taken a bag of money with him,
and will come home at the day appointed.

With her much fair speech she caused him to yield,
with the flattering of her lips she forced him.
He goeth after her straightway,
as an ox goeth to the slaughter.

At least he had a better time than the ox.

God's would-be advisers got back on track by declaring that ***wisdom is better*** 8 ***than rubies***. Perhaps that was because of her approach; ***I love them that love me; and those that seek me early shall find me.*** She was easy. The more mysterious claim was that ***Wisdom hath builded her house, she hath hewn out her seven*** 9 ***pillars***. We never did find out what those seven pillars were.

The wise are great self-improvers; ***Reprove not a scorner, lest he hate thee: rebuke a wise man, and he will love thee.*** Still, it's not how I'd suggest winning friends. Deeper insight came from the voice of folly pointing out that ***Stolen waters are sweet, and bread eaten in secret is pleasant***. Sin can be its own reward.

THE SAYINGS

Having examined wisdom, people were anxious to try to create it. They scattered 10 their putative pearls – some obvious, some dubious – in all directions.

As an example of the banal truism, there was ***A wise son maketh a glad father: but a foolish son is the heaviness of his mother.*** And of his father too, presumably. By contrast, Job might have raised an eyebrow at the suggestion that ***Blessings are upon the head of the just: but violence covereth the mouth of the wicked. The memory of the just is blessed: but the name of the wicked shall rot.*** I find history tends to ignore our moral judgments.

With platitudes we're on safer ground. ***Hatred stirreth up strifes: but love covereth all sins.*** Some seemed so evident, I thought they must be deep. ***The rich man's wealth is his strong city: the destruction of the poor is their poverty.*** Well, yes; the advantage of the rich is that they have more money. Or perhaps the idea is that money makes morality easier?

One piece of good advice is to get good advice. ***Where no counsel is, the people*** 11 ***fall: but in the multitude of counsellors there is safety.*** And as any financial adviser will tell you, ***He that is surety for a stranger shall smart for it.*** Never mind the stranger: even he that is surety for his children may live to regret it.

There was a quick encore for that favourite target, the wanton woman. ***As a jewel of gold in a swine's snout, so is a fair woman which is without discretion.*** Whose snout, I wonder, would a woman with discretion decorate? You shouldn't take your treasures for granted. ***He that trusteth in his riches shall fall: but the righteous shall flourish as a branch. He that troubleth his own house shall inherit the wind.***

Even a respectably married woman had a hard time of it, being either an 12 ornament or an ailment. ***A virtuous woman is a crown to her husband: but she that maketh ashamed is as rottenness in his bones.*** The overtones of ownership were uncomfortably strong, I thought. If you're going to be property, at least get character references; ***A righteous man regardeth the life of his beast: but the tender mercies of the wicked are cruel.***

The excursions into popular psychology were often quite successful. ***The way of a fool is right in his own eyes: but he that hearkeneth unto counsel is wise.*** So

13 get advice, even if you don't think you need it. Another insight was that ***Hope deferred maketh the heart sick: but when the desire cometh, it is a tree of life.*** In other cases the adages derived from wishful thinking, as with ***the way of transgressors is hard***, or even in saying ***The desire accomplished is sweet to the soul*** – it's sweet and sour, by my observation.

Generally the no-nonsense school had the upper hand. ***He that spareth his rod hateth his son: but he that loveth him chasteneth him betimes.*** Out of caning

14 distance, their stern demeanour was hard to take seriously. Of course they retorted that ***Fools make a mock at sin***, and they weren't amused if you promised to be serious about your sinning. The curse of the puritanical is to be sour, lonely, and depressed. ***The heart knoweth his own bitterness; and a stranger doth not intermeddle with his joy.*** No emotion of theirs was simple, or light. ***Even in laughter the heart is sorrowful; and the end of that mirth is heaviness.*** That was how I felt listening to them.

The simple believeth every word: but the prudent man looketh well to his going. They weren't really advocating open-mindedness; dour pragmatism was more like it. ***In all labour there is profit: but the talk of the lips tendeth only to penury.*** Self-expression had to be kept in check, because ***Righteousness exalteth a nation: but sin is a reproach to any people.***

15 Fortunately not everyone was so dreary. Some were gentle and good natured and knew a bit about diplomacy. ***A soft answer turneth away wrath: but grievous words stir up anger.*** They also knew about life, and the importance of happiness. ***A merry heart maketh a cheerful countenance: but by sorrow of the heart the spirit is broken.*** Remember what matters: ***he that is of a merry heart hath a continual feast. Better is little with the fear of the LORD than great treasure and trouble therewith. Better is a dinner of herbs where love is, than a stalled ox and hatred therewith.***

They had a string of aphorisms to promote diplomacy. ***A wrathful man stirreth up strife: but he that is slow to anger appeaseth strife.*** And more generally, ***a word spoken in due season, how good is it!*** I was amazed to hear someone declare that ***before honour is humility.*** Was self-righteousness on the way out?

16 ***The LORD hath made all things for himself: yea, even the wicked for the day of evil.*** God may be responsible for everything, but I don't think it's flattering to point it out. Similarly, I wasn't sure what to make of the statement that ***A man's heart deviseth his way: but the LORD directeth his steps.*** I thought it was the other way around. And what about the view that the king doesn't make mistakes? ***A***

divine sentence is in the lips of the king: his mouth transgresseth not in judgment.

Royals would do better to remember that ***Pride goeth before destruction, and an haughty spirit before a fall.*** Position is no substitute for age and wisdom. ***The hoary head is a crown of glory, if it be found in the way of righteousness. He that is slow to anger is better than the mighty; and he that ruleth his spirit than he that taketh a city.*** A touch of democratic morality, there. [17] ***Whoso mocketh the poor reproacheth his Maker: and he that is glad at calamities shall not be unpunished.***

Wisdom, or the lack of it, is revealed in personal relationships; ***he that repeateth a matter separateth very friends.*** Making the step from indiscretion to malice, ***Whoso rewardeth evil for good, evil shall not depart from his house*** – the evil already lives there, I'd say. ***A friend loveth at all times, and a brother is born for adversity.*** Sticking together through thick and thin, they should try to keep themselves cheerful. ***A merry heart doeth good like a medicine: but a broken spirit drieth the bones.***

The wise know when to be quiet. ***He that hath knowledge spareth his words: and a man of understanding is of an excellent spirit. Even a fool, when he holdeth his peace, is counted wise: and he that shutteth his lips is esteemed a man of understanding.*** To put it even more bluntly, [18] ***A fool's mouth is his destruction, and his lips are the snare of his soul.*** By the closed-mouth standard, wise people have generally been thin on the ground.

The spirit of a man will sustain his infirmity; but a wounded spirit who can bear? Damage to the family is also best avoided; ***A brother offended is harder to be won than a strong city: and their contentions are like the bars of a castle.*** But don't be afraid to leave the nest: ***Whoso findeth a wife findeth a good thing.*** A better thing than deserved, more often than not.

Widening the circle yet further, ***A man that hath friends must shew himself friendly: and there is a friend that sticketh closer than a brother.*** Someone was sufficiently cynical to note that [19] ***Wealth maketh many friends; but the poor is separated from his neighbour.*** Returning to the family, no prizes for guessing the sex of the person who declared that ***A foolish son is the calamity of his father: and the contentions of a wife are a continual dropping.*** The other side wasn't recorded.

He that hath pity upon the poor lendeth unto the LORD; and that which he hath given will he pay him again – just don't expect it to be in cash. Sobriety and self-control were also recommended. [20] ***Wine is a mocker, strong drink is raging: and whosoever is deceived thereby is not wise. ... It is an honour for a man to cease from strife: but every fool will be meddling.*** Be it meddling or not, though, ***Even a child is known by his doings, whether his work be pure, and whether it be right. The hearing ear, and the seeing eye, the LORD hath made even both of them.***

The homespun psychologists had an amusing commentary on bargaining. ***It is naught, it is naught, saith the buyer: but when he is gone his way, then he***

boasteth. Vendors, of course, are likely to tell fibs of their own – but they shouldn't get carried away. ***Bread of deceit is sweet to a man; but afterwards his mouth shall be filled with gravel.*** Gossip, too, is thoroughly unpleasant. ***He that goeth about as a tale-bearer revealeth secrets: therefore meddle not with him that flattereth with his lips.***

After the avuncular counsellors came the cynical floggers. ***The blueness of a wound cleanseth away evil: so do stripes the inward parts of the belly.*** Not soft words, but bribery, was their method of turning away wrath: ***A gift in secret pacifieth anger: and a reward in the bosom strong wrath.***

21

The misogynists weren't far behind. ***It is better to dwell in a corner of the housetop, than with a brawling woman in a wide house***, or less humorously, ***It is better to dwell in the wilderness, than with a contentious and an angry woman.*** Proverbs about violent menfolk were conspicuously absent.

22

A good name is rather to be chosen than great riches, assuming we are talking about character and not just reputation, that is actual as opposed to sham virtue. The procedure suggested was to ***Train up a child in the way he should go: and when he is old, he will not depart from it.*** I've seen a few parents who might report exceptions.

By contrast, it seems generally true that ***The rich ruleth over the poor, and the borrower is servant to the lender.*** Don't imagine that any revolutionary conclusions are going to follow, however. On the contrary, their sentiments were decidedly old-school. ***The mouth of strange women is a deep pit: he that is abhorred of the LORD shall fall therein. Foolishness is bound in the heart of a child; but the rod of correction shall drive it far from him.***

SPECIAL COLLECTIONS

A portion of ancient Egyptian wisdom literature, inserted into our own, was more broad-minded. It began:

Bow down thine ear, and hear the words of the wise,
and apply thine heart unto my knowledge.
For it is a pleasant thing if thou keep them within thee;
they shall withal be fitted in thy lips.
That thy trust may be in the LORD,
I have made known to thee this day, even to thee.
Have not I written to thee excellent things in counsels and knowledge,
That I might make thee know the certainty of the words of truth;
that thou mightest answer the words of truth to them that send unto thee?

The first few pieces of advice were prosaic, along the lines of ***Remove not the ancient landmark, which thy fathers have set. Seest thou a man diligent in his***

business? He shall stand before kings. But there followed a discussion of how to behave in strange company, featuring high anxiety at the dinner table: 23

When thou sittest to eat with a ruler,
consider diligently what is before thee:
And put a knife to thy throat,
if thou be a man given to appetite.
Be not desirous of his dainties:
for they are deceitful meat
Labour not to be rich:
cease from thine own wisdom.
Wilt thou set thine eyes upon that which is not?
for riches certainly make themselves wings;
they fly away as an eagle toward heaven.
Eat thou not the bread of him that hath an evil eye,
neither desire thou his dainty meats:
For as he thinketh in his heart, so is he:
Eat and drink, saith he to thee;
but his heart is not with thee.
The morsel which thou hast eaten shalt thou vomit up,
and lose thy sweet words.

Our people were also concerned about feasting. ***Be not among winebibbers; among riotous eaters of flesh: For the drunkard and the glutton shall come to poverty: and drowsiness shall clothe a man with rags.*** Anyone at such colourful extremes probably wasn't listening. It's the sort of thing parents would say, though, and you should ***Hearken unto thy father that begat thee, and despise not thy mother when she is old.*** Despise younger women instead. ***A whore is a deep ditch; and a strange woman is a narrow pit.*** Not what I would call delicate phraseology.

Of course if you get carried away, you can always blame the drink. ***Look not thou upon the wine when it is red, when it giveth his colour in the cup, when it moveth itself aright. At the last it biteth like a serpent, and stingeth like an adder. Thine eyes shall behold strange women, and thine heart shall utter perverse things.*** That's quite an advertisement.

24 ***A wise man is strong; yea, a man of knowledge increaseth strength.*** Keep in mind, though, that ***If thou faint in the day of adversity, thy strength is small.*** The wise are tough under pressure.

Rejoice not when thine enemy falleth, and let not thine heart be glad when he stumbleth. That didn't sound like the people I knew. Good judgment had its rewards, at least if you were suitably inclined; ***Every man shall kiss his lips that giveth a right answer.*** Honest dealing in general was encouraged. ***Say not, I will do so to him as he hath done to me: I will render to the man according to his work.*** Morality was bursting out all over.

25 Everyone liked to imagine that Solomon's hand could be detected in the suggestion book, and a further list of maxims was attributed to him. Fittingly enough, they include the claim that ***the heart of kings is unsearchable.*** Being both wisest and richest, he might well have said that ***A word fitly spoken is like apples of gold in pictures of silver.***

After that you have to speculate. ***Whoso boasteth himself of a false gift is like clouds and wind without rain***; was he rankled when a promised present didn't arrive? ***Withdraw thy foot from thy neighbour's house; lest he be weary of thee, and so hate thee***; perhaps his guests out-stayed their welcome.

Certainly there was some of that ingenious psychology for which Solomon was famous. ***If thine enemy be hungry, give him bread to eat; and if he be thirsty, give him water to drink: For thou shalt heap coals of fire upon his head, and the LORD shall reward thee.*** Getting the benefit both of humiliating and being merciful to the enemy is quite an achievement.

As cold waters to a thirsty soul, so is good news from a far country. Or any news at all, those living away from home might say. As a contrasting food metaphor, ***It is not good to eat much honey: so for men to search their own glory is not glory.***

26 He was ambivalent about how to deal with foolishness. ***Answer not a fool according to his folly, lest thou also be like unto him. Answer a fool according to his folly, lest he be wise in his own conceit.*** Foolishness was seen as a kind of addictive state. ***As a dog returneth to his vomit, so a fool returneth to his folly. Seest thou a man wise in his conceit? there is more hope of a fool than of him. The slothful man saith, There is a lion in the way; a lion is in the streets.*** It might be a novel excuse for missing work.

The sluggard is wiser in his own conceit than seven men that can render a reason. Weakness and wickedness rebound against the culpable person, however. ***Whoso diggeth a pit shall fall therein: and he that rolleth a stone, it will return upon him.***

27 Lack of candour is unwise, if only because it can lead to embarrassment. ***Boast not thyself of to morrow; for thou knowest not what a day may bring forth. Let another man praise thee, and not thine own mouth; a stranger, and not thine own lips.*** Frankness with other people is likewise essential, at least if you believe that ***Open rebuke is better than secret love. Faithful are the wounds of a friend; but the kisses of an enemy are deceitful. The full soul loatheth an honeycomb; but to the hungry soul every bitter thing is sweet.*** That proverb isn't about honesty, but I wanted to be open about the lack of organisation.

More persuasive than this straight-talking approach to personal relations is the maxim ***better is a neighbour that is near than a brother far off.*** You have to take care to act neighbourly, though, and keep the noise down. ***He that blesseth his friend with a loud voice, rising early in the morning, it shall be counted a curse to him. A continual dropping in a very rainy day and a contentious woman are alike.*** Better dripping water than a rasping file, I suppose. ***Iron sharpeneth iron;***

so a man sharpeneth the countenance of his friend.

Despite their pragmatic leanings, they weren't oblivious to the inner self. The guilty conscience, for example, could make it figuratively true that ***The wicked flee when no man pursueth: but the righteous are bold as a lion.*** And I imagine that spiritual impoverishment might explain why ***he that maketh haste to be rich shall not be innocent.*** The individual is so unreliable on the question of priorities in general, they believed, that ***He that trusteth in his own heart is a fool.*** 28

However dependent on authority their morality might have been, there's no denying the social cohesion they achieved. ***He that giveth unto the poor shall not lack: but he that hideth his eyes shall have many a curse.*** It enforced conformity as well as solidarity, of course, using such slogans as ***he that keepeth company with harlots spendeth his substance.***

I also admired their self-restraint and sense of collective responsibility. ***A fool uttereth all his mind: but a wise man keepeth it in till afterwards. If a ruler hearken to lies, all his servants are wicked.*** That does seem to me to go too far, however, given the lack of control people generally have over their rulers. 29

Nor am I convinced that ***The rod and reproof give wisdom: but a child left to himself bringeth his mother to shame.*** The more idealistic view was that ***Where there is no vision, the people perish.*** You have to distinguish the visionary from the autocrat, however, because ***A man's pride shall bring him low: but honour shall uphold the humble in spirit.***

The next collection of sayings, contributed by a sage named Agur, represented the wisdom of the East. It seemed appropriate that it should be launched with a paradox: ***Every word of God is pure ... Add thou not unto his words, lest he reprove thee, and thou be found a liar.*** 30

As the rich feel no need of God, while the poor tend to disgrace him by stealing, the request was to ***give me neither poverty nor riches; feed me with food convenient for me.*** Likewise the command ***Accuse not a servant unto his master*** seemed to be purely prudential, for the servant might find a way of getting his own back.

Augur offered both cryptic comments suitable for use in meditation – for example ***The horseleach hath two daughters, crying Give, give*** – and a whole set of gnomic observations.

There are three things that are never satisfied, yea,
four things say not, It is enough:
The grave; and the barren womb;
the earth that is not filled with water;
and the fire that saith not, It is enough.

Apparently he meant that a woman's desire, not infertility, is never satisfied, along with death, parched ground and fire.

After remarking in a brief aside that disrespectful children will have their eyes plucked out and eaten by birds, he went on:

There be three things which are too wonderful for me, yea,
four which I know not:
The way of an eagle in the air;
the way of a serpent upon a rock;
the way of a ship in the midst of the sea;
and the way of a man with a maid.

I could understand that he wouldn't know how to fly, float, or slither, but what didn't he know about men and women? Perhaps I should reflect on another of his intriguing comments: ***Such is the way of an adulterous woman; she eateth, and wipeth her mouth, and saith, I have done no wickedness.***

31 Another foreigner, king Lemuel, added what ***his mother taught him*** (reprovingly, I gathered):

Give not thy strength unto women,
nor thy ways to that which destroyeth kings.
It is not for kings, O Lemuel, it is not for kings to drink wine;
nor for princes strong drink:
Lest they drink, and forget the law,
and pervert the judgment of any of the afflicted.
Give strong drink unto him that is ready to perish,
and wine unto those that be of heavy hearts.
Let him drink, and forget his poverty,
and remember his misery no more.

The final contribution was a poem about the perfect wife.

Who can find a virtuous woman?
for her price is far above rubies.
The heart of her husband doth safely trust in her.

She works hard to feed her family, even buying and planting a vineyard. She is generous and always prepared.

Her husband is known in the gates,
when he sitteth among the elders of the land.
She maketh fine linen, and selleth it;
and delivereth girdles unto the merchant.
Strength and honour are her clothing;
and she shall rejoice in time to come.
She openeth her mouth with wisdom;

and in her tongue is the law of kindness.
She looketh well to the ways of her household,
and eateth not the bread of idleness.
Her children arise up, and call her blessed;
her husband also, and he praiseth her.
Many daughters have done virtuously,
but thou excellest them all.
Favour is deceitful, and beauty is vain:
but a woman that feareth the LORD, she shall be praised.
Give her of the fruit of her hands;
and let her own works praise her in the gates.

21

Ecclesiastes

In amongst the rest of the wisdom literature was a scorching critique of the be-good-be-glad-be-godly school. It reflects well on the people that it survived, without being tampered with too much.

1 The critic was called, appropriately, the Preacher. Sometimes he pretended to be Solomon, but his wisdom didn't need a big-name label. His main theme was the emptiness of life.

Vanity of vanities, saith the Preacher, vanity of vanities; all is vanity. What profit hath a man of all his labour which he taketh under the sun? One generation passeth away, and another generation cometh: but the earth abideth for ever. The sun also ariseth, and the sun goeth down, and hasteth to his place where he arose.

If life has any meaning, it's well disguised. The years go by in an unending cycle. ***All the rivers run into the sea; yet the sea is not full.*** There's never any result: ***the eye is not satisfied with seeing, nor the ear filled with hearing.*** Everyone is condemned to live out one more empty existence, ***and there is no new thing under the sun.***

Don't imagine that the memory of those who follow will provide you with immortality; it won't. ***There is no remembrance of former things; neither shall there be any remembrance of things that are to come with those that shall come after.*** As for the here and now, ***I have seen all the works that are done under the sun; and, behold, all is vanity and vexation of spirit. That which is crooked cannot be made straight: and that which is wanting cannot be numbered.*** As if to prove the point about the shallowness of history, the Preacher and pretend-Solomon referred to all who came before him on the throne in Jerusalem – apparently forgetting that there had only been David.

His great knowledge and understanding were insubstantial, perhaps worse than useless, ***For in much wisdom is much grief; and he that increaseth knowledge increaseth sorrow.*** It's no wonder that people prefer ignorance.

2 Experience taught an unhappy lesson. He had pursued pleasure – wine, women, and song – with great success. When he looked at what he had achieved, however, it was all empty. Satisfying your desires can be worse than having them.

Perhaps ***wisdom excelleth folly, as far as light excelleth darkness,*** but that didn't change the fact that both the wise and the foolish were heading for the same end: ***one event happeneth to them all.*** There's nothing to look forward to except death. ***And how dieth the wise man? as the fool.*** Not only that, but the achievements of the wise are quite likely to be inherited by the foolish. The only recourse is to live for the day, being properly grateful to God.

To every thing there is a season, and a time to every purpose under the heaven: 3
A time to be born, and a time to die;
a time to plant, and a time to pluck up that which is planted;
A time to kill, and a time to heal;
a time to break down, and a time to build up;
A time to weep, and a time to laugh;
a time to mourn, and a time to dance;
A time to cast away stones, and a time to gather stones together;
a time to embrace, and a time to refrain from embracing;
A time to get, and a time to lose;
a time to keep, and a time to cast away;
A time to rend, and a time to sew;
a time to keep silence, and a time to speak;
A time to love, and a time to hate;
a time of war, and a time of peace.

With things being so transitory, it's hard to distinguish people from animals; ***as the one dieth, so dieth the other; yea, they have all one breath; so that a man hath no preeminence above a beast.*** Both will vanish into dust.

The Preacher remarked that he had seen the oppression of the powerless, ***Wherefore I praised the dead which are already dead more than the living which are yet alive. Yea, better is he than both they, which hath not yet been, who hath not seen the evil work that is done under the sun.*** I think he couldn't quite decide whether existence was meaningless or just atrocious. 4

He offered a number of proverbs, presumably to help people making the best of a bad job. Competitiveness is vain and unattractive; ***Better is an handful with quietness, than both the hands full with travail and vexation of spirit.*** Because the solitary pursuit of prosperity is pointless, we should remember that ***Two are better than one,*** or for that matter that ***a threefold cord is not quickly broken.*** Maybe not, but it can come unravelled.

Clearly he hadn't given up on wisdom altogether. ***Better is a poor and a wise child than an old and foolish king, who will no more be admonished.*** Perhaps the child knows how to be seen and not heard: something more adults should master, ***for God is in heaven, and thou upon earth; therefore let thy words be few.*** Try not to bore him. 5

Be careful, in particular, not to make promises you can't keep. ***Better is it that thou shouldest not vow, than that thou shouldest vow and not pay. Suffer not thy mouth to cause thy flesh to sin; neither say thou before the angel, that it was an error:*** I might be sympathetic, but don't expect God to be.

Some people confuse ends and means, pursuing wealth they don't need. ***He that***

loveth silver shall not be satisfied with silver; nor he that loveth abundance with increase. It's not uncommon to find that ***The sleep of a labouring man is sweet, whether he eat little or much: but the abundance of the rich will not suffer him to sleep.*** Such self-torment seems pointless when you consider that ***As he came forth of his mother's womb, naked shall he return to go as he came, and shall take nothing of his labour, which he may carry away in his hand.*** Better to enjoy the moment.

6 Unless you enjoy life, you're worse off than a stillborn babe. What's the point in struggling to be wise or wealthy? ***For who knoweth what is good for man in this life, all the days of his vain life which he spendeth as a shadow?*** I wish I had an easy answer, but I don't.

WORLDLY WISDOM

7 On the whole, the most fortunate are those who have put it all behind them – ideally with their reputations intact. ***A good name is better than precious ointment; and the day of death than the day of one's birth. It is better to go to the house of mourning, than to go to the house of feasting***. Well, let's not get carried away here. I know that ***as the crackling of thorns under a pot, so is the laughter of the fool***, but you have to keep things in perspective.

Better is the end of a thing than the beginning thereof, and don't be nostalgic; ***Say not thou, What is the cause that the former days were better than these?*** Take things as they come. ***In the day of prosperity be joyful, but in the day of adversity consider:*** God is just keeping you guessing.

The proper response is not to be too predictable yourself. ***Be not righteous over much; neither make thyself over wise: why shouldest thou destroy thyself? Be not over much wicked, neither be thou foolish: why shouldest thou die before thy time?*** I was surprised to hear the Preacher advising people to be good and bad in moderation, but then he never claimed to be an angel.

He went on to say that ***there is not a just man upon earth, that doeth good, and sinneth not***. His experience with women had been even less happy, it seems. ***I find more bitter than death the woman, whose heart is snares and nets, and her hands as bands***. In fact, looking for worthy individuals, ***one man among a thousand have I found; but a woman among all those have I not found. Lo, this only have I found, that God hath made man upright; but they have sought out many inventions***. I'd have to say that his standards were a little severe.

8 The quest for meaning seemed to be doomed. ***Who knoweth the interpretation of a thing?*** Man has no control over his future, ***neither hath he power in the day of death: and there is no discharge in that war***. Not a cheerful prospect. ***Then I commended mirth, because a man hath no better thing under the sun, than to eat, and to drink, and to be merry:*** that's all he gets.

9 Because the fate of everyone is the same, being alive is the only thing that counts. ***For to him that is joined to all the living there is hope: for a living dog is***

better than a dead lion. For the living know that they shall die: but the dead know not any thing, neither have they any more a reward; for the memory of them is forgotten. Some of the living are forgotten too, I might say.

Go thy way, eat thy bread with joy, and drink thy wine with a merry heart; for God now accepteth thy works. Anticipating a later remark, he recommended having a good time with the one you love on the grounds that as meaningless experiences go, it's one of the best.

The moral is to make the most of it, even if the world doesn't work on merit. ***Whatsoever thy hand findeth to do, do it with thy might; for there is no work, nor device, nor knowledge, nor wisdom, in the grave, whither thou goest. I returned, and saw under the sun, that the race is not to the swift, nor the battle to the strong, neither yet bread to the wise, nor yet riches to men of understanding, nor yet favour to men of skill; but time and chance happeneth to them all.***

10

Wisdom, unfortunately, is spoiled by even occasional foolishness, just as ***Dead flies cause the ointment of the apothecary to send forth a stinking savour.*** Remember, too, that ***He that diggeth a pit shall fall into it.***

His world-weary wisdom extended to politics. Notwithstanding his earlier comment that a poor wise youth was preferable to a foolish old king, he declared that someone from the lower orders – a child, you might say – wouldn't know how to behave. ***Woe to thee, O land, when thy king is a child, and thy princes eat in the morning!*** It's best not to complain too loudly, though, about large breakfasts or anything else, because walls have ears – and cash is what counts. ***A feast is made for laughter, and wine maketh merry: but money answereth all things. Curse not the king, no not in thy thought; and curse not the rich in thy bedchamber: for a bird of the air shall carry the voice, and that which hath wings shall tell the matter.*** Very prudent, if perhaps a little paranoid.

11

Though everyone needs money, that isn't to say that it should be hoarded. On the contrary, ***Cast thy bread upon the waters: for thou shalt find it after many days.*** In any case, we have to take matters as we find them, and get on with it; ***in the place where the tree falleth, there it shall be. He that observeth the wind shall not sow; and he that regardeth the clouds shall not reap.***

The very uncertainty of fate is a reason not to be fatalistic; you must try, and then try again, to impose your will on events. ***In the morning sow thy seed, and in the evening withhold not thine hand: for thou knowest not whether shall prosper, either this or that, or whether they both shall be alike good.***

The Preacher didn't set out to be miserable; he declared that ***Truly the light is sweet, and a pleasant thing it is for the eyes to behold the sun.*** By the sound of it he longed for the days before his realisation of life's futility. ***Rejoice, O young man, in thy youth;*** you'll discover soon enough that everything is empty. Old age will creep up, and your strength will start to fail. To drive home the point, he spun an elaborate metaphor around the idea of the body as a house, with hands, teeth, eyes, ears, etc. as its occupants.

Remember now thy Creator in the days of thy youth, while the evil days come not, nor the years draw nigh, when thou shalt say, I have no pleasure in them; While the sun, or the light, or the moon, or the stars, be not darkened, nor the clouds return after the rain: In the day when the keepers of the house shall tremble, and the strong men shall bow themselves, and the grinders cease because they are few, and those that look out of the windows be darkened, And the doors shall be shut in the streets, when the sound of the grinding is low, and he shall rise up at the voice of the bird, and all the daughters of musick shall be brought low; Also when they shall be afraid of that which is high, and fears shall be in the way, and the almond tree shall flourish, and the grasshopper shall be a burden, and desire shall fail: because man goeth to his long home, and the mourners go about the streets: Or ever the silver cord be loosed, or the golden bowl be broken, or the pitcher be broken at the fountain, or the wheel broken at the cistern. Then shall the dust return to the earth as it was: and the spirit shall return unto God who gave it. Vanity of vanities, saith the preacher; all is vanity.

I'd have to say that this was a hard message for people to swallow. As they said, ***The words of the wise are as goads, and as nails fastened by the masters of assemblies***. Those who felt more threatened preferred to dismiss it altogether, grumbling ***of making many books there is no end; and much study is a weariness of the flesh. Let us hear the conclusion of the whole matter: Fear God, and keep his commandments: for this is the whole duty of man. For God shall bring every work into judgment, with every secret thing, whether it be good, or whether it be evil.*** The sheep decided to follow the shepherd wherever he might lead. If the destination turned out to be the dinner table, you can't say that the Preacher hadn't warned them.

22

The Song of Solomon

The song of songs, which is Solomon's – though why or in what sense isn't clear; yet another instance of the poor fellow's name being taken in vain, I fear. Still, Solomon, unlike God, does at least get a mention in the song. Then, too, it's the kind of thing the great lover would have liked: pure eroticism from start to finish. 1

The woman opened by musing, apparently to her companions, ***Let him kiss me with the kisses of his mouth: for thy love is better than wine. ... I am black, but comely, O ye daughters of Jerusalem, as the tents of Kedar, as the curtains of Solomon***. The man responded, and I'd have to say that he could have done with lessons in flattery. ***O thou fairest among women ... I have compared thee, O my love, to a company of horses in Pharaoh's chariots.*** Unoffended by the equine simile, she cooed ***A bundle of myrrh is my well-beloved unto me; he shall lie all night betwixt my breasts.*** I trust it was a warm night, because the man seemed to have something alfresco in mind; ***our bed is green. The beams of our house are cedar, and our rafters of fir.***

The amorous banter continued, starting with her: 2

I am the rose of Sharon,
and the lily of the valleys.

As the lily among thorns,
so is my love among the daughters.
As the apple tree among the trees of the wood,
so is my beloved among the sons.
I sat down under his shadow with great delight,
and his fruit was sweet to my taste.
He brought me to the banqueting house,
and his banner over me was love.
Stay me with flagons, comfort me with apples:
for I am sick of love.
His left hand is under my head,
and his right hand doth embrace me.

Steamy stuff. One morning the man came to announce that spring had come:

Rise up, my love, my fair one, and come away.
For, lo, the winter is past,

the rain is over and gone;
The flowers appear on the earth;
the time of the singing of birds is come,
and the voice of the turtle is heard in our land.

The lady's companions tried to introduce a note of pastoral caution, warning about the grapes, but she felt that her lilies were up to it.

Take us the foxes, the little foxes,
that spoil the vines: for our vines have tender grapes.

My beloved is mine, and I am his:
  he feedeth among the lilies.
Until the day break, and the shadows flee away,
  turn, my beloved.

3 Once asleep, though, her dreams were troubled by fear of losing him.

By night on my bed
I sought him whom my soul loveth:
I sought him, but I found him not.

She asked the nightwatchmen if they had seen her lover; finally, she caught up with him.

I found him whom my soul loveth:
I held him, and would not let him go,
until I had brought him into my mother's house,
  and into the chamber of her that conceived me.

Didn't she have a bedroom of her own? This is one for the analysts.

4 The man continued to compliment his partner, coming out with such priceless efforts as ***thy hair is as a flock of goats, that appear from mount Gilead.*** He improved as he descended:

Thy two breasts are like two young roes that are twins,
  which feed among the lilies.
Until the day break, and the shadows flee away,
I will get me to the mountain of myrrh,
  and to the hill of frankincense.
Thou art all fair, my love;
  there is no spot in thee.

It sounds as if he would know.

He added, very gallantly, ***how much better is thy love than wine! and the smell of thine ointments than all spices!*** (though pushing his luck a bit with ***the smell of thy garments is like the smell of Lebanon***). He compared her to a private garden, with a sealed fountain.

She was happy to invite him in:

Awake, O north wind; and come, thou south;
blow upon my garden, that the spices thereof may flow out.
Let my beloved come into his garden,
and eat his pleasant fruits.

Needless to say, the invitation was accepted. 5

I am come into my garden, my sister, my spouse:
I have gathered my myrrh with my spice;
I have eaten my honeycomb with my honey;
I have drunk my wine with my milk.

Once more, though, she had a troubling dream. He knocks on the door, ***saying, Open to me, my sister, my love, my dove, my undefiled***. She hesitates, but ***My beloved put in his hand by the hole of the door, and my bowels were moved for him.*** When she opens the door, however, he has gone. Again she searches the city for him, and this time the watchmen beat her: ***they smote me, they wounded me; the keepers of the walls took away my veil from me.*** Back to the analyst, I'd say.

Now it was her turn to describe him. She had trouble with the hair, too, appearing not even to know whether it was blond or black. ***His head is as the most fine gold, his locks are bushy, and black as a raven.*** Her confidence also seemed higher further down; ***his belly is as bright ivory overlaid with sapphires. His legs are as pillars of marble, set upon sockets of fine gold.*** His appearance brought to mind a cedar. All a bit physical, but the conclusion was touching:

His mouth is most sweet: yea, he is altogether lovely.
This is my beloved, and this is my friend,
O daughters of Jerusalem.

If her lover had really disappeared, it seems that he hadn't gone far. 6

My beloved is gone down into his garden,
to the beds of spices,
to feed in the gardens, and to gather lilies.
I am my beloved's, and my beloved is mine:
he feedeth among the lilies.

He paused from feeding for long enough to repeat his compliments, noticing this time her piercing eyes. ***Who is she that looketh forth as the morning, fair as the moon, clear as the sun, and terrible as an army with banners?*** Her attention was obviously being monopolised, because her companions cried ***Return, return, O Shulamite; return, return, that we may look upon thee.*** The man was only 7 warming up, though, in singing her praises. This time he proceeded from the bottom up, but that didn't save him from blathering when he reached her eyes and nose.

How beautiful are thy feet with shoes,
O prince's daughter!
the joints of thy thighs are like jewels,
the work of the hands of a cunning workman.
Thy navel is like a round goblet,
which wanteth not liquor:
thy belly is like an heap of wheat
set about with lilies.
Thy two breasts are like two young roes
that are twins.
Thy neck is as a tower of ivory;
thine eyes like the fishpools in Heshbon,
by the gate of Bath-rabbim:
thy nose is as the tower of Lebanon
which looketh toward Damascus.

Perhaps realising that he was going from bad to worse, he hurried on to describe just what he had in mind – which from her answer seemed to coincide with her own plans.

This thy stature is like to a palm tree,
and thy breasts to clusters of grapes.
I said, I will go up to the palm tree,
I will take hold of the boughs thereof:
now also thy breasts shall be as clusters of the vine,
and the smell of thy nose like apples;
And the roof of thy mouth like the best wine for my beloved,
that goeth down sweetly,
causing the lips of those that are asleep to speak.

I am my beloved's, and his desire is toward me.
Come, my beloved, let us go forth into the field …
there will I give thee my loves.
The mandrakes give a smell,
and at our gates are all manner of pleasant fruits,

new and old,
which I have laid up for thee, O my beloved.

These outdoor pursuits were becoming uncomfortable, however. The woman wished the man were her brother, so they could be together without creating a scandal. Then she would take him home, where – well, it hardly needs spelling out. ***I would cause thee to drink of spiced wine of the juice of my pomegranate.*** All credit to the imagination. 8

Having both dwelt on the raw passion, the man did, just at the end, have a few words to say about the emotional side.

Set me as a seal upon thine heart,
a seal upon thine arm:
for love is strong as death;
jealousy is cruel as the grave:
the coals thereof are coals of fire,
which hath a most vehement flame.
Many waters cannot quench love,
neither can the floods drown it.

The woman's brothers didn't seem to appreciate quite how far things had gone, perhaps because they never realised that she had grown up. ***We have a little sister, and she hath no breasts: what shall we do for our sister in the day when she shall be spoken for?*** You might notice ***my breasts like towers***, she commented, and everything is well, thank you. Then, with a call to her lover, the song ends.

Make haste, my beloved,
and be thou like to a roe or to a young hart
upon the mountains of spices.

Let's rut away together.

The way the song was interpreted as a sacred allegory and elevated to the rank of scripture continues to amuse me. It's an X-rated classic, and the best is that the people who squirm the most are generally those who take everything literally on principle.

23

Isaiah

1 Isaiah was a messenger of doom: not the first, but arguably the most influential. He called the nation a seedbed of evil, a body beaten too often; ***the whole head is sick, and the whole heart faint.*** The country was being overrun, and Jerusalem ***the daughter of Zion is left as a cottage in a vineyard, as a lodge in a garden of cucumbers, as a besieged city.***

In keeping with the prophetic vocation, Isaiah was a puritan. According to him, God was fed up with ceremony. ***To what purpose is the multitude of your sacrifices unto me? saith the LORD: I am full of the burnt offerings of rams, and the fat of fed beasts; and I delight not in the blood of bullocks, or of lambs, or of he goats.*** It's not that he was becoming a vegetarian, I think, just that the rigmarole was starting to depress him. ***Bring no more vain oblations; incense is an abomination unto me; ... Your new moons and your appointed feasts my soul hateth***; clearly we had an unhappy God on our hands.

To my mind, he was simply tired of his cosy congregation, and wanted them to go out and do good works. ***Learn to do well; seek judgment, relieve the oppressed, judge the fatherless, plead for the widow. Come now, and let us reason together, saith the LORD: though your sins be as scarlet, they shall be as white as snow; though they be red like crimson, they shall be as wool.*** There would be dire penalties for anyone unwilling to be laundered; God knew how to make his case persuasive.

2 The good news was that one day God would put the world to rights from his seat in Jerusalem, teaching people to follow his path. What that meant, I was surprised to hear, was that ***they shall beat their swords into plowshares, and their spears into pruninghooks: nation shall not lift up sword against nation, neither shall they learn war any more.*** Animal welfare, socialism, and now pacifism: whatever next?

The bad news was that before this time came, God planned to launch a holy terror. ***In that day a man shall cast his idols of silver, and his idols of gold, which they made each one for himself to worship, to the moles and to the bats.*** Isaiah told them to disdain each other's company: ***Cease ye from man, whose breath is in his nostrils: for wherein is he to be accounted of?*** Very little, apparently.

3 Isaiah was confident that the end was nigh, ***For, behold, the Lord, the LORD of hosts, doth take away from Jerusalem and from Judah the stay and the staff, the whole stay of bread, and the whole stay of water.*** In line with his new radicalism God condemned the ruling class as oppressive and exploitative. ***What mean ye***

that ye beat my people to pieces, and grind the faces of the poor? His progressive credentials took a knock, however, from a long tirade in which he promised to smite women in a variety of unpleasant ways, ***Because the daughters of Zion are haughty, and walk with stretched forth necks and wanton eyes, walking and mincing as they go, and making a tinkling with their feet.***

To start with, he proposed to strip them of their personal ornaments – by the sound of it in a garage – mentioning ***their round tires like the moon, The chains, and the bracelets, and the mufflers, The bonnets***, etc. To complete the degradation they would be left smelly, bald, and branded, dressed (if at all) in sackcloth, abandoned sitting on the ground. ***And in that day seven women shall take hold of one man***, each begging him to take her on any terms. I gathered that he found independent women rather threatening. 4

God recounted a story: ***My wellbeloved hath a vineyard in a very fruitful hill*** – the vineyard being his people. Every possible care had been taken of this plot, despite which ***it brought forth wild grapes.*** This being so, said God, ***I will tell you what I will do to my vineyard:*** I will wreck it. He was dismayed by abuse of power, not to mention the creation of private monopolies; ***he looked for judgment, but behold oppression; for righteousness, but behold a cry. Woe unto them that join house to house, that lay field to field, till there be no place, that they may be placed alone in the midst of the earth!*** 5

The political agenda was again combined with complaints about personal behaviour. ***Woe unto them that rise up early in the morning, that they may follow strong drink; that continue until night, till wine inflame them!*** I'd agree that anyone taking a liquid breakfast has a problem, but in God's view the people were just rotten. They tugged their wickedness along like tethered animals; ***Woe unto them that draw iniquity with cords of vanity, and sin as it were with a cart rope ... Woe unto them that call evil good, and good evil.*** As if being arrogant and corrupt wasn't enough, they even mixed their drinks. ***For all this his anger is not turned away, but his hand is stretched out still***: an invading army would be on its way.

How Isaiah became a prophet

Isaiah took a break from these omens to describe how he came to be a prophet. ***In the year that king Uzziah died I saw also the Lord sitting upon a throne, high and lifted up, and his train filled the temple. Above it stood the seraphims: each one had six wings; with twain he covered his face, and with twain he covered his feet, and with twain he did fly. And one cried unto another, and said,*** 6

Holy, holy, holy, is the LORD of hosts:
the whole earth is full of his glory.

Naturally a scene like that can be somewhat intimidating, and Isaiah said ***Woe is me! for I am undone; because I am a man of unclean lips, and I dwell in the midst of a people of unclean lips: for mine eyes have seen the King, the LORD of hosts.*** Instead of washing his mouth out with soap one of the seraphim flew over and touched his lips with a burning coal, which took care of the problem.

Isaiah continued his story. ***I heard the voice of the Lord, saying, Whom shall I send, and who will go for us? Then said I, Here am I; send me.*** Obviously a compulsive volunteer, but I had to feel sorry for him. He was to tell the people that, although they were too dull-witted to do anything about it, their position was hopeless. Isaiah was crestfallen. ***Then said I, Lord, how long? And he answered, Until the cities be wasted without inhabitant, and the houses without man, and the land be utterly desolate.*** That's where over-eagerness will get you.

7 I wasn't surprised that Isaiah – who often spoke in riddles – had a hard time persuading people, and some of the resultant misunderstandings were serious. Isaiah told the king of Judah, then under pressure from Israel and Syria, that ***the Lord himself shall give you a sign; Behold, a virgin shall conceive, and bear a son, and shall call his name Immanuel*** ('God is with us'). Now in fact he only mentioned a 'young woman', and the later confusion about virginity arose from an unfortunate mistranslation.

At any rate, the idea was simply that ***before the child shall know to refuse evil, and choose the good,*** the king's enemies would have suffered defeat. They were indeed overcome a couple of years later, but it seemed a convoluted way of getting the message across. He was also fond of unusual metaphors. ***In the same day shall the Lord shave with a razor that is hired***: not himself, I hasten to say, but the heads and bodies of the unfortunate people, with Assyria serving as the razor.

8 A child was born, in fact – to Isaiah's own wife. Instead of 'Immanuel', however, God came up with the longest name (indeed, the longest word) in this whole saga: Mahershalalhashbaz, meaning 'speed spoil hasten plunder'. All very interesting as an outlook for Israel and Syria, but not calculated to make childhood any easier. God had it in mind to serve ***for a stone of stumbling and for a rock of offence to both the houses of Israel.*** People would consult spirits, and ***wizards that peep, and that mutter***, but their doom was inescapable.

9 Looking on the bright side, Isaiah saw a better day coming with the advent of an ideal king. ***The people that walked in darkness have seen a great light: they that dwell in the land of the shadow of death, upon them hath the light shined.*** They could look forward to the joy of victory, peace and stability,

For unto us a child is born, unto us a son is given:
and the government shall be upon his shoulder:
and his name shall be called
Wonderful, Counsellor, The mighty God,
The everlasting Father, The Prince of Peace.

Of the increase of his government and peace
there shall be no end ...
The zeal of the LORD of hosts will perform this.

In the meantime he wanted to get a handle on something else: pride. ***Therefore the LORD will cut off from Israel head and tail, branch and rush, in one day. The ancient and honourable, he is the head; and the prophet that teacheth lies, he is the tail.*** God wasn't even going to have any mercy on widows and orphans, every one of whom, so he claimed, was evil and foul-mouthed. If there's going to be a crackdown on vice, I'm all for starting with the widows.

The instrument of his punishment would be the Assyrian army. Naturally he would then have to punish the Assyrians for being too proud themselves, with the result ***that his burden shall be taken away from off thy shoulder, and his yoke from off thy neck***. Isaiah even prophesied – incorrectly, as it turned out – the path of the Assyrian invasion. 10

Back to the glad tidings, though, and the emergence of a perfect king from the house of Jesse (David's father). 11

And there shall come forth a rod out of the stem of Jesse,
and a Branch shall grow out of his roots:
And the spirit of the LORD shall rest upon him,
the spirit of wisdom and understanding,
the spirit of counsel and might,
the spirit of knowledge and of the fear of the LORD.

He would be able to slay the wicked with a word, being armed with faith and justice. Happily, though,

The wolf also shall dwell with the lamb,
and the leopard shall lie down with the kid;
and the calf and the young lion and the fatling together;
and a little child shall lead them.
And the cow and the bear shall feed;
their young ones shall lie down together:
and the lion shall eat straw like the ox.
And the suckling child shall play on the hole of the asp,
and the weaned child shall put his hand on the cockatrice' den.
They shall not hurt nor destroy in all my holy mountain:
for the earth shall be full of the knowledge of the LORD,
as the waters cover the sea.

God would bring the exiles back home. Looking forward to this day, ***the LORD JEHOVAH is my strength and my song; he also is become my salvation.*** 12

BAD NEWS FOR FOREIGNERS

13 Isaiah launched into a long series of oracles on the fate of nations present and future, starting with Babylon, which in his day was no more than a province in the Assyrian empire. That being the case, people must have been perplexed when he foretold its fall.

And I will punish the world for their evil, and the wicked for their iniquity; and I will cause the arrogancy of the proud to cease, and will lay low the haughtiness of the terrible. The punishment would be fairly distributed, not just restricted to the guilty; ***Their children also shall be dashed to pieces before their eyes; their houses shall be spoiled, and their wives ravished.*** Babylon would be turned over to the wild beasts, not to mention ***dragons in their pleasant palaces.***

14 Gloating over the fallen king didn't have to be done tastefully; ***the worm is spread under thee, and the worms cover thee. How art thou fallen from heaven, O Lucifer, son of the morning!*** It would be our turn to mock; ***Is this the man that made the earth to tremble, that did shake kingdoms ...?***

Isaiah had similar prophecies of doom for Assyria, Philistia, and Moab. Towards the last of these he showed some sympathy – ***Wherefore my bowels shall sound like an harp for Moab*** – unless he was trying to suggest what he really thought of them. (15, 16)

17 Damascus, too, was on its way to becoming ***a ruinous heap.*** With everyone fighting everyone else at one time or another, ***The nations shall rush like the rushing of many waters.*** Isaiah having turned to the subject of Africa, God declared that ***I will set the Egyptians against the Egyptians; and they shall fight every one against his brother, and every one against his neighbour; city against city, and kingdom against kingdom.*** He always did give them a hard time. (18, 19)

20 Being a prophet wasn't an easy job with God in charge. For example, he obliged Isaiah to walk ***naked and barefoot three years for a sign and wonder upon Egypt and upon Ethiopia.*** Wonder they did, I'm sure, but the exhibition was merely to signal that Assyria would lead away captives from these nations, ***young and old, naked and barefoot, even with their buttocks uncovered, to the shame of Egypt.*** There must have been a better way.

21 Isaiah was a specialist in gloom and doom; he described the coming fall of Babylon, as I said, before it had even had a chance to rise. ***The burden of the desert of the sea. As the whirlwinds in the south pass through; so it cometh from the desert, from a terrible land.*** In a nightmare vision of upheaval, a voice cries ***Babylon is fallen, is fallen; and all the graven images of her gods he hath broken unto the ground*** – a few decades too late to save Jerusalem, unfortunately.

The oracle concerning Edom was wonderfully mysterious.

Watchman, what of the night?
Watchman, what of the night?

The watchman said, The morning cometh, and also the night:
if ye will enquire, enquire ye: return, come.

That would keep them guessing.

Isaiah might have been xenophobic, but he didn't discriminate: Jerusalem would share the fate of the rest. The way people reacted to trouble annoyed him. Instead of grovelling in the dust being mindful of God, they would say ***let us eat and drink; for to morrow we shall die***. Any excuse for a party. 22

Isaiah heaped abuse on one particular servant of the royal household, declaring as he put forward his own candidate that ***I will fasten him as a nail in a sure place***. Political carpentry wasn't his bag, though, and the person came unstuck.

One final state came under prophetic fire, that of ***Tyre, the crowning city, whose merchants are princes***. He saw it being destroyed; ***Howl, ye ships of Tarshish: for your strength is laid waste***. They were in good company: he had pronounced more or less the same sentence on every place in the known world. 23

Having condemned the nations individually, he continued by cursing them collectively, announcing the end of the world. 24

Behold, the LORD maketh the earth empty,
and maketh it waste, and turneth it upside down,
and scattereth abroad the inhabitants thereof.
And it shall be, as with the people, so with the priest;
as with the servant, so with his master;
as with the maid, so with her mistress; ...
The land shall be utterly emptied, and utterly spoiled:
for the LORD hath spoken this word.

As a sign of the apocalypse ***There is a crying for wine in the streets***, though I'm not sure it takes the end of the world to produce that – just the end of a night out.

SOME GOOD NEWS, SOME BAD NEWS

The predicted destruction notwithstanding, Isaiah paid tribute to God, ***For thou hast been a strength to the poor, a strength to the needy in his distress, a refuge from the storm, a shadow from the heat***. A great party was in the offing; ***in this mountain shall the LORD of hosts make unto all people a feast of fat things, a feast of wines on the lees, of fat things full of marrow, of wines on the lees well refined***. Might as well empty the cellar. 25

Perhaps, though, the celebration was to come after the disaster, not before; ***He will swallow up death in victory; and the Lord GOD will wipe away tears from off all faces; and the rebuke of his people shall he take away from off all the***

earth. Whether he just meant that survivors would be compensated, or that they could look forward to immortality, wasn't clear. The fact that Isaiah went straight on to describe what God would do to a particular enemy – ***Moab shall be trodden down under him, even as straw is trodden down for the dunghill*** – made me inclined not to read too much into it.

26 The victory song only added to the confusion. It started off well enough:

Open ye the gates,
that the righteous nation which keepeth the truth may enter in.
Thou wilt keep him in perfect peace, whose mind is stayed on thee:
because he trusteth in thee.

Next there was a declaration that the dead are dead, and will stay that way:

They are dead, they shall not live;
they are deceased, they shall not rise.

Moreover the people struggled to no great effect:

We have been with child, we have been in pain,
we have as it were brought forth wind.

But then out of the blue:

Thy dead men shall live, together with my dead body shall they arise.
Awake and sing, ye that dwell in dust:
for thy dew is as the dew of herbs,
and the earth shall cast out the dead.

All in all, I think the song itself offered the best advice.

Come, my people, enter thou into thy chambers,
and shut thy doors about thee:
hide thyself as it were for a little moment,
until the indignation be overpast.

When in doubt, keep your head under the covers.

27 Concluding his vision of the apocalypse, Isaiah declared that ***In that day the LORD with his sore and great and strong sword shall punish leviathan the piercing serpent, even leviathan that crooked serpent; and he shall slay the dragon that is in the sea***. Unfortunately it wasn't always so easy to tell when he was being allegorical.

28 Isaiah didn't think much of his rivals in Judah, nor did they of him. He claimed

that ***the priest and the prophet have erred through strong drink ... all tables are full of vomit and filthiness, so that there is no place clean.*** They in turn mocked his teaching: ***For precept must be upon precept, precept upon precept; line upon line, line upon line; here a little, and there a little.*** Isaiah retorted that ***Because ye have said, We have made a covenant with death, and with hell are we at agreement***, God will take awful vengeance; so nasty will your fate be, ***it shall be a vexation only to understand the report.***

29 Later Isaiah seemed to soften, saying that he had only been speaking figuratively; ***they are drunken, but not with wine; they stagger, but not with strong drink. For the LORD hath poured out upon you the spirit of deep sleep, and hath closed your eyes.*** God would sort them out when the time came.

30 Isaiah was just as interested in the contemporary political scene as in the fate of nations. The alliance of convenience that Judah had made with Egypt was a particular *bête noire*, ***For the Egyptians shall help in vain, and to no purpose: therefore have I cried concerning this, Their strength is to sit still. Now go, write it before them in a table, and note it in a book, that it may be for the time to come for ever and ever: That this is a rebellious people, lying children, children that will not hear the law of the LORD: Which say to the seers, See not; and to the prophets, Prophesy not unto us right things, speak unto us smooth things, prophesy deceits.*** If a preference for good news religion is a crime, it won't be just the Egyptians who are in trouble.

God's complaint was that the people had tried to take matters into their own hands. You should have trusted me, he said, ***in quietness and in confidence shall be your strength.*** Now that folly would be punished, but ***though the Lord give you the bread of adversity, and the water of affliction ... thine ears shall hear a word behind thee, saying, This is the way, walk ye in it.*** When the new day comes, the people will be reformed; the graven images, ***thou shalt cast them away as a menstruous cloth.*** Everything will be sweetness and light: too much so, perhaps, since ***the light of the moon shall be as the light of the sun, and the light of the sun shall be sevenfold.*** So shame on the doubters; God will destroy Assyria all by himself. 31

32 When the golden age arrives

Behold, a king shall reign in righteousness,
and princes shall rule in judgment.
And a man shall be as an hiding place from the wind,
and a covert from the tempest;
as rivers of water in a dry place,
as the shadow of a great rock in a weary land.

33 Isaiah relentlessly alternated his prophecies of perdition and paradise; the notion of a world good and bad in parts didn't interest him.

34 Thus, he would announce that because ***the indignation of the LORD is upon all***

nations, a great slaughter was imminent, in which ***their stink shall come up out of their carcases, and the mountains shall be melted with their blood.*** Indeed, even the heavens would be emptied and rolled up. No human would remain on the land, ***And thorns shall come up in her palaces, nettles and brambles in the fortresses thereof: and it shall be an habitation of dragons, and a court for owls.*** That was the bad news.

35 The good news was completely the reverse. ***The wilderness and the solitary place shall be glad for them; and the desert shall rejoice, and blossom as the rose.*** Therefore ***Strengthen ye the weak hands, and confirm the feeble knees,*** because God ***will come and save you.***

> ***Then the eyes of the blind shall be opened,***
> ***and the ears of the deaf shall be unstopped.***
> ***Then shall the lame man leap as an hart,***
> ***and the tongue of the dumb sing:***
> ***for in the wilderness shall waters break out,***
> ***and streams in the desert.***

Along the holy highway ***the wayfaring men, though fools, shall not err therein***; it will be rather for God's people to ***come to Zion with songs and everlasting joy upon their heads: they shall obtain joy and gladness, and sorrow and sighing shall flee away.*** Isaiah could be depressing or cheerful, as the occasion demanded.

36 I've already described how Isaiah played a starring role when Hezekiah was king of Judah. Emissaries from Assyria had come to point out that ***Lo, thou trustest in the staff of this broken reed, on Egypt,*** as well as in a god no more powerful

37 than any other. A worried Hezekiah prayed ***Incline thine ear, O LORD, and hear,*** and Isaiah was able to tell him that God didn't plan to be insulted. The Assyrian army was destroyed.

38 I don't know why we bothered, Hezekiah being such an ungrateful coward. Even after God extended his life, he grumbled in a poem that ***I shall go softly all***

39 ***my years in the bitterness of my soul.*** As for his response to Isaiah's prophecy that his sons would be eunuchs in Babylon – ***Good ... For there shall be peace and truth in my days*** – it was a disgrace.

ISAIAH'S VOICE CHANGES

40 So much for the old Isaiah. He had another side, but it came out in talking about events that happened so much later you wouldn't have thought it could be the same person at all.

Anyway, the new Isaiah celebrated the end of exile, and the coming return of the people to the land of Israel. He had acquired considerable poetic power, though I should declare an interest; notice how he quotes the angelic voice.

Comfort ye, comfort ye my people,
saith your God.
Speak ye comfortably to Jerusalem,
and cry unto her,
that her warfare is accomplished,
that her iniquity is pardoned:
for she hath received of the LORD's hand
double for all her sins.

The voice of him that crieth in the wilderness,
Prepare ye the way of the LORD,
make straight in the desert a highway for our God.
Every valley shall be exalted,
and every mountain and hill shall be made low:
and the crooked shall be made straight,
and the rough places plain:
And the glory of the LORD shall be revealed,
and all flesh shall see it together:
for the mouth of the LORD hath spoken it.

The voice said, Cry.
And he said, What shall I cry?
All flesh is grass,
and all the goodliness thereof is as the flower of the field:
The grass withereth, the flower fadeth:
because the spirit of the LORD bloweth upon it:
surely the people is grass.
The grass withereth, the flower fadeth:
but the word of our God shall stand for ever.

O Zion, that bringest good tidings,
get thee up into the high mountains;
O Jerusalem, that bringest good tidings,
lift up thy voice with strength;
lift it up, be not afraid;
say unto the cities of Judah,
Behold your God! ...
He shall feed his flock like a shepherd:
he shall gather the lambs with his arm,
and carry them in his bosom,
and shall gently lead those that are with young.

Before God the creator ***Behold, the nations are as a drop of a bucket, and are***

counted as the small dust of the balance. That didn't stop each side from claiming him as their own, of course.

Isaiah mocked human self-importance. To those who wanted to personalise God, or thought they could form a likeness of him, he asked ***Have ye not known? have ye not heard? hath it not been told you from the beginning? have ye not understood from the foundations of the earth? It is he that sitteth upon the circle of the earth, and the inhabitants thereof are as grasshoppers.*** Nothing of theirs is more durable than straw. ***But they that wait upon the LORD shall renew their strength; they shall mount up with wings as eagles; they shall run, and not be weary; and they shall walk, and not faint.*** He wasn't just referring to angels, either.

41 God launched into an exceedingly long monologue, mainly devoted to self-congratulation. In fairness he did recognise an occasional human contribution, for example ***They helped every one his neighbour; and every one said to his brother, Be of good courage.*** He also mentioned his 'servant', which might have been the

42 whole people or a particular individual. Either way, the servant was expected to tread carefully; ***A bruised reed shall he not break, and the smoking flax shall he not quench: he shall bring forth judgment unto truth.*** God made it clear, though, that his servant was not coming up to the mark.

43 None the less, he promised to bring about the fall of Babylon, and to set his

44 people free. In view of these efforts, the continued production of graven images galled him. It seemed an incredible thing for any sensible person to do; he imagined someone cutting down a tree, using some of the wood for a roast, some for heat: ***yea, he warmeth himself, and saith, Aha, I am warm, I have seen the fire: And the residue thereof he maketh a god.*** Quite a good joke, I thought – for God, anyway.

45 Proclaiming his own omnipotence, God made an astonishing confession. ***I form the light, and create darkness: I make peace, and create evil: I the LORD do all these things.*** Given the state of the world, I realise that it would have been hard to claim to be both all-powerful and supremely benevolent, but I was intrigued that he chose to emphasise might, not right. He clearly preferred the image of the universal boss to that of the beleaguered crusader.

Nor did he offer any apologies. ***Woe unto him that striveth with his Maker! ... Shall the clay say to him that fashioneth it, What makest thou?*** So no more questions.

46 Returning to the subject of idols, God contrasted the fact that they had to be carried with the way he himself carried his people. Since a lot of the carrying was into exile, I don't think I'd have mentioned it, myself. He did promise, though, that ***my salvation shall not tarry.***

47 Picturing the future enemy as a young woman, God described what he had in mind for her.

Come down, and sit in the dust,
O virgin daughter of Babylon ...

thou shalt no more be called tender and delicate.
Take the millstones, and grind meal:
uncover thy locks, make bare the leg,
uncover the thigh, pass over the rivers.
Thy nakedness shall be uncovered, yea,
thy shame shall be seen: I will take vengeance.

Most unpleasant. More fitting, perhaps, was his challenge ***Let now the astrologers, the stargazers, the monthly prognosticators, stand up, and save thee from these things that shall come upon thee. Behold, they shall be as stubble; the fire shall burn them; they shall not deliver themselves from the power of the flame.*** I'd be content with burning the horoscopes; the astrologers can always be redeployed as economists.

God had tested the people ***in the furnace of affliction*** in order to safeguard his honour. ***O that thou hadst hearkened to my commandments! then had thy peace been as a river, and thy righteousness as the waves of the sea.*** But had they been more deserving of punishment than everyone else? He stuck to his point: ***There is no peace, saith the LORD, unto the wicked.*** 48

MORE PROMISES OF GREATNESS

God again referred to the faithful as his servant, who would restore the glory of Israel. Moreover, he said, ***I will also give thee for a light to the Gentiles, that thou mayest be my salvation unto the end of the earth.*** The people hadn't been abandoned. ***Can a woman forget her sucking child, that she should not have compassion on the son of her womb? yea, they may forget, yet will I not forget thee.*** 49

Certainly no one was going to forget him. ***I will feed them that oppress thee with their own flesh; and they shall be drunken with their own blood, as with sweet wine.*** That should give them a hangover. Despite all the tribulations, God's servant remained confident. 50

After all, God was explicit: ***the redeemed of the LORD shall return, and come with singing unto Zion; and everlasting joy shall be upon their head.*** At the moment, it was true, they were prostrate, having tasted divine wrath; ***thou hast drunken the dregs of the cup of trembling, and wrung them out.*** Everything would soon change, however. ***Therefore hear now this***: the poisoned chalice would be passed to their enemies. 51

Pleasant as vengeance is, I was glad to hear instead about the joys of return, through the image of a messenger to Jerusalem being greeted by a watchman. 52

How beautiful upon the mountains are the feet of him
that bringeth good tidings, that publisheth peace;

that bringeth good tidings of good, that publisheth salvation;
that saith unto Zion, Thy God reigneth!
Thy watchmen shall lift up the voice;
with the voice together shall they sing:
for they shall see eye to eye,
when the LORD shall bring again Zion.
Break forth into joy, sing together,
ye waste places of Jerusalem:
for the LORD hath comforted his people,
he hath redeemed Jerusalem.

Isaiah went back to the theme of God's servant. I suspect that the image was still meant to represent the faithful of Israel, but the servant was so sharply personified that some listeners thought he was referring to a specific individual from the recent past. Subsequently other people took it as a description of the messiah, God's anointed liberator.

If applying literally to a person, then evidently the individual would be seriously disfigured, perhaps a leper. Because ***his visage was so marred more than any man, and his form more than the sons of men***, people would shudder and avoid him. At any rate, this is what was said:

53 ***Who hath believed our report?***
and to whom is the arm of the LORD revealed?
For he shall grow up before him as a tender plant,
and as a root out of a dry ground:
he hath no form nor comeliness; and when we shall see him,
there is no beauty that we should desire him.
He is despised and rejected of men;
a man of sorrows, and acquainted with grief:
and we hid as it were our faces from him;
he was despised, and we esteemed him not.
Surely he hath borne our griefs, and carried our sorrows:
yet we did esteem him stricken, smitten of God, and afflicted.
But he was wounded for our transgressions,
he was bruised for our iniquities:
the chastisement of our peace was upon him;
and with his stripes we are healed.
All we like sheep have gone astray;
we have turned every one to his own way;
and the LORD hath laid on him the iniquity of us all.
He was oppressed, and he was afflicted,
yet he opened not his mouth:
he is brought as a lamb to the slaughter,

and as a sheep before her shearers is dumb,
so he openeth not his mouth.
He was taken from prison and from judgment:
and who shall declare his generation?
for he was cut off out of the land of the living:
for the transgression of my people was he stricken.

Vicarious suffering is always affecting. I was even reminded of Moses: ***he was numbered with the transgressors; and he bare the sin of many, and made intercession for the transgressors.***

God made a grudging confession: ***For a small moment have I forsaken thee; but with great mercies will I gather thee.*** Just as he swore to Noah never again to flood the earth, so he would now swear never again to lose his temper with them; ***my kindness shall not depart from thee, neither shall the covenant of my peace be removed.*** I'll leave the subsequent history of the Hebrew people to speak for itself. 54

At any rate, he extended a general invitation to find spiritual fulfilment in the promised land. 55

Ho, every one that thirsteth, come ye to the waters,
and he that hath no money; come ye, buy, and eat;
yea, come, buy wine and milk without money and without price.
Wherefore do ye spend money for that which is not bread?
and your labour for that which satisfieth not?

There, the children of Israel would act as a latter-day David, for ***Behold, I have given him for a witness to the people, a leader and commander to the people.*** So likewise would they rally nations yet unknown, attracted by God's glory.

By way of preparation, a display of repentance was called for.

Seek ye the LORD while he may be found,
call ye upon him while he is near:
Let the wicked forsake his way,
and the unrighteous man his thoughts:
and let him return unto the LORD, and he will have mercy upon him;
and to our God, for he will abundantly pardon.
For my thoughts are not your thoughts,
neither are your ways my ways, saith the LORD.

Of that I had no doubt.

And so the people would be led back through the wilderness to the land of their fathers. ***The mountains and the hills shall break forth before you into singing, and all the trees of the field shall clap their hands. Instead of the thorn shall***

come up the fir tree, and instead of the brier shall come up the myrtle tree. The new landscaping would be a reminder of God's greatness.

On to the New Jerusalem

56 At this point Isaiah went through another transformation, considering nitty-gritty problems from a perspective that shifted to the time when the people had returned from exile.

The first task was to reassure the eunuchs – more than a few had come back from Babylon – that they wouldn't be forgotten. God promised that if they were obedient, ***I will give them an everlasting name, that shall not be cut off*** – perhaps an unfortunate choice of words.

If God was hospitable to eunuchs and strangers, he wasn't turning soft just yet. Politicians put him in a foul mood; he described the new leadership as ignorant, 57 indolent, greedy, drunken dogs. ***The righteous perisheth, and no man layeth it to heart.*** The fun really started when he spotted some of the less orthodox, ***sons of the sorceress, the seed of the adulterer and the whore.***

Who do you think you are, he asked, ***Enflaming yourselves with idols under every green tree, slaying the children in the valleys under the clifts of the rocks?*** But never mind infanticide; it was women who produced the most agitation. The thought of one lustily enjoying herself on a wide bed, naked but for the perfume in her hair, had him fuming. I wasn't so sure that she was in it for the money, but he maintained that she procured partners from everywhere; ***thou … didst send thy messengers far off, and didst debase thyself even unto hell.***

After a time God cooled off, saying ***Peace, peace to him that is far off, and to*** 58 ***him that is near.*** He turned to the required fasts, which were being observed in a mechanical way. To benefit, he declared, you have to show genuine contrition.

Is not this the fast that I have chosen?
to loose the bands of wickedness,
to undo the heavy burdens,
and to let the oppressed go free,
and that ye break every yoke?
Is it not to deal thy bread to the hungry,
and that thou bring the poor that are cast out to thy house?
when thou seest the naked, that thou cover him;
and that thou hide not thyself from thine own flesh?
Then shall thy light break forth as the morning,
and thine health shall spring forth speedily.

God the radical had reappeared, arguing that observance is a matter of righting social as well as personal wrongs.

Estranged from his people, God put the blame on them; apart from anything else, ***they make haste to shed innocent blood ... wasting and destruction are in their paths***. So he had noticed. 59

God gave people something to look forward to: the new Jerusalem. ***Arise, shine; for thy light is come, and the glory of the LORD is risen upon thee***. Everyone would gather in the city on which the sun and moon would no longer set, the city illuminated by the glory of God. ***A little one shall become a thousand, and a small one a strong nation: I the LORD will hasten it in his time.*** 60

The prophet was becoming inspired. 61

The Spirit of the Lord GOD is upon me;
because the LORD hath anointed me
to preach good tidings unto the meek;
he hath sent me to bind up the brokenhearted,
to proclaim liberty to the captives,
and the opening of the prison to them that are bound;
To proclaim the acceptable year of the LORD,
and the day of vengeance of our God;
to comfort all that mourn;
To appoint unto them that mourn in Zion,
to give unto them beauty for ashes,
the oil of joy for mourning,
the garment of praise for the spirit of heaviness.

The people had seen hard times, but in future everyone would recognise that God had blessed them. The land would no longer be called forsaken, but Beulah – married – because ***as the bridegroom rejoiceth over the bride, so shall thy God rejoice over thee.*** 62

He reappeared in a more warlike vein as God the avenger. It reminded me of a question-and-response song: ***Who is this that cometh from Edom, with dyed garments from Bozrah?*** God thunders that it is he. Why do you look like someone who has been treading grapes? 63

I have trodden the winepress alone;
and of the people there was none with me:
for I will tread them in mine anger,
and trample them in my fury;
and their blood shall be sprinkled upon my garments,
and I will stain all my raiment.

What a mess.

After that, it's not surprising that Isaiah seemed ambivalent in asking for a renewal of God's attention: ***where is thy zeal and thy strength, the sounding of***

thy bowels and of thy mercies toward me? are they restrained? I should hope so.

64 The prophet wasn't long on self-esteem; ***we are all as an unclean thing, and all our righteousnesses are as filthy rags; and we all do fade as a leaf.*** While grovelling in the dust, however, he made the sly remark that ***we all are the work of thy hand***, neatly raising the question of whether the clay or the potter is to blame for the misshapen pot.

65 God had another grumble about the unorthodox. They say ***Stand by thyself, come not near to me; for I am holier than thou. These are a smoke in my nose***, he added. I know how unpleasant that can be.

He announced the coming of a new age: ***behold, I create new heavens and a new earth***. There will be no more sorrow, and everyone will live to be a hundred – a statement that later seemed uncomfortably at odds with claims that death would be abolished altogether. That's gratitude for you: offer the moon, and they'll want the stars too. But to continue the vision:

And they shall build houses, and inhabit them;
and they shall plant vineyards, and eat the fruit of them.
They shall not build, and another inhabit;
they shall not plant, and another eat ...
They shall not labour in vain.

No more working for the benefit of ungrateful offspring, with any luck.

66 Perhaps the fault lay with the prophets, but God often seemed to send out mixed signals. He would say, for example, ***As one whom his mother comforteth, so will I comfort you***, and then the next moment he'd be describing how he'd descend like fire on anyone ***eating swine's flesh, and the abomination, and the mouse***. On reflection, though, I suppose most mothers would be upset if they caught you with a rodent between your teeth.

The conclusion was pure horror. God blessed his people, telling them that in the new Jerusalem they would come to worship at every new moon, at every sabbath.

And they shall go forth,
and look upon the carcases of the men that have transgressed against me:
for their worm shall not die,
neither shall their fire be quenched;
and they shall be an abhorring unto all flesh.

With a sight like that in store each week, I imagine that fasting should come easily in paradise.

24

Jeremiah

A century later, an even greater pessimist came along: the prophet Jeremiah. Through the reigns of the last few kings of Judah he carried out his mission – and had the unusual gratification of living to see his prophecies fulfilled, with Babylon triumphant. 1

When the call came, Jeremiah was reluctant to accept God's commission. Needless to say he was talked into it. Jeremiah described how ***the LORD put forth his hand, and touched my mouth. And the LORD said unto me, Behold, I have put my words in thy mouth. See I have this day set thee over the nations and over the kingdoms, to root out, and to pull down, and to destroy, and to throw down, to build, and to plant.*** A boy can't do better than that.

God was unhappy; Israel had been like a camel on heat, ready to go with all comers. ***In vain have I smitten your children; they received no correction***, he complained. Violence is so unreliable in education. ***Can a maid forget her ornaments, or a bride her attire? yet my people have forgotten me days without number.*** God's self-comparison to a wedding dress isn't one that would have occurred to me. 2

He protested to Jeremiah ***Hast thou seen that which backsliding Israel hath done? she is gone up upon every high mountain and under every green tree, and there hath played the harlot.*** God said that he would take her back if she repented, and smash the place to bits if she didn't. Send for the social worker, I thought. 3 4

Extending the fornication metaphor, God complained that the people ***were as fed horses in the morning: every one neighed after his neighbour's wife.*** Or rather, couldn't say nay. He was upset that his power hadn't been recognised. 5

Hear now this, O foolish people, and without understanding;
    which have eyes, and see not;
    which have ears, and hear not:
Fear ye not me? ...
But this people hath a revolting and a rebellious heart;
    they are revolted and gone.

God wasn't even happy with the religious leaders. ***The prophets prophesy falsely, and the priests bear rule by their means; and my people love to have it so: and what will ye do in the end thereof?*** A good question: who knows whom to believe? On the same theme, God asserted that ***They have healed also the hurt*** 6

of the daughter of my people slightly, saying, Peace, peace; when there is no peace. He didn't think much of faith healers, physical or spiritual.

God's advice was simple. ***Stand ye in the ways, and see, and ask for the old paths, where is the good way, and walk therein, and ye shall find rest for your souls.*** Take the wrong road and find unrest for your bodies, he might have added.

7 God told them repeatedly to ***Amend your ways and your doings,*** but disaster seemed inevitable. The people couldn't win; when he took them to task for giving undue attention to ritual, he claimed ***I spake not unto your fathers, nor commanded them in the day that I brought them out of the land of Egypt, concerning burnt offerings or sacrifices.*** Who was he trying to kid? Moses could have written a cookbook after all their talks.

8 As always, God had a good line in horror. He declared that when doomsday came they would bring all the bones out of the graves and lay them before the sun and the moon, whom they had worshipped. The prophet sounded resigned; ***The harvest is past, the summer is ended, and we are not saved. ... Is there no balm in Gilead ...?*** I'm afraid they were going to need more than balm.

9 Jeremiah was so depressing, he depressed even himself. ***Oh that I had in the wilderness a lodging place of wayfaring men; that I might leave my people, and go from them! for they be all adulterers, an assembly of treacherous men.*** For their part, they must have wished that they could steer clear of God, who was warning ***I will feed them, even this people, with wormwood, and give them water of gall to drink.*** Not content with poisoning, he would scatter and batter them, until they were finished off.

10 After making all these dire threats, God ridiculed his rivals as idols made with hammer and nails, capable of doing neither good nor harm. What more advertisement did they need, I ask.

11 Everyone was angry with everyone else. God accused the people of breaking the covenant, and told them to expect the worst. Jeremiah was so unpopular that 12 his own neighbours plotted to kill him. Asked by the prophet why he allowed the evil to prosper, God irritably replied that life was a picnic, compared to what it would become: ***If thou hast run with the footmen, and they have wearied thee, then how canst thou contend with horses?***

13 God compared the people to everything from a useless girdle to wine bottles about to be broken. It seems the intention was less to warn than to abuse, given the hopelessness of reform: ***Can the Ethiopian change his skin, or the leopard his spots? then may ye also do good, that are accustomed to do evil.*** He railed against their adulteries, lewdness, whoredom, abominations, and so on, but they had heard it all before.

14 The suffering caused by a drought didn't soften him. Indeed, he told Jeremiah not to pray for the people; ***When they fast, I will not hear their cry; and when they offer burnt offering and an oblation, I will not accept them: but I will consume them by the sword, and by the famine, and by the pestilence.*** And he wondered why they were rebellious?

He insisted that the people would be torn apart and devoured; like a fainting woman, ***her sun is gone down while it was yet day***. Jeremiah seemed depressed not so much by these predictions, as by the fact that no one liked him. ***Woe is me, my mother, that thou hast borne me a man of strife and a man of contention to the whole earth!*** Perhaps he should have chosen another employer. 15

His terms of service were unattractive, I'm bound to say. God told him ***Thou shalt not take thee a wife, neither shalt thou have sons or daughters in this place.*** Now I wouldn't envy any woman who had to live with Jeremiah, but he could have done with cheering up after a hard day prophesying death and destruction. 16

That said, God needed humouring even more. I suppose the people had been meant to act as spouse, but he maintained that ***The sin of Judah is written with a pen of iron, and with the point of a diamond***. They were on the brink of a messy divorce. 17

God found a song – some of which had been composed in Egypt centuries earlier – that expressed how he felt.

Cursed be the man that trusteth in man,
and maketh flesh his arm,
and whose heart departeth from the LORD.
For he shall be like the heath in the desert,
and shall not see when good cometh;
but shall inhabit the parched places in the wilderness,
in a salt land and not inhabited.
Blessed is the man that trusteth in the LORD,
and whose hope the LORD is.
For he shall be as a tree planted by the waters,
and that spreadeth out her roots by the river,
and shall not see when heat cometh,
but her leaf shall be green;
and shall not be careful in the year of drought,
neither shall cease from yielding fruit.

He did sound, I must say, like a lover betrayed: ***The heart is deceitful above all things, and desperately wicked: who can know it?*** Justice will be done, however. ***As the partridge sitteth on eggs, and hatcheth them not; so he that getteth riches, and not by right, shall leave them in the midst of his days, and at his end shall be a fool.***

Jeremiah seemed to want two things from God, protection and revenge, saying ***thou art my hope in the day of evil. Let them be confounded that persecute me ... destroy them with double destruction.*** I felt uncomfortable when prophets treated him like a mob boss, but God has to take some of the blame. He described the house of Israel as clay in his hands, so that like a potter he could make or unmake it as he chose. Since in his view ***the virgin of Israel hath done a very horrible*** 18

thing – why a virgin, I wonder – Jeremiah didn't hesitate to wish ghastly punishments on his enemies: the men killed, their children starved, the women widowed and childless.

19 It was hardly surprising that the prophet wasn't winning prizes for popularity. He went into the valley of Ben-Hinnom – which under the name 'Gehenna' became a synonym for hell – and told the people what God had in store for them: violent death, or if not ***I will cause them to eat the flesh of their sons and the flesh of their daughters***.

20 Such talk earned Jeremiah a night in the stocks. He didn't hesitate to convey a message from God to the priest responsible: ***I will make thee a terror to thyself, and to all thy friends***. Despite – or because of? – this threat, Jeremiah escaped further punishment.

21 During the final siege of Jerusalem the king asked Jeremiah if God had some good news for them. The prophet relayed word that, on the contrary, God intended to play an active part against Judah in the coming disaster. Anyone wanting to live should surrender quietly to the forces of Babylon.

22 The previous king had had no better luck. ***O earth, earth, earth, hear the word of the LORD***, Jeremiah had said: ***Write ye this man childless ... no man of his seed shall prosper, sitting upon the throne of David.*** His genealogy shows that he wasn't childless, so God must have been bluffing. It would have been bad news for later pretenders if that line of descent from David really had been extinguished.

23 God didn't make it easy for people. He vehemently condemned the followers of false prophets, but without offering criteria for distinguishing the good from the
24 bad. It wasn't easy to predict the distinctions he did make, either. Following his initial conquest, Nebuchadnezzar had sent the powerful and prosperous as captives to Babylon, while leaving the rest of the population in Judah. I might have expected God to favour the common folk still in the promised land, but in fact he compared them to a basket containing ***very naughty figs, which could not be eaten*** – unlike the high-class figs no longer present. As the group remaining was marked for destruction, the moral was to go quietly into exile, you naughty old fig, you.

25 When it came to calamity, I'm not sure that he made any distinctions at all. Babylon would be punished, he promised, though not before Jerusalem was destroyed and the people subjected to seventy years of servitude. God proceeded to press his cup of fury on a long list of nations, and finally on ***all the kingdoms of the world, which are upon the face of the earth ... Drink ye, and be drunken, and spue, and fall, and rise no more, because of the sword which I will send among you.*** You can't be more even-handed than that.

SCENES FROM THE PROPHET'S LIFE

26 It was hard not to feel some sympathy for Jeremiah. The poor fellow was nearly
27 executed once, being the bearer of bad news, and God made him do the most

outlandish things, such as trudging around wearing a yoke to urge submission to Babylon. A rival prophet who did him the favour of breaking the yoke had his life shortened by God as a result. 28

Jeremiah didn't confine himself to prophesying in Judah; he also sent messages to the exiles, telling them to settle and be patient. He wasn't uniformly gloomy, either; he occasionally held out hope of better times to come. ***In those days they shall say no more, The fathers have eaten a sour grape, and the children's teeth are set on edge. But every one shall die for his own iniquity*** – no need to keep such a close eye on the parents. God actually promised an entirely new covenant to the people of Israel and Judah, one so firmly imprinted that no one would need to be taught to know him. I wasn't aware that he needed much introduction. 29 30 31

As if being arrested wasn't bad enough, Jeremiah was even called upon to squander his money on God's business. Just when Judah was about to be taken over, Jeremiah paid 17 shekels of silver for a field he could never use. God promised that in due course ***I will plant them in this land assuredly with my whole heart and with my whole soul.*** How better to make the point than to have his prophet throw away some cash? 32

God was a strong believer in the reformative effects of punishment. Once the people had been cleansed by disaster his protection could be restored, and the house of David would furnish kings galore. Though generally finding the people's wickedness exaggerated, in one instance I had to agree that they behaved badly. With Jerusalem under siege they freed their slaves, and then revoked the emancipation proclamation when it appeared that the immediate danger had passed. Very sordid. 33 34

Jeremiah held up other tribes as role models for the people. The nomadic Rechabites, for example, obeyed an ancestral command not to drink wine, and you don't get more obedient than that. By contrast, God asserted, ***I have spoken unto you, rising early and speaking; but ye hearkened not unto me.*** It's awful to get up early for nothing. 35

After Jeremiah had been a prophet for over two decades, God told him to ***Take thee a roll of a book, and write therein all the words that I have spoken unto thee.*** That was a lot of words, but as the document was read aloud no fewer than three times in one day Jeremiah must have edited considerably. At the last reading the king burned the whole work, for which sacrilege God promised to expose his corpse to the elements. Jeremiah and his secretary rewrote everything that had gone up in smoke, ***and there were added besides unto them many like words.*** I know what sort of words I'd add if I had to rewrite an entire book. 36

During the final siege of Jerusalem Jeremiah was imprisoned for sedition – reasonably enough, given that he had been urging people to surrender rather than fight. Mind you, I rather liked his remark that he was in prison for being right, and what had the king done with the prophets who claimed that the Babylonians wouldn't attack? 37

An Ethiopian eunuch saved Jeremiah's life by hauling him out of the dungeon, 38

39 with the king's permission, to put him somewhere healthier. When Jerusalem fell the leading citizens were killed or taken captive, but Nebuchadnezzar ordered his commander to protect Jeremiah and to ***do unto him even as he shall say unto thee***, which no doubt confirmed for many that he had been a traitor all along. At any rate the helpful eunuch had made a wise choice, being given God's promise that he would escape with his life.

40 Jeremiah declined the opportunity to go to Babylon, chosing instead to join a collaborator who had been appointed governor in Judah. The policy of business as usual under Babylonian rule wasn't accepted by everyone, and the governor was 41 assassinated. Although they chased the killer away, some of the remaining Judaeans feared reprisals from Babylon and decided to flee to Egypt.

42 Jeremiah transmitted God's view that it was safe to stay, whereas going to Egypt 43 would result in unpleasant death. Accusing him of lying, and of wanting to turn them over to the Babylonians, the remnant of Judah set off regardless. For some reason Jeremiah went too; I couldn't see that he'd get much satisfaction from being right at his own funeral.

Once there he prophesied that Nebuchadnezzar would come to rule Egypt and 44 destroy its temples. He continued to fulminate against his own people, particularly those women who had been worshipping the queen of heaven, i.e. the goddess of nature. The women weren't afraid to answer back, saying that they had every intention of carrying on. For so long as offerings had been made to the goddess, ***then had we plenty of victuals, and were well, and saw no evil. But since we left off to burn incense to the queen of heaven, and to pour out drink offerings unto her, we have wanted all things, and have been consumed by the sword and by the famine.*** Naturally Jeremiah didn't accept that view of events, but I was entertained to see the tables turned.

45 God's advice was summed up in an earlier message to Jeremiah's secretary: ***And seekest thou great things for thyself? seek them not: for, behold, I will bring evil upon all flesh***. Encouraging he wasn't.

46 After that it was back to foreigners: when it came to a divine smiting, no one would be left out. Egypt was in big trouble, as always. The Philistines, another old 47 favourite, could look forward to an invasion. (The prophet was moved to ask ***O thou sword of the LORD, how long will it be ere thou be quiet?***) Not to be forgotten, 48 ***Moab also shall wallow in his vomit.*** God continued down the list, providing a 49 bad word for Ammon, Edom, Damascus, Kedar, and Elam. Just living in that part of the world was a mistake.

50 Last and far from least was Babylon, which having served as his flogger must now take its turn to be flogged, and at great length. Its forces had a horrible fate in 51 store; ***they shall become as women***, God said. The king of the Medes would be doing his will, ***and with thee will I break in pieces old and young; and with thee will I break in pieces the young man and the maid;*** and everyone else from the soldier to the shepherd.

In short, God announced, ***I will bring them down like lambs to the slaughter;***

Babylon would end up desolate and uninhabited. If God invites you to punish his people, my advice is to decline politely.

That more or less concluded what Jeremiah had to say. The fall of Jerusalem, the fate of the king, the exile of the remaining people – I've described all that already. A few of the details changed in the retelling, but let that pass. 52

25

Lamentations

The fall of Jerusalem brought the people to their lowest ebb; with the destruction of Israel and Judah, they had lost their inheritance. Apparently God was no longer their protector. In fact, of course, it was just a stage they were going through, another level up the rising spiral of sin, sacrifice and redemption. Forgiveness would ultimately follow each period of punishment, and indeed God generally promised to raise them higher than before.

1 None of this was so clear from the people's perspective, however, and they lacked confidence that Zion could be redeemed. Long laments were composed. Several, in later years, were ascribed to Jeremiah, but I don't remember him being the author. All except the last were acrostics, and he wasn't the type to play word games.

They were sad, and imagined that Jerusalem was, too.

How doth the city sit solitary,
that was full of people!
how is she become as a widow!
she that was great among the nations,
and princess among the provinces,
how is she become a tributary!
She weepeth sore in the night,
and her tears are on her cheeks:
among all her lovers she hath none to comfort her.

Personified as a fallen woman, degraded and despised, she cried out ***Is it nothing to you, all ye that pass by? behold, and see if there be any sorrow like unto my sorrow***. While confessing her sin, she wept at the loss of her children.

2 To all appearances God was cutting off the divine nose to spite the celestial face; it was his own temple that was desecrated, his own city that was destroyed, his own people whose infants were dying of starvation and whose mothers were eating their babies.

The young and the old lie on the ground in the streets:
my virgins and my young men are fallen by the sword;
thou hast slain them in the day of thine anger;
thou hast killed, and not pitied.

To voice the unspoken doubt: did the punishment fit the crime?

The poet complained that ***My strength and my hope is perished from the LORD: Remembering mine affliction and my misery, the wormwood and the gall.*** No sooner had he said it, though, than optimism got the better of him. Patience was a virtue, and anyway, ***It is good for a man that he bear the yoke in his youth.*** Try telling that to the youth. 3

Disaster seemed to have drained the aggression from them. ***He giveth his cheek to him that smiteth him***, hoping that God would eventually take notice. They were simply resigned to whatever came: God might do anything. ***Out of the mouth of the most High proceedeth not evil and good?***

Still, they each continued to appeal to his sense of justice, praying ***O LORD, thou hast seen my wrong: judge thou my cause***, and calling his attention to the scorn of the enemy: ***Behold their sitting down, and their rising up; I am their musick.*** (Better their music than their dinner, I suppose.) But if God had allowed their foes to prevail, some people must have wondered, was it realistic to expect that he would now ***Persecute and destroy them in anger***?

Whatever doubts were raised by the graphic descriptions of famine, of women boiling their own children to eat, their declared belief was that ***The punishment of thine iniquity is accomplished, O daughter of Zion; he will no more carry thee away into captivity***. I just wish it had been true. 4

Faithful as they were, the people couldn't escape the memory of what had happened to Jerusalem. The horror could only be explained as a punishment for the sins of previous generations. 5

They ravished the women in Zion,
    and the maids in the cities of Judah.
Princes are hanged up by their hand:
    the faces of elders were not honoured.
They took the young men to grind,
    and the children fell under the wood.

God might redeem them yet, ***But thou hast utterly rejected us;*** you wouldn't want to hold your breath.

26

Ezekiel

1 As Jeremiah was approaching the end of his career, God decided to appoint a younger man to carry on the work of spreading gloom and doom. Although this was several years before the final fall of Jerusalem, the man he chose was already in Babylon, being one of the captives taken in the initial conquest. His name was Ezekiel.

God liked to impress new prophets, and he was improving with practice. There was no mere burning bush when Ezekiel received the call, but a storm cloud wreathed in light, within which were four cherubim bathed in fire, forming a square. Each had four wings and four faces, those of a man, an eagle, a lion and an ox, facing outward, inward, right and left respectively. The cherubim moved together, but only in straight lines; even that took practice, I believe.

There was also a wheel on each side, ***and their appearance and their work was as it were a wheel in the middle of a wheel.*** Set at right angles, the rims of these wheels were filled with eyes: it certainly created an effect. God himself rode on top, appearing in the likeness of a man on a throne, shimmering with fire above the waist and a rainbow below.

2 Ezekiel had by this time fallen on his face, but a voice said ***Son of man, stand upon thy feet, and I will speak unto thee.*** Expressing displeasure at the people's rebelliousness, God gave Ezekiel his commission as prophet. He handed Ezekiel a scroll to eat, secret-agent style, ***and there was written therein lamentations, and***
3 ***mourning, and woe.*** It didn't sound very appetising, but I was wrong. Ezekiel recounted that ***he said unto me, Son of man, cause thy belly to eat, and fill thy bowels with this roll that I give thee. Then did I eat it; and it was in my mouth as honey for sweetness.*** I wonder what more cheerful words would have tasted like.

Like Isaiah, Ezekiel was told that people wouldn't listen to him. He was simply to act as a watchman, passing on warnings from God. It would be his fault if the people were not alerted, but theirs if they took no notice. God wasn't in a forgiving mood; he planned to punish even a righteous man who had gone astray, regardless of his good deeds.

4 Eating the scroll was only the first challenge. Next Ezekiel had to build a little model of Jerusalem under siege, complete with towers, ramps, battering rams, etc. Playing besieger was supposed to serve as a sign to the people.

Then God told him to lie on his left side for a very long time (either 190 or 390 days – there was some confusion on this score), where each day would represent a year that Israel would be in exile. That completed, he was to spend another 40 days on his right side to signify Judah's exile.

During this whole period God allowed him only a small ration of bread and water, with baking to be done in public view using human manure for fuel. Ezekiel balked at this last requirement, and God substituted cow dung. Let no one say he wasn't reasonable.

5 To complete the games, Ezekiel had to shave off his hair and beard with a sharp sword – not a good example to the children. He divided the pile of hair, apparently meant to represent the people, into three parts. Following God's instructions he burnt one third in his model city, hacked up another third around its borders, and scattered the remainder to the winds.

God confirmed that the people's fate would not be pleasant. As punishment for their sins, ***the fathers shall eat the sons in the midst of thee, and the sons shall eat their fathers***. I suppose it would be a race to see who could finish first. Not only famine, but pestilence, death by the sword, and attacks by wild beasts were all in prospect.

6 Losing religious market share made God upset. ***I will lay the dead carcases of the children of Israel before their idols; and I will scatter your bones round about your altars.*** He would teach them respect; ***they shall know that I am the LORD.***
7 When he started to sound like that it was best to stay out of his way. He would swear that ***An end, the end is come upon the four corners of the land***, and then make turbid speeches promising death and destruction. Of course he was awfully gentle, really.

8 One day God took Ezekiel by the hair – it had grown back by then – and transported him in a vision to Jerusalem. In and around the temple people were worshipping every kind of pagan figure: idols, animals and reptiles, a nature god,
9 the rising sun. Having called up his shock troops, ***every man a slaughter weapon in his hand***, God took aside a figure ***clothed with linen, with a writer's inkhorn by his side***: it was I. He told me to go through the city putting a mark on the forehead of non-heathens.

I tried to give people the benefit of the doubt, it being all too clear what was coming. Even so, I was shaken to overhear his orders to the death squad: ***Go ye after him through the city, and smite: let not your eye spare, neither have ye pity: Slay utterly old and young, both maids, and little children, and women: but come not near any man upon whom is the mark; and begin at my sanctuary. Then they began at the ancient men which were before the house. And he said unto them, Defile the house, and fill the courts with the slain: go ye forth. And they went forth, and slew in the city.***

10 Jerusalem was a shambles shortly to be turned into a crematorium; God told me to bring some coals out from his chariot to scatter over the city. Ezekiel, possibly in a state of shock, could only stare at the wheels and cherubim on the divine vehicle. Although he claimed to recognise them from his previous encounter, he wrote in his diary that the four faces of each creature were those of a man, lion,

eagle – and cherub. I don't know how anyone could confuse a cherub and an ox.

11 Later, Ezekiel made another trip in spirit to Jerusalem. Without any apparent sense of irony he accused a group of people there of filling the streets with bodies, and of violating God's law. Distressingly, one of the leaders fell down dead on the spot. God told Ezekiel not to worry: the remnant would return from exile and be restored to the land. Those left in the city were expendable, I gathered.

12 Getting back to games, God made him act out a little drama to illustrate the future exile, by going out through a hole in the wall with a knapsack. ***The days are at hand***, he said to rebuke the sceptical, though an audience of exiles can't have been that difficult to persuade.

13 Occasionally God had me baffled. ***Son of man***, he told Ezekiel, ***prophesy against the prophets of Israel that prophesy, and say thou unto them that prophesy out of their own hearts ... Woe unto the foolish prophets***! Having picked on a pack of prophets, he proceeded to reproach female practitioners in particular. ***Woe to the women that sew pillows to all armholes, and make kerchiefs upon the head of every stature to hunt souls!*** String them up, I say. He was talking about sorcery, in case you're wondering.

14 God undertook to deal with false prophets personally. Singling them out seemed pointless to me, as everyone was going to be exposed to the sword, famine, wild

15 beasts and pestilence anyway. Why bother? He regarded the whole people as worse than useless, like a worthless vine that had been burnt.

THE FALL OF JERUSALEM

16 In the analogy God developed at greatest length, Jerusalem was a fallen woman. Abandoned at birth, she had come under God's protection. The day arrived when he noticed that she had reached womanhood, with firm breasts and long hair; ***behold, thy time was the time of love; and I spread my skirt over thee, and covered thy nakedness ... thou becamest mine***. Being deflowered by her guardian must have had a disturbing effect, and she became promiscuous.

That wasn't all, God was shocked to discover. ***Thou hast also taken thy fair jewels of my gold and of my silver, which I had given thee, and madest to thyself images of men, and didst commit whoredom with them***. So much less trouble than the real thing. He even claimed that she had sacrificed their children to these figures, which seemed hard to credit.

What horrified God was not just her fornication with Egyptians, Assyrians and Babylonians, but also the notion that she had paid them rather than the reverse: not feminine, presumably. ***Behold, therefore I will gather all thy lovers, with whom thou hast taken pleasure, and all them that thou hast loved, with all them that thou hast hated; I will even gather them round about against thee, and will discover thy nakedness unto them ... they shall strip thee also of thy clothes, and shall take thy fair jewels, and leave thee naked and bare. They shall also bring***

up a company against thee, and they shall stone thee with stones, and thrust thee through with their swords. All this would have a calming effect on him, God said.

From the curious idea that Jerusalem had a Hittite mother and an Amorite father, God declared that ***As is the mother, so is her daughter.*** Samaria was her elder sister, and Sodom her younger, but she was worse than either of them. None the less he would one day restore the covenant, although his idea of reconciliation was that she would ***never open thy mouth any more because of thy shame***. He wasn't easy to live with.

17

It was a refreshing change to hear a parable about eagles, cedars and vines, though the message condemned the last king of Judah for resisting the domination of Babylon. Even defending God's own land could be a mistake if he had punishment in mind. As I say, it was hard to stay in his good books.

18

I appreciated God's homily on the adage ***The fathers have eaten sour grapes, and the children's teeth are set on edge***. This should no longer apply, he declared; everyone will be judged as an individual. The righteous man – someone meeting every qualification from having not ***come near to a menstruous woman*** to having ***executed true judgment between man and man*** – will live. His wicked son – one who has ***defiled his neighbour's wife, Hath oppressed the poor and needy***, or whatever – will die. But if the son's son returns to the path of virtue, he will not be punished for his father's sins.

It was a major change of policy; no more visiting the iniquity of the fathers upon the children unto the third and fourth generation: on the contrary, ***The son shall not bear the iniquity of the father, neither shall the father bear the iniquity of the son***. Who would want to foist responsibility for his past onto a son? Not even God, I suspect.

The past didn't necessarily matter even for an individual; if you were good and turned bad, you would die in spite of your earlier virtue, but ***when the wicked man turneth away from his wickedness that he hath committed, and doeth that which is lawful and right, he shall save his soul alive***. His advice, therefore, was ***Repent ... and make you a new heart and a new spirit***. And try not to leave it too late.

19, 20

Ezekiel offered a couple of laments for the last kings of Judah (exactly which ones wasn't clear). God moved quickly back to centre stage, complaining that the people had been unfaithful to him right from the outset, in Egypt. Having wanted to destroy them ever since, he was amazed at his own moderation in waiting so long.

He finally lost patience, ***Wherefore I gave them also statutes that were not good, and judgments whereby they should not live***, and abandoned them to idolatry and child sacrifice. In other words, he provoked his own justification for punishing them: an astonishing confession. When he did restore the people it would be to protect his reputation, God said, not because they deserved another chance.

21

God announced that his sword was unsheathed. The enemy would reach a fork in the road, and when ***the king of Babylon stood at the parting of the way*** he would use divination to choose his direction. That choice – no surprise – would take them towards Jerusalem. ***I will overturn, overturn, overturn, it: and it shall be no more, until he come whose right it is; and I will give it him.*** The identity of this deserving king was a mystery, I'm afraid.

22 It was only right that God should spell out the sins for which they would soon suffer. Idolatry, of course, was high on the list, but he also mentioned abuse of power, lack of respect for parents, ill-treatment of widows and orphans, violation of sabbaths, and a whole host of sexual offences, including intercourse with menstruating women, daughters-in-law, and sisters. That his punishment would precipitate the rape, murder, or deportation of all the afore-mentioned struck me as unfortunate, but he felt obliged to melt the people down like impure silver in a furnace.

23 God's favourite image, regrettably, remained the wicked woman. There were two sisters ***in Egypt; they committed whoredoms in their youth: there were their breasts pressed, and there they bruised the teats of their virginity.*** The sisters were Samaria and Jerusalem, and notwithstanding their wild youth, God fathered his children on them. Because Samaria liked Assyrian men, and fornicated with as many as she could, he ***delivered her into the hand of her lovers***, who raped and murdered her.

Jerusalem, too, ***doted upon the Assyrians her neighbours, captains and rulers clothed most gorgeously, horsemen riding upon horses, all of them desirable young men.*** Not content to stop there, she recruited lovers in Babylon. ***And the Babylonians came to her into the bed of love, and they defiled her with their whoredom, and she was polluted with them.*** She was especially fond of their gigolos, who had virile organs as long as those of donkeys, and seminal emissions as copious as those of stallions.

Non-sadists might wish to skip her punishment, a gruesome torture-killing. Her nose and ears were cut off; she was stripped and raped; she was mocked and made to tear off her own breasts. And so ***ye shall know that I am the Lord GOD***; he had a way of making his point.

24 When the fall of Jerusalem finally came, God told Ezekiel to make a note of the date. Not that the poor fellow was in much danger of forgetting it: God ended his wife's life at the same time, and forbade him to mourn. By losing what is most precious, God said, he could serve as a symbol for the people's loss of the temple, and as an example of keeping a stiff upper lip. Wives can come in handy.

FOREIGNERS ARE PUNISHED, ISRAEL IS RESTORED

25 At last God wearied of flogging Judah and turned his attention to her neighbours. Ammon, Moab, Edom and Philistia might be gloating, but none would escape the

26 divine fury. Similarly, the island state of Tyre was due for destruction: God said that Nebuchadnezzar would wipe the city from the face of the earth. Perhaps he was having an off day, because in fact the Babylonians laid siege to Tyre for years

without success.

Ezekiel's premature lament for Tyre turned into a consumer catalogue listing goods of every kind in which they traded, mentioning two dozen places of origin like so many brand names. But the city was a sinking ship, he proclaimed; its cargo and crew would all be lost. The king of Tyre himself was condemned to ***die the deaths of the uncircumcised at the hand of strangers: for I have spoken it, saith the Lord GOD.*** 27 28

Next in line for destruction was Egypt, but I fear that God was losing his touch. ***I will make the land of Egypt utterly waste and desolate***, he proclaimed; ***No foot of man shall pass through it, nor foot of beast shall pass through it, neither shall it be inhabited forty years. ... I will scatter the Egyptians among the nations***. If anything like that happened, I missed it. 29

The agent of Egypt's calamity was supposed to be Nebuchadnezzar; God asserted that ***I will strengthen the arms of the king of Babylon, and put my sword in his hand: but I will break Pharaoh's arms, and he shall groan before him with the groanings of a deadly wounded man.*** It didn't quite work out that way; in Egypt life went on, while within fifty years Babylon had fallen. 30

As an aside, nature lovers will be comforted to hear that there will be trees in the underworld. God remarked that ***they are all delivered unto death, to the nether parts of the earth, in the midst of the children of men***. The Egyptians were headed more quickly in that direction; in telling them to ***go down, and be thou laid with the uncircumcised***, he wasn't just being rude. 31 32

Ezekiel's mission, God repeated, was to act as watchman for the children of Israel. If anyone ignored the prophet's warnings, ***his blood shall be upon his own head.*** Ezekiel had been rendered mute except when transmitting God's messages, but his speech was restored just as news of Jerusalem's fall reached Babylon. It's an ill wind that blows nobody good. 33

The shepherds of the people had not done their duty, God complained; they had exploited the sheep and not fed them. He promised to take over, gathering up the scattered flock and returning it to the fold in Israel. The big sheep had themselves been guilty, however, of oppressing the weaker ones. To provide the necessary guidance, ***I will set up one shepherd over them, and he shall feed them, even my servant David ... I the LORD will be their God, and my servant David a prince among them***. Under this prince among sheep they would henceforth live in comfort and tranquillity. 34

There were still scores to settle before paradise could be inaugurated. Edom, in particular, would have to run with blood while the whole world celebrated. God would restore the people to Israel, but not, he made it clear, for their sake: his reputation as the nation's god/father had suffered, and needed to be re-established. 35 36

Ezekiel received a dramatic preview of the coming restoration: ***The hand of the LORD was upon me, and carried me out in the spirit of the LORD, and set me down in the midst of the valley which was full of bones, And caused me to pass by them round about: and, behold, there were very many in the open valley; and,*** 37

lo, they were very dry. And he said unto me, Son of man, can these bones live? And I answered, O Lord GOD, thou knowest. Again he said unto me, Prophesy upon these bones, and say unto them, O ye dry bones, hear the word of the LORD.

Not only did they hear, they sat up and took notice. The bones rattled, gathered themselves together, and fitted one into another; sinews, flesh and skin appeared; the winds were summoned to breathe life into the bodies. This living army, God said, was the people of Israel; they thought that all was lost, and that they were as good as dead, but he would bring them out of their graves and back into their own land.

As an encore, God told Ezekiel to join two pieces of wood representing Israel and Judah. They would again be one nation, living in the promised land, ***even they, and their children, and their children's children for ever: and my servant David shall be their prince for ever.*** I presume he meant a new David, and not just the old one reassembled.

38 If anyone thought that living happily ever after presupposed peace and quiet, God set them straight. He was going to make those foreigners who sniggered that he couldn't look after his own eat their words once and for all. ***Son of man, set thy face against Gog, the land of Magog***, he told Ezekiel. Once everybody had been resettled, God planned to lure Gog, whoever he was, out of the north. The invaders would encounter a huge earthquake, so terrifying that ***every man's sword shall be against his brother***, not to mention disease and slaughter, ***an overflowing rain, and great hailstones, fire, and brimstone.***

39 That apocalypse would be the end of Gog and his mighty army; their bodies would be left to be eaten by scavengers, and their weapons would provide the Israelites with firewood for seven years. God then seemed to change his mind about the corpses, saying that the people should spend seven months burying them all.

THE NEW JERUSALEM

40 Fourteen years after the fall of Jerusalem, God gave Ezekiel a look at what he planned for the city. Or rather, he deputised me, measuring rod in hand, to lead the prophet on an architect's tour of the new temple. Ezekiel carefully (and tediously) noted the dimensions as we poked around in every corner. We examined the outer wall, the gates, the main courtyard, tables for slaughtering animals, the Holy of

41 Holies, adjacent buildings, and elements of the decor, including carved cherubim of the two-faced (human and lion) variety.

42 We trailed through the refectories, where priests would ***eat the most holy things***, and the vestries, where – because the holiness of the sanctuary had rubbed off on their clothes – they would change. The whole enclosure was separated by a wall from the profane area outside.

43 God made an impressive entrance into the temple, bringing a message for the people: ***Now let them put away their whoredom, and the carcases of their kings,***

far from me, and I will dwell in the midst of them for ever. He was tired of royalty cluttering up his house with tombs; I can't say that they've taken much notice.

The consecration of the altar would require the usual amounts of sacrificial blood. Ezekiel learned about various restrictions: the gate through which God entered the temple should never be opened again, foreigners would never be allowed inside, and the Levites were to be relegated to minor duties as punishment for their faithlessness. Only descendants of Zadok could perform priestly functions. 44

Priests themselves were constrained, of course. They were allowed to marry only virgin Israelites, or the widows of other priests. Even so, contact with a dead wife would pollute the bereaved holy man. Bodies of a parent, child, brother or unmarried sister might be touched, but not that of a spouse.

God laid down a miscellany of rules on the assignment of territory, weights and measures, ceremonial duties, feasts and sacrifices. Being a staunch defender of old money and the social order, he ruled out redistribution of land. The ruling prince could give property to his sons and it would be theirs to keep, but if he made such a gift to a slave, it would revert to the prince when the slave was freed. 45 46

The best part of the visit I saved for last. Water flowed from a spring underneath the temple towards the east. As I measured out the distances, Ezekiel splashed in the growing river; after little more than a mile it was too fast and deep to ford. I told him that the water would run into the Dead Sea, bringing it back to life with every kind of fish. Production of salt could continue around the pools and marshes, however. The people would be able to have their fish and keep them too. 47

God sketched out the future boundaries of Israel. He unexpectedly offered a radical innovation: the land should be shared with non-Israelites. ***And so it shall come to pass, that ye shall divide it by lot for an inheritance unto you, and to the strangers that sojourn among you, which shall beget children among you: and they shall be unto you as born in the country among the children of Israel; they shall have inheritance with you among the tribes of Israel.*** It still seems a novel idea.

Land was parcelled out among the twelve tribes in contiguous rectangles: a risky way of defining borders. The priests would occupy an area, wholly sacred, surrounding the temple. I know I said that the land outside the temple walls was profane; there was some confusion about the matter. 48

The dawn of a new age being a major occasion, ***the name of the city from that day shall be, The LORD is there***: Jehovah-shammah. Personally I preferred Jerusalem, but so far it's a moot point.

27

Daniel

1 ***In the third year of the reign of Jehoiakim king of Judah came Nebuchadnezzar king of Babylon unto Jerusalem, and besieged it.*** Which is odd because according to my recollection Nebuchadnezzar hadn't even reached the throne then, much less the gates of Jerusalem. Be that as it may, the Babylonians took captives, some of whom were chosen to be trainee wise men in the royal service, including a certain Daniel and three other young Judaeans.

The first problem they faced in exile was the food, polluted as it was. ***Now God had brought Daniel into favour and tender love with the prince of the eunuchs.*** This official, responsible to the king for their well-being, feared that a ritually acceptable diet might be bad for their health and in consequence bad for his own. Daniel proposed a trial period on vegetables and water, ***And at the end of ten days their countenances appeared fairer and fatter in flesh than all the children which did eat the portion of the king's meat.*** The vegetarians had prevailed; Daniel would go on to vanquish other carnivores.

At the end of their apprenticeship the four young men were brought to court, ***And in all matters of wisdom and understanding, that the king enquired of them, he found them ten times better than all the magicians and astrologers that were in all his realm.*** In my experience of magicians and astrologers, that's not saying much. Anyway, Daniel didn't have to wait for an opportunity to demonstrate his skills.

2 Nebuchadnezzar had had a troubling dream, and summoned all his wise men and mystics to interpret it. He insisted, however, that they describe the dream as well as its meaning, on pain of gory death. Their protests that he was asking the impossible only provoked him into ordering the execution of all the wise men in the country.

Being reduced to small pieces along with the rest of the profession sounded to Daniel like a poor way to start his career. Fortunately God revealed all, and he was able to go to the king with the answer. The dream, he said, had been of a giant figure, and his ***head was of fine gold, his breast and his arms of silver, his belly and his thighs of brass, His legs of iron, his feet part of iron and part of clay.*** A falling stone struck these feet of clay, and the entire figure crumbled into dust, which then blew away. Finally ***the stone that smote the image became a great mountain, and filled the whole earth.***

Nebuchadnezzar was the head of gold, Daniel stated, and each lower element succeeding kingdoms. Latterly there would be mixed marriages, but like iron and clay the mixture would not hold. In the end God would establish an everlasting kingdom to supplant all the others.

The king was much impressed, telling Daniel that ***your God is a God of gods, and a Lord of kings, and a revealer of secrets***. By way of reward he made him provincial ruler and chief wise man, appointing his three compatriots to senior positions at Daniel's request. Joseph himself couldn't have done any better.

3

Still, life in Babylon was not without problems for the nice young men from Judah. Nebuchadnezzar erected an enormous golden image, some nine storeys high, with instructions that ***To you it is commanded, O people, nations, and languages, That at what time ye hear the sound of the cornet, flute, harp, sackbut, psaltery, dulcimer, and all kinds of musick, ye fall down and worship the golden image that Nebuchadnezzar the king hath set up: And whoso falleth not down and worshippeth shall the same hour be cast into the midst of a burning fiery furnace***. That was enough encouragement for most people, but the Jews ignored it.

Daniel's three friends were brought before a furious Nebuchadnezzar. They calmly stated that God could save them if he wished, but that in any case they had no intention of worshipping anyone or anything else. At this the king ordered that the furnace be heated to seven times its normal temperature. He was playing with fire: when it came time to toss in the recalcitrant threesome the flames leapt out and devoured their guards.

None the less, ***these three men, Shadrach, Meshach, and Abednego, fell down bound into the midst of the burning fiery furnace***. Having left matters rather late, God sent me down into the furnace to look after them. The king was flabbergasted to see not three but four figures, all walking around in the midst of the fire. He called into the furnace, ***Shadrach, Meshach, and Abednego, ye servants of the most high God, come forth, and come hither***. They stepped out unscathed, ***nor was an hair of their head singed***; I noticed that they had even kept their coats on.

The king was moved to praise God, ***who hath sent his angel, and delivered his servants that trusted in him***. Commanders always get the credit; the rest of us feel lucky to be mentioned in dispatches. Nebuchadnezzar ingratiatingly issued a decree that anyone saying a word against God ***shall be cut in pieces, and their houses shall be made a dunghill***. Praise the Lord – or else.

4

Daniel reappeared when the time came to interpret another of Nebuchadnezzar's dreams. He had seen a great tree cut down, leaving only the stump and a man tethered like a beast. Daniel hesitated to bring bad news, but told the king that he was the tree, and the man as well; he would lose his sanity, and live like an ox for seven (unspecified) units of time. God wanted to show who was in charge.

A year later ***the thing fulfilled upon Nebuchadnezzar: and he was driven from men, and did eat grass as oxen, and his body was wet with the dew of heaven, till his hairs were grown like eagles' feathers, and his nails like birds' claws***. On finally returning to his right mind he praised God, which is always a wise thing to do.

5 The pinnacle of Daniel's career as a (mis)fortune teller came towards the end of his life. ***Belshazzar the king made a great feast to a thousand of his lords,*** and foolishly decided to bring out the gold and silver cups taken from the temple in Jerusalem. As he sat with his concubines, toasting the graven images round about, ***In the same hour came forth fingers of a man's hand, and wrote over against the candlestick upon the plaister of the wall of the king's palace.*** Poor old Belshazzar was so frightened ***that the joints of his loins were loosed, and his knees smote one against another.***

The writing on the wall posed the usual problem: none of the wise men could make sense of it. Daniel chastised the king for failing to show God the respect that his father Nebuchadnezzar had been taught, but agreed to help. He announced ***this is the writing that was written, MENE, MENE, TEKEL, UPHARSIN. This is the interpretation of the thing: MENE; God hath numbered thy kingdom, and finished it. TEKEL; Thou art weighed in the balances, and art found wanting. PERES; Thy kingdom is divided, and given to the Medes and Persians.***

Belshazzar didn't even survive the night. ***Darius the Median took the kingdom,*** which must have come as a surprise to Cyrus the Persian, conqueror of Babylon. But then Nebuchadnezzar would have been surprised to hear that he had a son named Belshazzar. It was all very confusing.

6 While Daniel kept his high office under the new ruler, envious subordinates devised a scheme to remove him. They flattered Darius by proposing that during a period of thirty days all appeals should be made to the king alone, with any violators thrown to the lions: ***Now, O king, establish the decree, and sign the writing, that it be not changed, according to the law of the Medes and Persians, which altereth not.*** Sign he did, though why he should want to make work for himself escaped me.

Naturally Daniel took no notice of the new decree, and carried on saying his prayers three times a day just as before. The conspirators pounced: obliging the king to apply the law, ***they brought Daniel, and cast him into the den of lions.*** Darius was unhappy about losing one of his chief ministers, and consoled Daniel with the hope of divine intervention before sealing the mouth of the pit with a stone. Employees do appreciate these little words of encouragement.

As soon as the sun came up the next morning Darius went to the pit and, in much trepidation, called out to Daniel. The answer came back ***O king, live for ever. My God hath sent his angel, and hath shut the lions' mouths, that they have not hurt me.*** Frankly I didn't have much trouble holding the lions back: being at the very least eighty years old, he didn't look especially tasty. ***So Daniel was taken up out of the den, and no manner of hurt was found upon him, because he believed in his God*** – and his God believed in delegating.

Even the lions had their due. Daniel's enemies, and naturally their wives and their children, were tossed to the hungry beasts, who tore the bodies to pieces before they hit the ground. Happy endings are so satisfying.

PROPHETIC VISIONS

Daniel did more than just interpret dreams and run the country; he had visions himself. Very complex they were too: four great beasts came up from the sea: a lion with eagle's wings, which it then lost; a bear with three ribs between its teeth; a leopard with four wings and four heads; and finally a destructive creature with ten horns, three of which were pushed out by a little horn having eyes and a mouth. Thrones appeared, 7

and the Ancient of days did sit,
whose garment was white as snow,
and the hair of his head like the pure wool:
his throne was like the fiery flame,
and his wheels as burning fire.
A fiery stream issued and came forth from before him:
thousand thousands ministered unto him,
and ten thousand times ten thousand stood before him:
the judgment was set, and the books were opened.

The fourth beast was destroyed, after which a man approached the throne and was given everlasting dominion over the world.

Fortunately someone was on hand to provide an explanation. The beasts were empires; ***But the saints of the most High shall take the kingdom, and possess the kingdom for ever.*** Although the fourth would be oppressive – especially the king represented by the small new horn – God's people would prevail in the end. Simple, really.

A couple of years later Daniel had another vision. A powerful two-horned ram was overcome by an even mightier goat flying out of the west. The goat's single horn snapped off, to be replaced by four new ones. Out of one of these grew a small horn which proceeded to cause havoc. Holiness was predicted to triumph, however, after hard times lasting for 2,300 evenings and mornings. 8

Faced with Daniel's perplexity, God said to my colleague, ***Gabriel, make this man to understand the vision.*** Gabriel explained to Daniel that it was a vision of the end: Greece, the goat, had defeated the Medes and Persians, the ram. The victorious kingdom was split into four parts. In the latter days a wicked king would appear in one of them, making life miserable until he was finally destroyed by a non-human force.

Gabriel told him to ***shut thou up the vision*** – it would have to be their own little secret – while Daniel said ***I was astonished at the vision, but none understood it.*** I understood it well enough: Alexander the Great did come flying out of the west, and his empire was divided between four generals. Antiochus Epiphanes, a successor to one of these, persecuted the Jews. That said, neither did the world come to an end, nor were our people put in charge. Events proved to be less exciting than the prophecy.

9 For his part, Daniel didn't have much confidence in God's promise through Jeremiah that the people would be restored after seventy years of exile. Putting on sackcloth and ashes to confess their sinfulness, he asked God to show mercy towards his sacred city. Gabriel flew in to reassure him. Everything would be rosy in seventy weeks, although he might have meant seventy weeks of years: almost five centuries. The last of these weeks would be very eventful, with the elimination of an anointed one and a full dose of horror. To be honest the message was barely comprehensible, even to me.

10 The last of Daniel's visions came after he had been fasting for three weeks. One of my colleagues appeared before him, eyes flashing and voice booming, to declare ***O Daniel, a man greatly beloved, understand the words that I speak unto thee, and stand upright,*** the poor fellow having collapsed. The messenger apologised for the delay, saying that the guardian angel of Persia had detained him for the past twenty-one days, ***but, lo, Michael, one of the chief princes, came to help me.*** Well, I hadn't saved Daniel from the lions just so that he could starve himself to death.

11 My celestial comrade launched into a description of things to come. Skipping quickly over the following couple of centuries, he went into uncanny detail on later events, eventually reaching the period of oppression under the ruler I subsequently recognised as Antiochus Epiphanes, desecrator of the temple. Up to that point the future had been as clear as history to him, but thereafter things didn't happen at all as he described. His prophetic gift must have deserted him.

12 I was flattered to be given a leading role in the apocalyptic finale:

And at that time shall Michael stand up,
the great prince which standeth for the children of thy people:
and there shall be a time of trouble,
such as never was since there was a nation even to that same time:
and at that time thy people shall be delivered,
every one that shall be found written in the book.
And many of them that sleep in the dust of the earth shall awake,
some to everlasting life,
and some to shame and everlasting contempt.

Major news – all off the record, unfortunately. ***But thou, O Daniel, shut up the words, and seal the book, even to the time of the end: many shall run to and fro, and knowledge shall be increased.*** The end was apparently coming in as little as three and a half years: three and a half something, at any rate.

Daniel confessed that he didn't follow, and asked God what would happen. ***And he said, Go thy way, Daniel: for the words are closed up and sealed till the time of the end. ... none of the wicked shall understand; but the wise shall understand.*** That put him in his place. Remarkably, God went on to be quite specific: the end would come 1,290 days after the desecration of the temple, and ***Blessed is he that waiteth*** a mere 45 days after that. People waited. People still wait. Blessed they might be, but Life – unlike life – goes on.

28

Hosea

1 In the days when the northern kingdom of Israel still existed, there was a prophet named Hosea. ***And the LORD said to Hosea, Go, take unto thee a wife of whoredoms and children of whoredoms: for the land hath committed great whoredom, departing from the LORD.*** If the people had been unfaithful to him, then he'd make the prophet marry an adulterous woman. To see him venting frustration on his own staff made me feel uneasy.

Even Hosea's children suffered, receiving names like 'Not pitied' and 'Not my people'. The day would come, however, when the children of Israel returned to favour, and ***it shall be said unto them, Ye are the sons of the living God.*** Not much consolation if your playmates call you 'Worthless'.

2 God tended to see himself as a wronged husband, and so Hosea wasn't just speaking for himself when he fumed that his errant wife should ***put away her whoredoms out of her sight, and her adulteries from between her breasts; Lest I strip her naked, and set her as in the day that she was born ... I will not have mercy upon her children; for they be the children of whoredoms.*** And this was a man who claimed to want a reconciliation.

3 Ultimately Hosea went and bought back his wife for fifteen pieces of silver and a quantity of barley, although he wasn't going to sleep with her. While Israel was likewise condemned to live for a time without conjugal support, God apparently intended to resume normal relations with her at some point. The female partner never did seem to have much choice in the matter.

4 Apart from his unusual personal life, Hosea was a normal prophet. He accused the people of every sin imaginable: ***there is no truth, nor mercy, nor knowledge of God in the land. By swearing, and lying, and killing, and stealing, and committing adultery, they break out, and blood toucheth blood.*** Even the priests had a lot to answer for, and when it came to punishment God's policy was ***like people, like priest.***

There was no favouritism; everyone was guilty. He thought that women behaved appallingly, but said ***I will not punish your daughters when they commit whoredom, nor your spouses when they commit adultery***, because the men were all out fornicating, too. Equal rights can be fun.

5 Hosea was inclined to blame those in authority for the general lack of orthodoxy. He expected God to punish the nation, and the people to repent. To them, however,
6 God was simply a force of nature, ruining and restoring by turns. ***After two days will he revive us; in the third day he will raise us up, and we shall live in his sight.***

... he shall come unto us as the rain, as the latter and former rain unto the earth.

Their attitude was reciprocated; God regarded Israel's virtue as transitory, like the morning dew. He doubted the sincerity of their observance; ***I desired mercy, and not sacrifice; and the knowledge of God more than burnt offerings.*** In his view the whole kingdom was corrupt. ***Woe unto them!*** Bad news was on its way. 7

Assyria was hovering; Israel would suffer, ***For they have sown the wind, and they shall reap the whirlwind.*** Their children would be massacred, but that wasn't enough for Hosea. ***Give them, O LORD: what wilt thou give? give them a miscarrying womb and dry breasts.*** What a creep. 8 9

As punishment for not listening to God, ***they shall be wanderers among the nations.*** Things might have been different: ***Sow for yourselves in righteousness, reap in mercy,*** but as ***Ye have plowed wickedness, ye have reaped iniquity.*** As far as I could see, though, the Assyrians were just as wicked, and they reaped success. We had to punish their children to make things even. 10

Looking back nostalgically, God recalled that ***When Israel was a child, then I loved him.*** The people drifted away, but ***I drew them ... with bands of love.*** Perhaps he was starting to feel a certain parental responsibility for the mistakes of his children. Whatever the reason might be, he confessed that ***mine heart is turned within me, my repentings are kindled together. I will not execute the fierceness of mine anger.*** The mood must have passed, because the people's situation went from bad to worse. 11

Endorsing his spokesman, God said ***I have multiplied visions, and used similitudes, by the ministry of the prophets.*** But which ones? The whole problem is that true and false prophets make the same claims. 12

The thought of idols made God's temper rise again, and he resolved to set upon the people like a wild beast. His rejection of any pardon – save them? he asked rhetorically: be executioner, more like – wasn't always understood. 13

I will ransom them from the power of the grave;
I will redeem them from death:
O death, I will be thy plagues;
O grave, I will be thy destruction:
repentance shall be hid from mine eyes.

Any possible ambiguity, though, was quickly eliminated.

Samaria shall become desolate;
for she hath rebelled against her God:
they shall fall by the sword:
their infants shall be dashed in pieces,
and their women with child shall be ripped up.

He had a knack for clearing up misunderstandings.

14 Hosea did add that if they repented, God would stop being angry. Some of them tried, I think, but the results were disappointing.

29

Joel

1

Joel specialised in the apocalypse; no one was more interested in the end of the world. When a plague of locusts arrived he feared the worst. The devastation was indeed total; ***That which the palmerworm hath left hath the locust eaten; and that which the locust hath left hath the cankerworm eaten; and that which the cankerworm hath left hath the caterpiller eaten.*** Even the vines were ruined: a real disaster.

Joel called for repentance, with as much sackcloth and breast-beating as possible. He took it for granted that they had something to repent – why else would they be suffering? – but neglected to say what. In good prophetic voice he proclaimed ***Alas for the day! for the day of the LORD is at hand, and as a destruction from the Almighty shall it come.*** The end hasn't come yet, but perhaps the sin tally wasn't quite so bad as he thought.

2

Or maybe we're just waiting for the signal. ***Blow ye the trumpet in Zion***, and the apocalypse will begin. Gather everyone to repent; let ***the bride out of her closet***: one wonders what she was doing there in the first place. God promised to give back what the people had lost, saying ***I will restore to you the years that the locust hath eaten, the cankerworm, and the caterpiller, and the palmerworm, my great army which I sent among you.*** They would be expected to praise him for this; I admired the way he avoided blame for causing torment, while taking credit when it stopped.

Restoring the former prosperity would be only the beginning; God had a surprise in store. Everyone would start to act like a prophet: ***it shall come to pass afterward, that I will pour out my spirit upon all flesh; and your sons and your daughters shall prophesy, your old men shall dream dreams, your young men shall see visions***. He would even enlighten the slaves, which was possibly not their top priority.

3

When I say 'everyone', of course God was only talking about our people. He planned to annihilate the other nations on the day of judgment. After all, ***they have cast lots for my people; and have given a boy for an harlot, and sold a girl for wine***. He'd let them die in battle, though. Reversing Isaiah's vision of universal peace, he told them to ***Beat your plowshares into swords, and your pruninghooks into spears***.

Once conveniently gathered together, the infidels would be crushed like grapes in a wine press. ***Multitudes, multitudes in the valley of decision: for the day of the LORD is near in the valley of decision*** (rather like December shopping). Foreigners would no longer pose a problem in Jerusalem, because there wouldn't be any. But for our people it would be paradise, the mountains running with wine and the hills with milk. After what was supposed to happen to the Gentiles, I'd think twice before drinking from any wine-coloured rivers.

30

Amos

1 Though originally a shepherd, Amos was a prophet's prophet. He had it all: the puritanical passion, the paranormal visions, the zeal for justice. When it came to predicting doom, he had something for everyone.

First he denounced every nation in turn for some characteristic sin: Syria for cruelty to prisoners, Philistia and Tyre for slave trading, Edom and Ammon for barbarism and greed, Moab for abusing the dead. 2 God would send down fire on them all. But then, without pausing for breath, he condemned Judah in exactly the same way.

Israel was cursed at greatest length, ***because they sold the righteous for silver, and the poor for a pair of shoes ... and a man and his father will go in unto the same maid ... and they drink the wine of the condemned in the house of their god.*** The last straw was telling prophets to keep quiet; I knew then that he was going to be hard on them.

3 Amos asked a series of rhetorical questions, leading to the menacing conclusion that they deserved what was coming: ***Can two walk together, except they be agreed? ... Shall a trumpet be blown in the city, and the people not be afraid? shall there be evil in a city, and the LORD hath not done it?*** Evidently not. Israel would be devoured as completely as the sheep whose ***shepherd taketh out of the mouth of the lion two legs, or a piece of an ear.***

4 The wealthy women of Samaria would be led away like cattle, with rings through their lips. As for the ordinary people, God expressed amazement that after everything he had done (to wit sending famine, drought, blight, locust, plague and destruction) they still didn't show him the proper respect. Some people are just ungrateful.

> ***I have overthrown some of you,***
> ***as God overthrew Sodom and Gomorrah,***
> ***and ye were as a firebrand plucked out of the burning:***
> ***yet have ye not returned unto me, saith the LORD.***
> ***Therefore thus will I do unto thee, O Israel:***
> ***and because I will do this unto thee,***
> ***prepare to meet thy God, O Israel.***

5 Amos lamented the fate of the nation. God, who was mighty enough to put Orion in the sky, would unleash his wrath; there would be crying in the streets. Anyone

foolish or vain enough to look forward to judgment day was in for a shock. ***Woe unto you that desire the day of the LORD!***

In fact, God was fed up with religious activists. ***I hate, I despise your feast days, and I will not smell in your solemn assemblies***; he wouldn't let the roast beef tempt him. It wasn't sacrifices and singing he wanted, but justice and virtue.

6 Indeed, the powerful and prosperous would be the first to suffer in the coming doom. There would be so many deaths that survivors would say ***Hold thy tongue: for we may not make mention of the name of the LORD***, for fear of attracting God's attention.

7 Amos started to have visions; in the first two the land was being destroyed by locusts or fire when ***The LORD repented for this***, and let Israel survive. But then God appeared again to Amos, ***and, behold, the Lord stood upon a wall made by a plumbline, with a plumbline in his hand.*** (I think Amos actually saw someone else in his vision, but I treasure the image of God standing on the wall dangling a string.) What this signified, it seems, was that God wouldn't pass them by a third time.

These predictions didn't endear Amos to the authorities, and a priest who served king Jeroboam told him to go back to Judah where he belonged. You don't talk to God's prophet like that and get away with it. ***Therefore thus saith the LORD; Thy wife shall be an harlot in the city, and thy sons and thy daughters shall fall by the sword, and thy land shall be divided by line; and thou shalt die in a polluted land: and Israel shall surely go into captivity***. The wives and children never had much luck.

8 A vision of a basket of summer fruit confirmed that Israel was ripe for destruction. When the day of the LORD came, the oppressors of the poor would be punished – but then everyone would be punished, so the warning wasn't very effective.

9 In his last vision, Amos saw God standing by an altar, bringing the roof crashing down on the heads of the worshippers: there would be no escape. Just to underline how little they meant to him, God taunted ***Are ye not as children of the Ethiopians unto me, O children of Israel?*** The black-skinned Ethiopians were considered inferior, but I wouldn't want you to think that God was racially prejudiced. Some of his favourite entertainers were coloured.

Israel wasn't left without hope. No sooner had God said ***I will destroy it from off the face of the earth***, than he promised to ***raise up the tabernacle of David that is fallen ... I will build it as in the days of old***. It was odd, though, that Amos should prophesy the restoration of something still in existence.

What's more, he suddenly seemed excited by the idea that material prosperity would return. In the past Amos had been distinctly sniffy about wealth, as opposed to spiritual welfare. I suppose the prospect of years and years in exile softened him up; no doubt he was simply a few centuries ahead of his time.

31

Obadiah

Obadiah was a single-issue prophet; in fact, he had less to say in all senses than any of them. Edom was the sole object of his wrath. As the putative descendants of Esau, their exploitation of Israel's disaster was particularly irksome. Still, it was a bit much when he declared that ***For thy violence against thy brother Jacob shame shall cover thee, and thou shalt be cut off for ever.*** By my recollection, the grievances were mostly on the other side.

Although Amos had warned against looking forward to judgment day, Obadiah took it for granted that God was on his side. Edom would be sorry, ***For the day of the LORD is near upon all the heathen: as thou hast done, it shall be done unto thee: thy reward shall return upon thine own head*** – with interest, apparently, as ***there shall not be any remaining of the house of Esau.*** These people took their xenophobia seriously.

32

Jonah

1 There was a tradition of reluctant prophets, but Jonah went overboard in attempting to avoid the call – in fact he got carried away. It all started when God told him to go to Nineveh, capital of Assyria, to berate its people for their wickedness.

The mission sounded potentially suicidal, so I wasn't altogether surprised when Jonah tried to disappear in the opposite direction. Quite how he hoped to escape I don't know; perhaps he thought that God would just use another conscript in his place. What a mistake.

God sent a tempest to intercept the ship that Jonah had boarded. At first the sailors followed conventional procedure: praying to an assortment of gods, throwing things over the side, and so on. Jonah was sleeping through all this down in the hold, which must have been a considerable annoyance. He was awakened and told to help with the praying.

As matters became desperate, the sailors said ***Come, and let us cast lots, that we may know for whose cause this evil is upon us. So they cast lots, and the lot fell upon Jonah.*** Under questioning he confessed to being a Hebrew on the run from his god, maker of the land and the sea. Things didn't look good.

Jonah volunteered to be tossed over the side, but to the sailors' credit they struggled to row back towards land. It was useless, however, and in the end they decided that Jonah would have to go. No sooner had he been pitched into the deep than the storm subsided, so impressing the crew that they joined God's admirers on the spot.

Now the LORD had prepared a great fish to swallow up Jonah. And Jonah
2 ***was in the belly of the fish three days and three nights.*** During that time he prayed, as you might imagine, though he seemed to take it for granted that God would rescue him. As it happened, he was right: ***the LORD spake unto the fish, and it vomited out Jonah upon the dry land.***

3 God repeated his instructions about going to Nineveh, and this time Jonah did as he was told. No doubt he still expected to be torn limb from limb, but at least it would be on dry land. What happened instead was unbelievable. Jonah announced ***Yet forty days, and Nineveh shall be overthrown. So the people of Nineveh believed in God, and proclaimed a fast, and put on sackcloth, from the greatest of them even to the least of them.***

Well, I was astonished. Hebrew prophets never had it so good at home, and here Jonah was in Assyria. The king even ordered that all the livestock fast and wear sackcloth: a whole new concept in animal sacrifice. Perhaps he couldn't stand to be worse off than a goat. Anyway, you can't argue with success. ***God repented of the evil, that he had said that he would do unto them; and he did it not.***

4 Jonah was disgusted, whether because he wanted to see Nineveh destroyed, or just resented having his credibility undermined, I wasn't sure. He declared that he'd prefer to be dead, and went and sulked under a shelter outside the city.

God caused a large plant to spring up and provide some shade for him, only to kill it the next day, much to Jonah's annoyance. If the prophet felt sorry for a plant, God said, shouldn't he himself feel compassion for a city of 120,000 persons ***that cannot discern between their right hand and their left hand; and also much cattle?*** Quite so, but Jonah was concerned about his own well-being, not the plant's. He was lucky it didn't swallow him.

33

Micah

1 Like most peasants, Micah thought that cities were wicked places. He regarded Samaria and Jerusalem as little better than Sodom and Gomorrah, and likely to meet a similar fate.

2 His main concern, however, seemed to be social injustice rather than depravity. He remarked that the powerful take what they want, and will be punished by being 3 dispossessed. The nation's leaders ***eat the flesh of my people, and flay their skin from off them; and they break their bones, and chop them in pieces, as for the pot***. Micah wasn't afraid to express himself.

4 Although Jerusalem was heading for destruction, God would ultimately return to make peace among all nations. Having beaten their swords into plowshares – yet more work for the blacksmiths as defence policy changes again – ***they shall sit every man under his vine and under his fig tree; and none shall make them afraid ... For all people will walk every one in the name of his god, and we will walk in the name of the LORD our God for ever and ever.*** Religious toleration: paradise indeed.

Assyria was the enemy in Micah's day, so it must have been mystifying to hear that ***thou shalt go even to Babylon; there shalt thou be delivered***. But then no one seemed to pay much attention to prophets anyway – the entire population of Nineveh excepted, of course.

5 Micah prophesied the coming of a victorious leader, like himself from the wholesome countryside, though to be fair David was the real model. Micah warned David's clan, ***But thou, Beth-lehem Ephratah, though thou be little among the thousands of Judah, yet out of thee shall he come forth unto me that is to be ruler in Israel***. There'd be no more problem with the Assyrians in the time to come; he had that right.

6 In common with his fellow prophets, Micah was suspicious of ritual observance. It wasn't what God wanted.

Will the LORD be pleased with thousands of rams,
or with ten thousands of rivers of oil?
shall I give my firstborn for my transgression,
the fruit of my body for the sin of my soul?
He hath shewed thee, O man, what is good;
and what doth the LORD require of thee,

but to do justly, and to love mercy,
and to walk humbly with thy God?

Greater honesty in commerce would be a good start, Micah suggested. His denunciation of the traders seemed rather personal, as if he had had a bad experience in the market.

Micah declared that everyone was wicked, that no one could be trusted. He looked forward to the day when his enemies were trampled down like mud; ***They shall lick the dust like a serpent, they shall move out of their holes like worms.*** Moderation wasn't high on the list of prophetic virtues. 7

34

Nahum

1 Nahum had just one concern: the doom of Nineveh. True, he made his start by exalting the vengefulness of God in general, but storm, drought, earthquake, fire and flood need a target. Theory isn't enough.

2 The people of Nineveh were not in for a happy time. ***She is empty, and void, and waste: and the heart melteth, and the knees smite together, and much pain is in all loins, and the faces of them all gather blackness.*** I was perplexed; hadn't God decided to spare them? Jonah's visit can't have been such a success after all. ***Behold, I am against thee, saith the LORD of hosts,*** lest there be any doubt about the matter.

3 ***Woe to the bloody city! it is all full of lies and robbery; the prey departeth not.*** Mostly it is full of corpses, as far as I could make out, and all ***Because of the multitude of the whoredoms of the wellfavoured harlot, the mistress of witchcrafts, that selleth nations through her whoredoms.*** I cringed whenever the prophets spoke to a family audience.

Once Nahum had his hands on the wanton woman metaphor – which anyway was gratuitous when applied to Assyria; why should she have been faithful? – the sex and violence became unpleasant. God said that he would strip her and expose her to the world, ***And I will cast abominable filth upon thee, and make thee vile.***

It takes some nerve for a muck thrower to call the target vile, I'm bound to say. According to Nahum everyone would clap hands at the news; that might be true, but it wouldn't be pretty.

35

Habakkuk

Habakkuk tried to cope with the Big Problem: failure of divine justice. As often as not evil triumphed over virtue, and the prophet asked God straight out why he put up with it. God's response was to be contrary: he was going to let the forces of Babylon go on the rampage.

Despite this slap in the face, Habakkuk persisted in his rationality. It's all very well to use Babylon as an instrument of chastisement, he said, but what's the point of punishing wickedness with greater wickedness? How did giving success to merciless infidels serve justice? Mystified, he climbed a watchtower to wait for the reply.

God told him to ***Write the vision, and make it plain upon tables, that he may run that readeth it.*** Run by all means, but where are you going to hide? There was an appointed time for what was to come; ***though it tarry, wait for it; because it will surely come, it will not tarry.*** But don't stay up, would be my advice; I found God rather relaxed about time keeping.

The just would live by their faithfulness, he continued; the oppressors wouldn't live at all. They would be punished for their greed and pretensions, not to mention their orgies. ***Woe unto him that giveth his neighbour drink, that puttest thy bottle to him, and makest him drunken also, that thou mayest look on their nakedness!*** Perhaps from the effect of the alcohol, things got a bit wild; ***drink thou also, and let thy foreskin be uncovered ... and shameful spewing shall be on thy glory.*** Sounds exciting. As further encouragement to sobriety, the idol worshippers were reminded that ***the LORD is in his holy temple: let all the earth keep silence before him.***

Everyone would be punished in due course, and although that didn't sound like much of an answer to me, Habakkuk sang a hymn to God anyway. He would come on the storm, bringing pestilence and plague with him; his wrath would descend on the enemies of his people. Even if the crops failed and the herds vanished, ***Yet I will rejoice in the LORD, I will joy in the God of my salvation.*** A touching comment, though I doubt he bargained for quite as much opportunity to celebrate in the face of adversity as he was going to get – if he lived long enough, that is.

36

Zephaniah

1 When it came to gloom and doom, no one could outdo Zephaniah. His great preoccupation was the day of the LORD, judgment day, when God would demonstrate that what he had created, he could destroy.

I will utterly consume all things from off the land, saith the LORD. I will consume man and beast; I will consume the fowls of the heaven, and the fishes of the sea. I know that mankind had been a disappointment, but it seemed a shame to wipe out everything else. ***The great day of the LORD is near, it is near, and hasteth greatly.*** Apparently it wasn't so near as all that, but preachers like to create excitement, and the idea that the end is nigh is a perennial crowd pleaser.

Zephaniah's description of the apocalypse was sonorous, if lacking in detail.

That day is a day of wrath,
a day of trouble and distress,
a day of wasteness and desolation,
a day of darkness and gloominess,
a day of clouds and thick darkness,
a day of the trumpet and alarm.

As for people, ***their blood shall be poured out as dust, and their flesh as the dung.*** All in all, not a good day for a picnic.

2 Having given the impression that judgment would be impartial, the prophet proceeded to curse the traditional targets: the Philistines, Moab, Ammon, and Assyria, with Ethiopia thrown in for good measure. ***The LORD will be terrible unto them: for he will famish all the gods of the earth; and men shall worship him, every one from his place.*** Animals, people, and now gods were queuing up for elimination; it was going to be a busy time.

3 Zephaniah was far from making an exception of Jerusalem, I should say. ***Woe to her that is filthy and polluted, to the oppressing city!*** God repeated that ***all the earth shall be devoured with the fire of my jealousy.*** He wasn't making it easy to stay cheerful.

After being so gloomy, Zephaniah said things that didn't sound like him at all. Israel was supposed to shout for joy, because God was eliminating her enemies; everything would be just as in the good old days. I think the prophet knew better than to assume that God was on his side, whatever words had been put in his mouth.

37

Haggai

1

The prophetic line didn't expire in exile; when Darius permitted Jerusalem to be rebuilt, there were prophets ready to tell everyone what to do. One of these was Haggai.

Although the people struggled just to survive in the ruined city, Haggai thought that their priorities were wrong. ***Ye have sown much, and bring in little; ye eat, but ye have not enough; ye drink, but ye are not filled with drink; ye clothe you, but there is none warm; and he that earneth wages earneth wages to put it into a bag with holes.*** What they should be doing, he said, was to rebuild the temple.

To me that didn't sound more important than, say, avoiding starvation, but when God let drop that he would make their lives miserable until he had a proper house, I could see Haggai's point. The people did too, and they got to work.

2

God acknowledged that, especially for anyone who remembered the previous temple, the task seemed enormous. Still, they shouldn't be despondent. He was going to shake up the world, filling his house with gold and silver, making it even better than before.

Somewhat cryptically, Haggai pointed out that when the holy and the polluted come into contact, both end up unclean. My guess is that he was making a disparaging reference to the Samaritans, the local people of mixed heritage. They were keen to help out, but the leadership wouldn't tolerate fraternisation with the natives.

The new foundations having been laid, God promised to bless them from that day forward. Amazingly, he even named Zerubbabel, governor of the province and descendent of David, as his chosen saviour, the messianic king. ***I will destroy the strength of the kingdoms of the heathen ... In that day, saith the LORD of hosts, will I take thee, O Zerubbabel, my servant, the son of Shealtiel, saith the LORD, and will make thee as a signet: for I have chosen thee.*** An embarrassing mistake, of course, but there was always next time.

38

Zechariah

1 Haggai had a contemporary, Zechariah. God complained to this new prophet that the people had never been very obedient, obliging him to flex his muscles. ***Your fathers, where are they? and the prophets, do they live for ever?*** They had been forced to admit that ***according to our doings, so hath he dealt with us.***

Zechariah's main aim, however, wasn't to demand repentance – they had served their time – but to offer encouragement. That said, the visions he described were too obscure to incite dancing in the streets. Even I often had difficulty in seeing their point, and I appeared in them.

Zechariah's first vision was of horses of different colours, returned from patrolling the world. It was disappointing that ***all the earth sitteth still, and is at rest***; after all, God had promised to shake things up. I was able to pass on the word that he still intended to make Jerusalem great again.

A vision of four horns (the enemy) being beaten down by four smiths with divine 2 powers gave place to a more peaceful prospect of Jerusalem without walls, protected by God. He called the people out of exile – and did I hear sleigh bells? ***Ho, ho, come forth, and flee from the land of the north, saith the LORD: for I have spread you abroad as the four winds of the heaven.*** He would join them in ***the holy land, and shall choose Jerusalem again.***

3 Satan put in one of his rare appearances in the fourth vision, standing before God as accuser of Joshua, the high priest. As defence counsel, I made sure that Joshua got a new suit of clothes to replace his filthy old ones; looking innocent is half the battle. God was convinced, and promised ***I will bring forth my servant the BRANCH.*** That was good news, I gathered.

4 The identity of this offshoot became apparent. Haggai had tipped us off that Zerubbabel was God's chosen one, and I had a message for him: ***Not by might, nor by power, but by my spirit, saith the LORD of hosts.*** The highest mountain is flat, next to the greatness of Zerubbabel. Having laid the foundation of the temple he would also complete it; perhaps its beginnings seemed modest (***For who hath despised the day of small things?*** most people, probably) but the result would be imposing.

The vision itself was somewhat confused, especially as regards a seven-branched lampstand. The olive trees on either side, though, appeared to represent Joshua and Zerubbabel, the spiritual and temporal leaders. ***These are the two anointed ones, that stand by the Lord of the whole earth.*** Maybe it would still have been a damp squib, but I think Zerubbabel should have changed his name.

It's hard to be messiah when it sounds as if you're a racehorse.

In his sixth vision Zechariah saw a ***flying roll***: not the remains of lunch, but a huge scroll inscribed with curses on thieves and liars sailing from house to house, demolishing those of the guilty. Next to feature was a flying barrel. It contained a woman, wickedness personified, who was being carried off to a purpose-built temple in Babylon. I don't imagine you'd want to be around when she was let out of the barrel. 5

The four horses of different colours, pulling chariots this time, reappeared in the eighth and final vision. They would strike out on the four points of the compass to do God's work. The navigation, mind you, left something to be desired, with Babylon (to the east) being referred to as ***the north country***. 6

God commanded that a crown be set on the head of – whom? It was supposed to be Zerubbabel, I'm sure, but somehow it ended up being Joshua, the high priest. Still, it hardly matters; neither came close to messianic status. The problems might have been avoided if God hadn't been so allusive; his words were ***Behold the man whose name is The BRANCH; and he shall grow up out of his place, and he shall build the temple of the LORD ... and he shall bear the glory, and shall sit and rule upon his throne***. All quite thrilling: too bad the choice was such a fiasco.

Some people wondered whether it was still necessary to keep the fasts that they had observed since the fall of Jerusalem. God grumbled that the rituals were for their own benefit; all he asked was that they ***Execute true judgment, and shew mercy and compassions every man to his brother***. He'd have to scourge anyone who forgot it. 7

God proposed to let bygones be bygones. Answering the original question, he declared that the fasts would henceforth be ***cheerful feasts***. Jerusalem would become a magnet, not just for returning exiles, but for people from all over the world. They ***shall take hold of the skirt of him that is a Jew, saying, We will go with you: for we have heard that God is with you***. That would be something to see. 8

At this point Zechariah seemed to undergo a transformation. First he prophesied the destruction of the usual enemies in the usual terms: ***a bastard shall dwell in Ashdod, and I will cut off the pride of the Philistines*** – ouch – and so on. Then, abruptly, he described the messianic king: 9

Rejoice greatly, O daughter of Zion;
shout, O daughter of Jerusalem:
behold, thy King cometh unto thee:
he is just, and having salvation;
lowly, and riding upon an ass ...
and he shall speak peace unto the heathen:
and his dominion shall be from sea even to sea,
and from the river even to the ends of the earth.

God just as suddenly went back to business. The exiles, those ***prisoners of hope***, should return to triumph over their enemies, a victory that would leave them soaked
10 in blood, like the corners of the altar. God lingered over the images of fighting; he was an action fan.

11 Zechariah offered an allegory of unrivalled obscurity. In it he was a shepherd responsible for fattening a flock for slaughter, who gradually abandoned his position. First he sent away three other shepherds and told the sheep to do what they liked, breaking his staff called Grace as sign that the covenant was broken. Having asked to be paid off, he reported that ***they weighed for my price thirty pieces of silver***, insulting him with a slave's compensation. At that he broke his other staff, Union, signalling the separation of Israel and Judah.

God told him to act the part of a worthless shepherd, one who didn't take care of his sheep at all. In consequence he was wounded with a sword, losing the use of an arm and an eye. Later on we heard that the flock was scattered, with only a third surviving. In due course the remnant would return to God.

12 Fortunately I wasn't called upon to interpret, which had been my job for the previous visions, and God went back to predicting military victories in which ***they shall devour all the people round about***. Despite the triumph, our side would look with remorse on him ***whom they have pierced, and they shall mourn for him***. Whether this martyr was a particular person, and if so whom, I couldn't tell.

13 God was looking forward to the day when there would be no more prophets; I know the feeling. It only needed a little parental discipline; anyone who persisted in prophesying would be killed by his own mother and father. To avoid family tiffs prophets would repudiate the vocation, even advertising their years of youthful carnality. That way should someone notice marks and scratches (self-inflicted by pagan prophets) and ask ***What are these wounds in thine hands? Then he shall answer, Those with which I was wounded in the house of my friends*** – during periods of high excitement, if you catch my drift. You'd think they could dream up a less embarrassing explanation.

14 If Zechariah had set out to be reassuring, God wasn't giving him much help: ***I will gather all nations against Jerusalem to battle; and the city shall be taken, and the houses rifled, and the women ravished; and half of the city shall go forth into captivity***. At that point, finally, he would get around to fighting. At least he was going to pull out all the stops: splitting the Mount of Olives down the middle, abolishing the night, causing rivers to flow west as well as east out of Jerusalem. Naturally he would win, and ***in that day shall there be one LORD***.

To tidy up he would make the whole country as flat as a pancake, with only the city rising above it. People who had been on the wrong side were in for a spot of bother, as God decided to let them rot: ***Their flesh shall consume away while they stand upon their feet, and their eyes shall consume away in their holes, and their tongue shall consume away in their mouth***. He didn't even spare the animals in the enemy armies.

And it shall come to pass, that every one that is left of all the nations which

came against Jerusalem shall even go up from year to year to worship the King, the LORD of hosts, and to keep the feast of tabernacles. Any group declining to attend would receive a drought. After God's final victory, people will be holy, or else.

39

Malachi

1 Those remarks implying that God had had his fill of prophets must have had an effect: only one more came forward, and even then anonymously. He was simply known as Malachi, which means 'my messenger', and the secret of his identity is safe with me. Malachi lived around the time of Nehemiah's return, prophesying some sixty years or more after Haggai and Zechariah thrilled the people just back from Babylon with visions of a great future.

Generations on, with life as hard as ever, everyone was fed up. God's support, it seemed, was all talk and no action. God could only reply that people he disliked were in real trouble. ***I loved Jacob, And I hated Esau, and laid his mountains and his heritage waste for the dragons of the wilderness. … They shall build, but I will throw down.*** Very entertaining, I'm sure, but the people were looking for something more constructive.

Malachi criticised them, and the priests in particular, for their cynical approach to sacrifices. They were offering God animals that were injured, lame, and diseased, not the best of the flock. Even the heathen showed more appreciation.
2 So, God told the priests, ***I will even send a curse upon you … I will corrupt your seed, and spread dung upon your faces.*** That was an assignment I hoped to avoid.

The people also received a lecture on keeping faith with one another. ***Have we not all one father? hath not one God created us?*** Apparently some women, at least, were more equal than others, because he condemned men who ***hath profaned the holiness of the LORD which he loved, and hath married the daughter of a strange god. The LORD will cut off the man that doeth this.*** That will teach him. In fairness, though, God seemed to be thinking particularly of men who deserted their wives in favour of foreign women – and he declared that divorce is hateful.

Unfortunately God was losing credibility, with justice not yet in evidence. He
3 was tired of the questions, and could only repeat ***Behold, I will send my messenger, and he shall prepare the way before me: and the Lord, whom ye seek, shall suddenly come to his temple.*** Lest anyone assume that this was good news for all, he added ***But who may abide the day of his coming? and who shall stand when he appeareth? for he is like a refiner's fire, and like fullers' soap.*** Not your average household god, clearly.

He announced that, as well as purifying the priests, ***I will be a swift witness against the sorcerers, and against the adulterers, and against false swearers, and against those that oppress the hireling in his wages, the widow, and the fatherless, and that turn aside the stranger from his right, and fear not me.*** There could be something of the social crusader about him: a touch puritanical, certainly, but with a radical banner.

That's not to say that he didn't know how to engage in mutual back-scratching. ***Return unto me, and I will return unto you.*** Because they were robbing him of tithes and offerings, they had been cursed. A few well placed shekels would see them right.

Quite a few people weren't yet convinced that obeying God was worth the trouble; the wicked seemed to do well and to get away with it. God assured them that the names of the righteous were being noted, and that one day they would be glad to be on the list. ***For, behold, the day cometh, that shall burn as an oven; and all the proud, yea, and all that do wickedly, shall be stubble: and the day that cometh shall burn them up, saith the LORD of hosts, that it shall leave them neither root nor branch. But unto you that fear my name shall the Sun of righteousness arise with healing in his wings ... And ye shall tread down the wicked; for they shall be ashes under the soles of your feet.*** So keep your shoes on.

4

God told them to remember the law of Moses, winding things up with a promise and a threat. ***Behold, I will send you Elijah the prophet before the coming of the great and dreadful day of the LORD: And he shall turn the heart of the fathers to the children, and the heart of the children to their fathers ...*** And indeed, people still leave the door open for Elijah. God concluded ominously, however. I'd better give him the last word; I don't think I could get another job. Be nice to each other, he said, ***... lest I come and smite the earth with a curse.***

Appendix

The Story of the Bible

Having seldom been made aware of the results of biblical scholarship, lay people tend to lapse into a pre-modern conception of scripture. If your view of the Bible entails a divine hand writing on tablets of stone, it is not surprising that the entire critical enterprise seems essentially irreligious. Nothing could be further from the truth: Augustine, Maimonides, Luther and Calvin (to span Catholics, Jews and Protestants) were all important critics, willing where necessary to contest the words on the page. (At one point Luther even favoured throwing out the whole book of Revelation.) There is no need to adopt an all-or-nothing approach.

A good Bible commentary will provide an introduction to the achievements of textual and historical research, but it might be worth highlighting a few rudimentary points. The Bible did not suddenly appear in its present form. A number of people over a very extended period turned out songs, stories, sayings and at some point writings. These existed and developed independently over the centuries before being gathered together as parts of a single sacred work. In that sense the Hebrew Bible is an anthology drawn from a millennium of religious life and literary creation.

In another sense, however, the very process of textual evolution has produced a work that is truly singular. Individual books have often been woven from separate strands, or stitched together from material of different ages. Certain sections relating to early events were written after other sections describing later events. A communal consciousness permeates the whole canon and helps it to cohere; related concerns hold everything together. Of course the unification of the various segments has itself made us look beyond the parts to see an integrated whole.

Any processing of a text such as translating or summarising will tend to make the new more uniform than the old. Any overview, such as this version supplies, will subordinate the elements, however distinct they might be. These are facts to be acknowledged, but not necessarily regretted: the Bible transcends its own diversity.

A few dates might help to make the history of the people and the book more concrete. Abraham is traditionally placed some four thousand years ago; the exodus from Egypt would have been in the 13th century BCE. David became king in Jerusalem just before the year 1000 BCE, with the division of the kingdom around 922 starting the downward slide to the fall of Israel in 721 and Judah in 587. The story continues to the time of Ezra and Nehemiah, closing about 425 BCE (on traditional dating) or a few decades later (on more recent analysis).

Looking now at the Bible, it seems likely that writing began in earnest when the kingdom was established, with some segments derived from earlier oral tradition. Activity continued through the centuries of monarchy, division, exile and restoration, with the latest books, Daniel and Esther, completed by 150 BCE. The five books of Moses were in their present form by about 400 BCE. The whole Hebrew canon was fixed by the end of the first century after the birth of Jesus.

As an aside, the division of the Bible into chapters and verses is not original. When the Vulgate was carved into chapters in the thirteenth century, the breaks were not always placed at what now seem the most appropriate points.

The present volume comprises the books of the Hebrew Bible; it does not include the Jewish scriptures written in Greek (described as 'deutero-canonical' and 'apocryphal' by Catholics and Protestants respectively), which are omitted from the biblical canon by Jews and Protestants. Neither, of course, does it include the books of the Christian New Testament, also written in Greek.

The order of the books follows the Christian convention, which allows the historical saga to unfold more or less chronologically from Genesis through to Esther. The traditional Jewish arrangement, better reflecting the evolution of the Bible itself, is in three sections: the Law (Torah), the Prophets, and the Writings. The first refers to the Pentateuch (the five books of Moses). The second contains the 'former' prophets (Joshua, Judges, Samuel and Kings) as well as the 'latter' prophets (Isaiah, Jeremiah, Ezekiel and the Twelve). The last includes everything else: poetry, wisdom literature, short stories (Ruth, Esther, Daniel), and some history (Chronicles, Ezra and Nehemiah).

Despite being the national (not to say nationalistic) literature of the Hebrew people, it is more concerned to criticise than to praise them. Other features may be even more surprising. The narrative rarely sets the scene, physically or psychologically. Clauses are chained by the conjunction 'and', leaving the link between events – sometimes, indeed, whether they are consecutive or simultaneous – in doubt. (Modern translations frequently sacrifice this ambiguity through the use of subordinate clauses introduced by 'because', 'in spite of', etc.)

This 'narrative minimalism', as it has been called, is not merely descriptive. Most episodes in the historical saga are recounted dispassionately, with no judgment being offered. The law and the prophets are a different matter, but even these seem positivist; questions of what should be done refer simply to facts about divine commands. Moral reflection is most evident in the wisdom literature, and yet here the considerations seem prudential and worldly – as in many proverbs – or remarkably unorthodox – as in much of Job and Ecclesiastes.

An interesting result of this paucity of analysis is that personality emerges where modern readers least expect it, in the figure of God. We find it difficult to think in terms that the earlier writers, at least, took for granted: the God of Israel had a name, and just as a name identifies each of us and marks us out from others, so he was distinguished from rival gods. This name came to be rendered as 'Jehovah', though it was probably closer to 'Yahweh'; ancient Hebrew being written without vowels or diacritical marks, we have simply the letters YHWH.

Over the course of time people conceived of God in ways that were increasingly universal and abstract. When 'YHWH' came to be viewed as too sacred to utter, they substituted another term for the ineffable name. Translators maintained the tradition, using 'LORD' rather than 'Jehovah'. While this practice is in accord with our current perspective, it is worth remembering that the original is more concrete.

To read, of course, is to interpret. The Bible comes to us across two to three thousand years of history, and our cultural spectacles are too thick to be set aside. None the less it helps occasionally to ponder what the original writers were trying to say as we consider what our civilisation has made of the Bible, as well as how our world has been made by it.

When Gutenberg made it possible for books to be printed in quantity rather than copied by hand, he provided the means of general access to scripture. Despite their initial reservations, the authorities had little choice but to accept the distribution of vernacular Bibles. Between the completion of Tyndale's New Testament in 1525 and the publication of the King James (or Authorised) Version in 1611, there was an English eruption in print: the Coverdale Bible, Matthew's Bible, the Great Bible, the Geneva Bible, the Bishops' Bible, the Douai Bible.

Scriptures in the vernacular no longer surprise us; indeed some people believe, the joke has it, that the Word came down from on high in King James' English. At one time, however, the whole enterprise was considered sacrilegious, if not impossible. *They will say it cannot be translated into our tongue, it is so rude. It is not so rude as they are false liars*, William Tyndale, 'father of the English Bible', robustly responded in 1528.

Producing a new version of the Bible has often been a thankless task. Even St Jerome, whose late fourth-/early fifth-century translation into Latin (the Vulgate) became the focus of Western scholarship for a thousand years, is said to have died disconsolate because of unfavourable comment from his contemporaries. The early English translators fared considerably worse. Having narrowly avoided the inquisitors Wycliffe managed to die in bed, but his grave was desecrated. Tyndale spent most of his life in exile, and ended it at the stake.

Tyndale's work provided the basis for a number of the subsequent translations, including the King James Version. Although the latter did not immediately sweep the field, it was soon accepted as the standard English Bible, and remained unchallenged in that position through four centuries. There has been another boom in Bible translation since the war, but competition from wholly new (as opposed to revised) versions is a comparatively recent phenomenon.

Quite apart from its religious significance, the Bible is an important piece of literature. Indeed, the King James Version is the single most influential work in English (rivalled only by Shakespeare, a product of the same age). Its classic formulations have passed into the folk memory. Moreover, in its preservation of the characteristics mentioned above, if not in literal correctness, the King James is superior to other translations. It retains both the allusiveness and the ambiguity often sacrificed in the search for everyday English.

Ironically, the history of the Bible contradicts its tendency to over-awe. The entire biblical project – from Moses and the prophets to their scribes and translators – is one of letting the people know, of bringing the word down to earth. It is a continuing compromise between old language and new: a permanent search for an alternative voice.

Index of Names